P9-DFZ-298

Listen Up

Voices from the Next Feminist Generation

edited by

Barbara Findlen

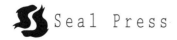 Seal Press

Copyright © 1995 by Barbara Findlen

All rights reserved. No part of this book may be reproduced in any form, except for the quotation of brief passages in reviews, without prior written permission from Seal Press, 3131 Western Avenue, Suite 410, Seattle, Washington 98121.

Cover photography by Alice Wheeler
Cover design by Kate Thompson
Text design by Clare Conrad

Grateful acknowledgment is made to the following for permission to reprint their copyrighted material: "One Less Bitch," by Tracy Curry / Andre Young / Lorenzo Patterson. Copyright © 1991 Sony Songs, Inc. (BMI) / Ruthless Attack Muzick (ASCAP). All rights on behalf of Sony Songs Inc. administered by Sony Music Publishing, 8 Music Square West, Nashville, TN 37203. All rights reserved. Used by permission. "She Swallowed It," by Lorenzo Patterson / Andre Young. Ruthless Attack Music (ASCAP). Used by permission. "Your Life As a Girl," by Curtis Sittenfeld reprinted by permission of Ms. magazine, copyright © 1993.

Library of Congress Cataloging-in-Publication Data
Listen up : voices from the next feminist generation / edited by Barbara Findlen.
Includes bibliographical references.
1. Feminism—United States. 2. Feminists—United States—Biography. I. Findlen, Barbara.
HQ1426.L57   1995   305.42'0973—dc20 94-42609

Printed in the United States in America
First printing, May 1995
10 9 8 7 6 5 4

Distributed to the trade by Publishers Group West
In Canada: Publishers Group West Canada, Toronto, Ontario
In the U.K. and Europe: Airlift Book Company, London, England

Acknowledgments

First, I want to thank the Findlens—Fred, Rosella, Pat, Kate and Fred—each of whom had a role in making me a young feminist.

I thank Holly Morris of Seal Press for initiating this project, for entrusting it to me and for gently guiding me through the process of creating an anthology. We shared a vision for this book from the beginning, and she has been a reassuring and steady influence throughout.

I appreciate the commitment and hard work of all the women who contributed their work to this anthology, as well as the dozens more whose submissions didn't make it into the book.

Kate Rounds, Judy Warner and Edite Kroll were instrumental in helping me get this project off the ground. One of the keys to making this book happen was outreach to young feminists wherever they could be found—high schools and colleges, community and youth groups, feminist bookstores and organizations, the Internet, you name it. Andrea Estepa of *New Youth Connections*, Susan Buttenwieser and Meghan O'Hara helped me find them.

Thank you to my pals who helped in the preparation of the manuscript: Randy Hawkins, Anastasia Higginbotham, Joan Philpott, Susanne Skubik and Erin Wade. Helen Bennett, Susan Buttenwieser, Sharon Lennon, Therese Stanton and Madhavi Sunder read the manuscript in various stages and offered valuable feedback.

For their boundless enthusiasm, constant cheerleading and unwavering encouragement, I am deeply grateful to Anastasia

Higginbotham, Sharon Lennon, Betty and Sam Carter and my colleagues at *Ms.* magazine.

My profound gratitude goes to Marcia Ann Gillespie, the editor in chief of *Ms.* The early encouragement she gave me to edit this book was just the beginning of the enormous support she offered throughout the project (imagine a boss who insists that you take time off from your day job to tend to your freelance work). An embodiment of feminist principles in action, Marcia truly lives the song she sings.

I want to offer a special thanks to Gloria Steinem. She was an inspiration and a role model to me long before I met her, and she has offered invaluable guidance and encouragement both in this project and in our shared work at *Ms.* magazine.

Finally, eternal thanks to Kristen Golden, my partner in everything, and most certainly a partner in this anthology. She shared every aspect of the creation of this book and performed each task, from stuffing envelopes to typing to sharing editorial advice, with the brilliance, humor and creativity she brings to everything. I am grateful for her unshakable faith in this book and in me.

For Kristen

Contents

Introduction

My feminism wasn't shaped by antiwar or civil rights activism; I was not a victim of the problem that had no name. Indeed, by the time I was discovering feminism, naming had become a principal occupation of feminists. Everywhere you looked feminists were naming things—things like sexual harassment, date rape, displaced homemakers and domestic violence—that used to be called, as Gloria Steinem pointed out, just life.

In fact, born in 1964, I became a part of a massive, growing, vibrant feminist movement at the age of eleven—something that literally had not been possible for Gloria Steinem, Kate Millett, my older sisters, my mother, or any of my other feminist role models. While feminism has been around for as long as patriarchy, I came of age during one of those moments in history when the feminist movement was becoming so large, so vocal and so visible that it could reach into and change the life of an eleven-year-old suburban girl.

It was a time of unlimited possibilities for women—or that was my impression, anyway. When I was eight, I cried as my father tried to explain to me why my brother could play Little League baseball, while I, who had just reached the age of eligibility, was still somehow ineligible. Two years later, my best friend Linda Brauer and I joined a nearby team, the ban on girls having magically disappeared. I knew that there was a feminist movement, but I hadn't learned about the grueling and sometimes humiliating struggle of the girl, Maria Pepe, two years older than me, who had sued Little League Baseball all the way to the New Jersey State Supreme Court in order to be allowed to play the game.

To me, feminism meant that women and men, girls and boys, were equal. Almost every woman has experienced the feeling of being mistreated, trivialized, kept out, put down, ignored, assaulted, laughed at or discriminated against because of her gender. To me, the existence of feminism—and a feminist movement—meant that the rage I felt was no longer impotent. When I was locked out of Little League, I didn't know what to do except cry. When I then was allowed to play, I realized that change was possible, although I didn't yet realize the struggles and risks inherent in making change.

The legacy of feminism for me was a sense of entitlement. The year after Linda and I joined our baseball team, we started to wonder why the "boys' yard" at our elementary school was the one with the basketball court, baseball field, football field and jungle gym, while the "girls' yard" offered only a hopscotch grid. We took our complaint to the principal, who eventually integrated recess.

A trivial matter? Perhaps, in the scheme of things. But the possibility of achieving redress, even if it starts on a small scale, is self-perpetuating. The more justice you think you can achieve, the more you try to achieve. If it had been 1955 instead of 1975, we wouldn't have questioned the unfairness, even if we resented it. In 1965, we may have asked for fair treatment, but we probably would have been laughed at. But because we were eleven at a time when there was a feminist movement creating awareness everywhere about sexism, we could not only identify an injustice in our world, we could right the wrong.

While this certainly is not the kind of experience every young woman, or even every young feminist, has had, the point is that it's the kind of experience *only* a woman of this generation could have had. We are the first generation for whom feminism has been entwined in the fabric of our lives; it is natural that many of us are feminists.

This anthology is about the experiences of women of this generation in the United States. We have been shaped by the unique events and circumstances of our time: AIDS, the erosion of reproductive rights, the materialism and cynicism of the Reagan and Bush years, the backlash against women, the erosion of civil rights, the skyrocketing divorce rate, the movement toward multi-culturalism and greater global awareness, the emergence of the lesbian and gay rights movement, a greater overall awareness of sexuality—and the feminist movement itself. During our early years, feminism was already a major social force. As we reached adolescence and adulthood, the feminist movement was challenging society's basic assumptions about gender. For the first time, there were significant numbers of girls and boys growing up in feminist families. But even those of us not lucky enough to be raised by feminists have found other avenues to discover and integrate feminism into our lives: women's studies, a huge body of feminist fiction and nonfiction, community- and school-based activist groups, the occasional sitcom.

Generation X, thirteenth generation, twentysomething—whatever package you buy this age group in—one of the characteristics we're known for is our disunity. Maybe we're not as unified as the generation that preceded us. Maybe we're just not as categorizable. In any case, I wonder whether the famous unity of the baby boomers might not be a bit mythical. Even in eras that offer unifying forces more momentous than *The Brady Bunch*, each individual's personal experiences define the time for her. Women's *experiences* of sexism have always been an important basis for political action. And our experiences of sexism are far from universal; they have always been affected by race, class, geographic location, disability, sexual identity, religion and just plain luck. How patriarchy crosses our paths and how we deal with that can also be determined by our families, school systems, the degree and type of violence in our communities and myriad other factors. So what may appear to be a splintering in this generation often comes from an honest assessment of our differences as each of us defines her place and role in feminism.

The writers in this collection have done a lot of thinking about their identities as young feminists. Several write about the ongoing process of integrating their feminist identities with ethnic, racial, religious, sexual, regional, class and other identities. Many women of color in particular struggle to promote the visibility and concerns of feminists in communities of color and at the same time ensure that feminist scholarship, activism and institutions fully integrate the lives and realities of women of color. This, of course, is not the responsibility of only women of color; as Christine Doza writes in this collection: "There is a system of abuse here. I need to know what part I'm playing in it."

Women in this book call themselves, among other things, articulate, white, middle-class college kid; wild and unruly; single mother; Asian bisexual; punk; politically astute, active woman; middle-class black woman; young mother; slacker; member of the Muscogee (Creek) Nation; well-adjusted; student; teacher; writer; an individual; a young lady; a person with a visible disability; androgynous; lapsed Jew; child of professional feminists; lesbian daughter; activist; zine writer; a Libra; and an educated, married, monogamous, feminist, Christian, African American mother. These identities all coexist (to varying degrees of comfort) with feminism. We are determined, as Sonja D. Curry-Johnson writes, "to bring our whole selves to the table."

Young feminists are constantly told that we don't exist. It's a refrain heard from older feminists as well as in the popular media: "Young women don't consider themselves feminists." Actually, a lot of us do. And many more of us have integrated feminist values into our lives, whether or not we choose to use the label "feminist." This is an important barometer of the impact of feminism, since feminism is a movement for social change—not an organization doing a membership drive.

But, as is made clear by several of the writers in this book, some young women do fear the feminist label, largely because of the stereotypes and distortions that still abound. If something or someone is appealing, fun or popular, it or she can't be feminist.

Feminists are still often assumed to be strident, man-hating, unattractive—and lesbian. I continue to be amazed at the power of that final "accusation," even though as a lesbian, I am well accustomed to the depth of the homophobia that pervades this country. The idea that all feminists are lesbians is scary enough for some women to stay away from the feminist label *and* movement even when their beliefs are basically feminist. When a young woman decides to identify as a feminist—a woman who stands up for herself and other women—she soon discovers at least two things: that women of all sexual identities are feminists, and that, even so, she will now be subject to the same stereotypes and dyke-baiting that may once have scared her away. But simply denying that all feminists are lesbians is not the way to right this wrong. We need to take the harder road of challenging the homophobia that gives this image its power.

One thing that becomes clear in reading these essays is that there's no singular "young feminist" take on the world. But more to the point, there's no one "feminist" take on the world, and there never has been. And that's one of the many ways in which there's more common ground than differences between young feminists and older feminists. The spirited voices in this collection are not "daughters" rebelling against the old-style politics of their "mothers." In fact, many of the writers in this anthology cite the writings and actions of older feminists as an integral part of their own development and beliefs. It is clear that the kinds of experiences that lead young women to feminism are often similar to those that have always led women into feminism, even though the personal circumstances and social context may differ.

If there is a troublesome legacy from the feminism that has come before, it's the burden of high expectations—of both ourselves and the world. Many young feminists describe growing up with the expectation that "you can do anything," whether that message came directly from parents or just from seeing barriers falling. But there's a point where you realize that while you may indeed feel capable of doing anything, you can be stopped—

because of sexism. Maybe you played Little League baseball but found yourself relegated to girls' softball at age thirteen. Maybe you were the smartest kid in your high school class, and were stunned the first time you heard a college professor say that women couldn't be great artists or mathematicians or athletes. Maybe your mother gave you *Our Bodies, Ourselves* and taught you to love your body, but that didn't stop you from being raped.

The moment when sexism steps into your path can be disappointing, humiliating, shocking. It can take away your breath, your hope, your faith in yourself, your faith in the world. The impact is even greater if you're not expecting it, if you have no framework for understanding that you are being mistreated because of your gender. Feminism is what helps us make sense of the unfairness by affirming that it's about political injustice, not personal failure. The feminist movement offers us strength to fight back.

This country hasn't heard enough from young feminists. We're here, and we have a lot to say about our ideas and hopes and struggles and our place within feminism. We haven't had many opportunities to tell our stories, but more of us are finding our voices and the tools to make them heard: books like this one, and also music, zines, newspapers, videos, the vote, letters to the editor, marches, conferences, the Net. This collection gives voice to young feminists' personal experiences because they have often been, and continue to be, our point of entry to feminism. But that's just the beginning. My hope is that this anthology—along with all the other platforms we are creating—will serve as a catalyst for consciousness, action and, ultimately, change in the lives of young women and those whose lives we touch.

Barbara Findlen
New York, New York
October 1994

Listen Up

Chicks Goin' at It

Anastasia Higginbotham

Aside from the occasional dream of being chased by a man throwing hot dogs at me, I consider myself a fairly well-adjusted feminist. Yes, I sometimes imagine myself alone, late at night, surrounded by candles; the scent of incense fills the air as I scribble on little slips of paper, "Howard Stern—AWAY," while a small doll, cut off at the waist and doused in gasoline, awaits its grim fate. . . . Still, for all intents and purposes, I think I coexist quite reasonably with the phalloexplosive media and institutions that surround me. Oh, there was that time I talked all through Thanksgiving dinner about why I consider the clitoris to be the jewel of human anatomy and the source of my strength and magic as a woman and feminist. But everyone was telling stories and I just wanted to participate.

I know now that I've overcome the angry stage. When the evening news made me cry and fraternity boys made me vomit. When I thought men who hate women were cowering assholes with too much testosterone and too little brain power. When I thought the fight to bring patriarchy to a screeching, jubilant halt was the only fight worth my time or anyone else's.

But, oh, I've changed from that bitter girl of seventeen. I'm now a bitter woman of twenty-three. I don't watch the news, and

I'm convinced that men who hate women are indeed cowering assholes with an exorbitant amount of testosterone and very little brain power, if any. I know that the fight to end patriarchy, to devour it, to deplete and dismember it in favor of a system that does not achieve cosmic orgasm through the oppression of others is a just and valiant fight. And I will continue to pursue this glorious end as long as my soul wanders the earth. Fraternity boys still make me vomit. But now I imagine vomiting on them rather than because of them. I've become a gastric avenger of sorts.

I wasn't always a feminist. In fact, I used to think feminists were sexually undesirable and perpetually angry. (Boy, was I wrong. Feminists are perpetually desirable, and I am sexually angry.) Prior to my feminist epiphany, I felt I was nothing more than big hair with a fellatio fetish, the worst part about this being that I thought I was pretty cool. In the time that has passed since then, I have grown from girl to woman, but more dramatically, I have been transformed from masochist to feminist.

The big hair, accompanied by moderately big breasts and a dancer's ass, all bundled into a squeezy purple dress, attracted all sorts of attention—all sorts dangerous. For one thing, I could have brought my high school to its knees on charges of sexual misconduct. My most serious encounter nearly led to an affair with a teacher who, despite the inappropriateness of his forty-seven-year-old affections for a fifteen-year-old girl, won me over somehow. Being near him made my stomach churn, my throat ache, my eyes blur. Though I wish it had been a temporary virus, I realize now it was probably terror, and at the time it seemed quite romantic. Another of my faculty suitors had a nasty habit of pressing his bulging manhood against my back as I sat in his class furiously taking notes to prove I was smart. They were charmers, all right.

It's appalling to me now, but at the time it felt normal and hardly bothered me. In fact, I thrived on making them all hard and then laughing in their faces at the obvious fact that they could never have me. I thought I was god's gift to men because I could play glam, sweetheart and harlot all in one shot. I had my pick, and like your typical fallen angel-to-be, I chose poorly.

I lost my virginity, or rather, rid myself of its intolerable presence. Virginity implied immaturity, stupidity and a dearth of passion—as such, I wanted no part of it. To me, virginity represented all the qualities of "girliness," none of which merited any respect at all from anyone, anywhere.

Furthermore, coming from a long line of passionate women, I felt drawn to the pleasures of flesh. But more than sexual contact, I wanted the hard edges that come from having a lot of sex with many lovers. My role models were the prostitutes in old Westerns who played poker with mean cowboys (and won). They swore in low, husky voices, were cynical but funny, carried guns in their garter belts and never needed men. I wanted to be scarred by love the way these women were. For what it's worth, I was successful in achieving my goal.

I began having vaginal intercourse—I'd already done everything else—with one of the men who, in middle school, had thrown my brother over a wall to prove his seventh-grade masculinity. Though he was never violent with me, I had yet to recognize a separation between sex/iness, violence and the romantic intrigue of scars. For example, I recall an incident in which my friends and I discussed going to see *The Accused*. They shared my sexually curious desire to see "the gang rape," as I said to them with a mischievous grin, "I heard they show it."

I left the movie theater the following weekend in tears, completely traumatized (scarred, in fact). I spent the next two days in exactly the same condition, crying for that woman, crying for myself and convinced that I would inevitably find myself pinned to a table by hovering, raping, evil men. My fear of rape and of men culminated in frequent nightmares about incest, murder and, of course, more rape.

The problem was not that I suffered an abusive childhood or bad luck, because I didn't. It was also not that I was weak or ill-prepared for life as a young adult in a world full of "adult" bookstores. It was simply that I was born a girl in a society that devalues women and girls. Bam. That easy. And because I lacked the words to describe my demons, I had no power to address them.

I know all kinds of words now. Words like revolution, equality, dignity, reproductive freedom. I've mistressed phrases like subvert the patriarchy, run with the wolves, and take back the night. Words of empowerment. The one word all phallocrats most fear (and well they should), I wear like a badge of honor, my pride, my work, my glowing, spiked tiara. That word is "feminist."

I became a feminist through other forms of activism—race education (my own) and gay rights. One shining moment of radicalization occurred in my Speech 105 class. I'd given a speech on gay, lesbian and bisexual rights—you know the ones I'm talking about. The right to not be beaten up, the right to not be thrown out of the house/church/military, the right to not die from a disease the ruling class chooses to ignore, that is, until they're the ones to get it, blah, blah, blah. Unreasonable demand after unreasonable demand.

So, I've just finished my tribute to queers everywhere, when a student raises his hand to ask me (the only question I received at all), "When you say 'homosexuals,' do you mean guys? Or chicks goin' at it, too?" Chicks goin' at it. Obviously, my rhetoric had sung its way into his tender, eager-to-be-enlightened heart. My calling into the world of gay activism.

Then there was the time I bought these hunky purple hiking boots, a look I'd admired from atop my three-and-a-half-inch heels for some time. I enhanced my purchase by wearing them with dresses, the nonclinging kind, and the most alarming thing happened. I began to walk differently. I no longer wobbled. I took bigger steps, surer steps, harder steps. A friend of mine wears boots anytime she waits tables to combat wobbliness in the face of the inevitable harassment endured by women in the service industry. It's clear to me now that every feminist, indeed every woman, needs a good, solid pair of boots. It's not just a symbolic assault on the patriarchy, it's a fashion statement. Like short hair.

I know because I cut the hell out of my long, curly hair. My mother loved it; my boyfriend hated it. (Duh.) He said it made him feel like he was making love to a boy. I found this particularly amusing since he had very long, very female hair, which provided just the touch I needed to reach orgasm with him. I suddenly realized why he was so upset. I apologized for not having warned him and told him I hoped that he would never cut his own hair. "I know exactly what you mean," I said.

So now we have the boots, the hair, the lesbian fantasy (more on this later), and, in my effort to dive headlong into the stereotypical/archetypal image of a feminist, I offer what was my next, triumphant step toward full-blown feminist liberation. Susan B. Anthony did it. Mary Ann Shadd Cary did it. Ida B. Wells did it, and so did Margaret Sanger. Heck, all the kids were doin' it. On the campus of Vanderbilt University, a place that quite resembles an old southern plantation crawling with J. Crew models and debutantes, I started a feminist newspaper with two womenfriends. The initiation, my rebirth—feminist at last.

We took on woman haters, Limbaugh lovers, date rapers, and the ever-popular, oh-so-predictable brothers (and sisters) of backlash. We lost sleep, I lost a three-year dean's list streak, we nearly went insane, and it was still some of the best fun I ever had in my life. Every heartbeat, every bit of energy, our very souls, we spent for that paper and for each other.

In my prefeminist incarnation, I was incapable of this kind of close relationship with women. Vanity, competition and superficial alliances more accurately describe my friendships with women then. But imagine my surprise as I took this intimacy even one step further when I ended up in bed with a dear friend and co-editor.

We only slept—that day. But we wrapped our bodies around one another and stayed that way, from early one Saturday afternoon to late in the evening. Some of the time I slept, some of the time I contemplated the curve of her hip, some of the time I imagined how we looked, lying there, me with this warm grin crawling across my face. We only slept. Anything more would have been redundant, excessive. I'd been introduced to a feeling I never knew existed. That moment of revelation satisfied me more than any sex ever could.

It also came as a shock to me, for about a minute. Then I put it into my own historical context. I had wondered whether or not I might be lesbian ever since the time the sound of k.d. lang's voice over my headphones made me blush. Plus, I consistently fantasized about women in order to get through sex with men. For, contrary to the much-publicized, rather unfortunate words of Naomi Wolf, the male body is neither home nor shelter to me. It's more like a really itchy blanket with some holes in it. And while I, too, have seen the word "love" trigger an erection, I have also seen the word "rape" inspire much of the same.

And though I know that my rejection of men is not what led me to the arms of women, my experiences with them certainly provided me with the impetus to go looking for something (and someone) else. Sleeping with men required more compromise and more effort than I was willing to make. Sleeping with women felt like just another extension of my sexuality and identity. It is also something I aspired to as a die-hard advocate for women. That's what troubled me.

My bedroom, as you might well expect, was full of politics. Ever since the moment I inherited the fiery skull of knowledge, my head and my bed swarmed with the power dynamics of sex: Who leads, who follows, when is it rape, when is it just bad sex and why do I so desperately hate it these days? But women, I thought, sex with women must be different.

It tormented me for months. I had these massive crushes on my best friend and my boss, and suddenly I was in angst over whether or not to tattoo a pink triangle on my forehead. But I worried (and still do occasionally) that I was taking on lesbianism out of loyalty to a cause, fearful that my capacity to sleep with the bad guys was bad for PR. Was I trying too hard to sleep with my politics? After all, with all my issues there was hardly room for anyone else in the bed. Why not take advantage? Or, worse yet, was I a wanna-be? A baby dyke? A lesbian chic groupie, flashing in the pan, wanting my fifteen minutes of fame on the cover of *Newsweek*? Or was I truly falling more in love with women, with spirited feminists and with my own womanhood than I had ever been with anyone?

Um . . . yes.

I figure you can fantasize about sleeping with women only so much before it stops being a fantasy and starts becoming a reality. And while I still have a bed full of feminist ideologies—combined with the world of women-loving women—I find they practically serve as erotica. "Tell me again in your sexiest voice how pathetic the Senate Judiciary Committee is while I light some candles and slip into my sleeveless 'Patriarchy Bites!' T-shirt." Rrowll.

Now, instead of arguing over the well-known fact (known by delinquent assholes) that "some women *like* hard-core S/M porn, eh, eh, whine, whine," I can argue over who knows more lines from *Thelma and Louise*. "You said you and me wuz gonna git outta town and for once jus' really let our hair down. Well, darlin', look out, 'cause my hair is comin' down."

So I'll tell you the truth: I still don't know if all of this makes me a lesbian. I'm definitely bisexual. And I only recently claimed that label for myself without fear of it implying indecisiveness, internalized all-out-lesbian homophobia or the perception that I'm just plain easy. I've known both straight and gay people who shunned it (the word, the deed and the person) for each of the biphobic reasons I just expressed. In the wake of this paranoia, on my part and theirs, I've allowed myself to conclude a few things.

I'm a Libra for goddess' sake. You better believe I'm indecisive! It's the only thing I know for sure at all! I can't even determine whether I'm right-handed or left-handed, just in case my left hand one day decides to assert itself. I'd feel terrible having given up on it before it was ready to come out—if you know what I mean. Needless to say, I only assumed I was straight all those years because nothing led me to believe otherwise. Hallelujah, I believe otherwise!

As far as fearing status as a true-blue lesbian, I'll tell ya, I came out two or three times in front of large audiences before it was even relevant to my personal life. In the heat of many a debate, we needed a lesbian, I took the bulldyke by the horns and BAM: instant lesbian. Short hair, raging feminist, swearing in front of faculty? As if they didn't already think it.

My campus environment proved just slightly less than fascist when it came to gay rights. I mean, it's not as if we had drag queens and biker dykes screamin' across the delicately manicured lawn. (If only we had! The mere thought makes my heart leap.) The atmosphere was more than hostile to even the most meager queer on campus. How can I say this without offending anyone? Do the words Bible-bangin' freaks all carryin' plastic fetuses in their backpacks mean anything to you? The only lesbians we had were these badass, underappreciated grad students and a philosophy professor. I think all the other lesbians transferred.

Besides, my alliance with lesbians, as a women-loving woman and feminist, has always been core to my political activism and identity. Feminists are routinely "accused" of being lesbians or man-haters (as if the two are synonymous). Straight feminists often scramble to defy this stereotype by proclaiming their unfailing love for men and their affinity for bikini waxes. Some subtly distance themselves from lesbians by wearing buttons that claim "straight but not narrow." This is bullshit to me. If being called a lesbian is an insult to me, then I am an insult to lesbians. Any feminist who fears being called lesbian, or who fears association with a movement demanding civil rights for gays, lesbians and bisexuals, is not worthy of being called feminist.

The only other reason that could prevent me from embracing my bisexual identity is the implication to others that I might be easy. Ain't no might about it. I am easy. But, as long as I'm safe, what the hell?

My favorite term (other than plain old "queer") is "bisexual lesbian." It just works for me. I don't expect a man to understand me; I don't applaud him if he does. My heart and my mind belong with other women-loving women.

So here I am. I have birthed of myself a wild and unruly feminist. I feast as often as possible with my womensisters under new and full moons. I am seriously in love with Susan B. Anthony, and I have the dearest little crush on Gloria Steinem (especially during her big hair stage—probably some kind of narcissistic throwback to my past). I don't think I could be prouder of the cause that fuels my existence. I certainly didn't expect this much support, encouragement and spiritual nourishment outside of the womb, but what a lovely surprise!

I offer my feminist flamboyance as a personal attack on the patriarchy. And to further hack at the roots of patriarchal power, I would like to co-opt a statement made by Sarah Grimké in 1838. (If there had been a Miss Feminist America Pageant in 1838, this answer to world peace would surely have taken the crown.) She wrote: "All I ask our brethren is, that they will take their feet from off our necks and permit us to stand upright on that ground which God designed us to occupy."[1] I'd like to reiterate (without the "God" part—whole other story), since apparently SOMEBODY wasn't in class that day. Give it up, would you? I'm so over it.

1. Gerda Lerner, *The Creation of Feminist Consciousness: From the Middle Ages to Eighteen-seventy* (New York: Oxford University Press, 1993), p. 162.

Ruminations of a Feminist Aerobics Instructor

Alisa L. Valdés

Just saying my title is enough to make most people laugh: feminist aerobics instructor. Huh? It's like being a fascist poet. People think you just can't. One day several years ago as I impelled my step class to eat whatever they wanted whenever they wanted, to love their thighs no matter what size, I was overwhelmed by all the uniquely American, female contradictions confronting me. The women in the class just stared at me with these blank, nearly hostile eyes. Hello? What part of "low-fat" didn't I understand? Couldn't I see how fat they were? What kind of aerobics instructor was I, anyway?

The answer was easy: a twenty-something, lower-middle-class musician/writer/social critic cum feminist aerobics instructor with big college loan payments and, therefore, a big, two-sided problem.

Part of the problem is this: In a lecture she gave at the Boston Public Library in 1991, the year of my emerging feminism, Gloria Steinem pointed out that women are a permanent underclass in the United States of America; because of our economic inequity, we comprise a third-world nation within the borders of our own developed country. There is no argument. In 1991, women still earned only seventy-one cents to every dollar earned by a man, and a college-educated woman could (and still can) expect to earn the same as or less than her male colleague with only a high school diploma. If we are ever going to progress, we are going to have to achieve economic equality. Period.

In New York City, aerobics instructors, feminist and otherwise, earn between thirty-five and forty-five dollars an hour.

The second part of my problem is roughly this: In 1986, nutritionist Laurel Mellin did a study through the University of California at San Francisco called "Why Girls as Young as Nine Fear Fat and Go on Diets To Lose Weight." Probably we don't need to know much more than the title to feel depressed, but in this study fifty percent of the nine-year-olds, and nearly eighty percent of the ten- and eleven-year-olds, had "put themselves on a diet because they thought they were too fat." According to some experts, eating disorders were "the disease" of the seventies and have only been getting worse since then, despite being eclipsed by AIDS since the mid-eighties. And this: Studies show that seventy-five percent of adult women in this country think we are too fat, though only twenty-five percent of us actually weigh more than the standards set forth by Metropolitan Life's weight tables. And of course, there's always America's favorite doll, Barbie, by Mattel. If a woman of Barbie's proportions existed, she wouldn't be able to walk, breathe or digest food.

When I first started teaching aerobics I was fifteen years old. I did it for extra money and for a free membership to a health club. I'm not going to lie: I also did it to counter the geek factor of my adolescent existence. I was teased endlessly as a child for being overweight (*fatty fatty two-by-four, can't fit through the kitchen door* was my name), and once I actually lost weight, my parents wouldn't let me be a high school cheerleader like my best friends, Staci and Nana. Instead, they insisted that I go into band. Being a teenage aerobics instructor was a way for me to fight back on both fronts.

Even then I made about eight dollars an hour, which was great compared to the three and change I had earned wearing a greasy orange-and-brown uniform as a cashier at a local restaurant.

In early 1988, at the age of seventeen, I moved to Boston to study saxophone at the Berklee College of Music. One of the first things I did after arriving was secure a job for myself as an aerobics instructor at New England Aerobics and Nautilus, a women's gym a few blocks from school. My peers at Berklee were eighty-five percent male, so it was a good balance for me to enter that sweaty female domain where I could stand in front of the class and command and connect. The gym was one of the few places on earth where I actually felt I possessed an irrefutable degree of power. It hadn't occurred to me yet to analyze why so many brilliant, professional women were wasting so many hours every week hopping around in leotards. All I knew then was that it was a great job with good money, lots of other women, loud music and a kind of ritualized dancing that I got to choreograph. As fun and American as lite beer, buffalo wings and fried cheese.

Gradually, and somewhat to my astonishment, I became a *professional* instructor. By my senior year of college I had actually carved out a secondary career for myself in the aerobics industry in Boston, which was good since not too many jazz saxophonists or poets were making enough bread to pay back a loan such as the twenty-three thousand dollars I suddenly owed after graduation (no thanks to Uncle Reagan). I was teaching at the city's top clubs—places populated by women who carried attaché cases and men in ties, places with names like the Sky Club, Healthworks, the Squash Club and Boston Health and Swim Club—and getting about twenty-five dollars an hour for my perspirational efforts. Other friends from school were working as cashiers at Tower Records or as security guards at the Hines Convention Center, barely breaking minimum wage. I felt lucky.

I even invested in a license to train other instructors for the Aerobics and Fitness Association of America, one of the two major certification organizations in the country, and was soon able to make about three hundred dollars an hour for private clinics. I taught step, funk, Latin, high- and low-impact, body sculpting and stretch. I even entered an aerobics competition in 1992 with a male partner, and we grinned and bounced our way to second place in the New England regionals.

Soon I was heading the aerobics program at a club near Tufts University; at twenty-three I had my own office, a good salary and power over a whole staff of instructors, and I was presenting a master class at the Boston MetroSports Fitness Expo. People in the industry knew my name. Disc jockeys made free tapes for my classes. Reebok invited me to sit on its instructor board to help design its 1993 line of shoes. Reebok, Nike and Rykä shoe companies gave me freebies, just for being a good instructor. And I could pay back my loans. Though I kept telling myself I was really still a feminist, a musician and a writer, I was becoming a career instructor—sweating more, practicing less, writing less—and it was almost comfortable.

Almost, except for the gnawing ache of betrayal. I had read Alice Walker. I knew better than to encourage women's obsession with their appearance, including my own. I knew better than to freak out at my own cellulite, staying late after work to pump iron to make it go away. I knew better than to stand skinny in front of a room full of self-doubting women and actually say to them, "Okay, let's tone up." I had betrayed myself, betrayed my dreams; most of all I had betrayed my gender. But it was almost as if I, who spent the first years of my life in a housing project and have been living hand-to-mouth ever since, had no choice. The world had rewarded "Hispanic female" me not for being a writer or musician, but for being an aerobics instructor. I was a cheerleader after all, and I hadn't even noticed. Like many other women who bought the fitness lie, I had been duped into believing there was strength in, well, fat loss. Eventually, my conscience got the better of me. I quit everything fitness-oriented in Boston, packed my bags and moved to New York City to try to be a feminist writer and musician for real. At first it was groovy, but it was only a matter of time before my credit was canceled and the phone company lawyers were threatening me.

I landed a prestigious unpaid internship at the *Village Voice*, but ended up having to leave early and quite sloppily because I was also teaching fifteen to twenty aerobics classes a week to pay my bills. Commuting two hours a day, practicing my saxophone, writing consistently and holding down two jobs was too much; I just couldn't handle the pressure. The physical and emotional stress overwhelmed me: I was physically sick all the time, I slept on the bus home, I craved several boxes of doughnuts at once. So I quit the *Voice* when I really wanted to quit teaching. But there was no money at the *Voice*, and women, remember, are a permanent, albeit fit, underclass in our society.

Before long, I was a full-time aerobics instructor again, this time in Manhattan, at places with names like the Jeff Martin Studio, Molly Fox Fitness and Crunch Fitness, places that had articles written about them in those "women's" magazines, right next to articles about sticking to your diet or ten ways to make Him find you sexy again. I watched as my lifelong dream of being a professional feminist writer slipped through my fingers and back into my spandex and sneakers, all because I needed to pay for a roof over my head and the food in my stomach. I realized that only the children of the rich are able to afford to be entry-level journalists for the progressive publications of our nation. The poor become, well, cheerleaders for the status quo. Give me a "Y"! (Why!)

And that is my problem.

I say I was a cheerleader after all, and a part of me grimaces. I've tried hard to hold on to a shred of feminist dignity in all this jumping around. I made it a goal to battle the common misconception about aerobics instructors—that we are nothing but airheads in thongs.

I rationalized this femifitness philosophy in many ways. I grew convinced that there is actually a great deal of raw, primal energy and force in a room full of women moving together in time; a few of the editors from the *Voice*, feminists all of them (well, Pagliaesque, cutesy, Voicey, Madonna feminists at any rate), took classes at one of the studios I worked for. In real life, I reminded myself, women take aerobics classes in shorts and T-shirts; it is only on television that they all wear tights and thongs. And only on the ESPN programs that air in sports bars at eleven in the morning do aerobics instructors grin wildly and stick their asses in the air.

That dignified instructor part of me thought men, including Woody Allen, had sexified and bubblefied the image of aerobics instructor in order to claim ownership of one of our society's few appealing areas where men simply are not welcome. I thought, What could honestly be more frightening to men than a room full of capable, professional women moving together, in sync, unaware of anything but themselves and each other? Only Hillary Rodham Clinton and a truly lesbian orgy, perhaps.

And I found intellectual polemics to support my misdirected theory. In 1989 Roberta Pollack Seid wrote that "ten years ago vigorous exercise was seen as the province primarily of young men. Today women have smashed the sex barrier that once excluded them from this 'male' domain."[1] Right on, part of me gurgled over the water fountain. Not only had we smashed the barriers, but through our organized dance exercise, we had also created a girls' club where women work for women and make money off of and for women (albeit with a sociopolitically skewed agenda).

Iris Marion Young, a professor from the University of Pittsburgh who has written extensively on gender differences in motility in our society, wrote that there are "certain observable and rather ordinary ways in which women in our society typically comport themselves and move differently from the ways that men do."[2] She documents that we take proportionally shorter steps than men do, keep our arms in close to us when we walk (whereas men swing freely) and stand with our legs closer together. She argues that the cliché way boys and girls throw a ball differently is an outward manifestation of an across-the-board social conditioning to female inferiority; and she adds that until a human can trust her body to actually comport itself in the direction of its possibilities, the possibilities will remain overlooked. The aerobics studio, then, I told myself, is one of the few places women let go of these inhibitions and trust their bodies to move *big*. By hopping and squatting hundreds of women throughout the week, I was moving women toward self-realization.

Young also writes that in everyday life women "fail to summon the full possibilities of our muscular coordination, position, poise, and bearing."[3] I knew the high of that endorphin-assisted moment in the middle of each class when women summon the very core of their strength, and I had seen it shine. Maybe that's why I taught, because seeing and directing a room full of women who were summoning their full possibilities was a charge, even if the motive was ultimately less than feminist.

Finally, both Young and my hero Robin Morgan have argued that consciousness as a human being is related not to the intellect alone, but also to the body; the body is the vehicle through which everything comes to and goes from us. I think that maybe this is why I taught, as well: to dance, to connect with my body in a tangible way so that I could better connect with my intellect and assist others in doing the same. The process of strengthening the body could also strengthen women's ability to achieve our goals. Never mind that often those goals—to achieve a flat tummy, to fit into that tiny wedding dress, to lose ten pounds before going to Club Med to find Mr. Right—do not exactly subvert patriarchy. Creating a psychological space where women could move, really move, was the thrill. Teaching was my way of doing battle with the one idea expressed by Simone de Beauvoir that I vehemently disagreed with: that the female body is ultimately a burden. I tried to bring joy and movement into that body. In a word, I backwardly justified what I did as empowerment.

Interestingly, Young points out that her research does not include "movement that does not have a particular aim—for example, dancing." Ah. But dancing, aerobic dancing in particular, does have an aim, and this is where all of my aerobi-feminist convictions have turned on me. The aim, usually, is to be thin and beautiful, or as one of my fifty-year-old clients wrote on her release form, "to be 21 years old, 115 pounds, and Beautiful [sic]."

Women's fitness as we now know it truly is our newest patriarchal religion, based in principle as much on ritualized pain and suffering as any of the Judeo-Christian ones that came before it. No wonder nobody trusts Jane Fonda anymore. Fitness is a rigid religion of style, as debilitating and oppressive for many as a corset. Anorexics fill my classes like worshipers in a church, and no one stares. Other instructors starve themselves and do cocaine for energy with a regularity that would surprise many of their admirers. *She's so thin*, the members whisper admiringly in the locker room, *she looks great*. "In earlier centuries," writes Seid, "people who exhibited such mastery over hunger were categorized either as saints or as possessed by the devil, or, like the sixteenth-century Fasting Girl of Couflens, they were regarded as marvels whom travelers flocked to see. Today, that awe has become a horrified fascination, not because of the rarity of the phenomenon, but because of its increasing commonplaceness."[4]

So by the time I reached twenty-three, I really began to think about my priorities. Might it be worth going into debt to attend graduate school, just so that one day I could pull myself away from the contradictions? I thought about myself, about my assisting other women to betray their potential. And it was a great relief to finally recognize the female obsession with thinness and fitness as an extension of the hurt we suffer at the hands of a patriarchal society, a society that even convinces us to hurt ourselves, so that we are kept from the real business of our lives.

I had to battle the hurt. I'd go into debt. I did. I am. Two years later I owe nearly forty thousand dollars in loans, but I have a gig as a staff writer for the *Boston Globe*, because my graduate degree from Columbia, while it might not have helped my writing, convinced some editors I was made of the right stuff.

This debt, the one I will have to feed from my bank account for the next couple of decades, is what happened to me because of my second-class citizenship and economic disadvantage. I was distracted for a time from the more serious pursuit of actually hustling to make a living as a writer and musician.

The *Globe* has given me a biweekly fitness column, something

I find ironic but challenging. I try to avoid fueling fitness obsession. I've written columns on kid-friendly gyms, community centers that have programs for seniors, how to use objects in the home to strengthen muscles—anything that doesn't evoke spandex. I understand now that the gym has really become just another painful way we are all distracted from the serious business of our lives.

It seems that no matter how close I have gotten to empowerment through the modern fitness industry—women bosses and coworkers, good salary, the opportunity to connect with and help other women—there is still the knowledge that none of us, instructors or members, will ever reach our real goals playing by the rules of that industry, no matter how many inches we shed, no matter how much money we make.

1. Roberta Pollack Seid, *Never Too Thin: Why Women Are at War with Their Bodies* (New York: Prentice Hall, 1989), p. 8.

2. Iris Marion Young, *Throwing Like a Girl and Other Essays in Feminist Philosophy and Social Theory* (Bloomington: Indiana University Press, 1990), p. 143.

3. Young, p. 145.

4. Seid, p. 21.

Betrayal Feminism

Veronica Chambers

It was a sinking feeling in the pit of my gut. Not anger really, but disappointment. I am talking about the first time feminism broke my heart. I was a college student in the late eighties, espousing feminism with the fervor and delight with which I had espoused black studies. Being black and female all my life, I had felt a double invisibility, like the double veil that W.E.B. Du Bois wrote about in *The Souls of Black Folk*. When I discovered black studies and women's studies, I felt that I had learned to speak all over again. There was a context for my particular existence. A vocabulary for my situation. An agenda to empower myself and others.

Little did I know that women's studies and black studies were not too different from those old water faucets where both hot water and cold water run, but never shall the two meet. Growing up in the black community, I knew that sexism often accompanied an Afrocentric perspective. What I was not ready for was the racism of white women, women who called themselves progressive, liberal, even radical. And when the trust I put in these women—and in what increasingly felt like *their* movement—was betrayed, I felt hurt and confused. It would not be the last time.

Recently I went to the library to research black women feminists. I typed the words "African American," "women" and "feminists" into the reference computer. The machine searched all the recent magazine articles that included all three words. I found three articles—two by bell hooks, one by Rebecca Walker. It's not that there aren't black feminists, but the journals and periodicals that they appear in tend to be small and underfunded and don't make it into the *Reader's Guide* database. In larger and more mainstream media, coverage for and about feminists too often focuses on white women feminists. As a result, the presence of black women has been all but erased by the media and, in turn, the history books.

To be a young, black feminist today, I believe, is to feel unsure that your needs and interests can be fully addressed in any one camp. It seems that for sanity's sake you must choose sides—your skin color versus your gender, blacks (implicitly male) versus women (implicitly white). Because of the pressing problems in the community—poverty, drugs, men's absence from many of our families—most young black women choose to play the game like boys on a b-ball court. When it comes down to picking teams— skins vs. shirts—most of us opt to play skin, shedding our gender questions like a layer of clothing that becomes tedious and superfluous on a hot ghetto day.

As rapper Heavy D. put it, "Picking cotton was hard, but we picked it together." In the United States, in 1995, black women and black men are not together—in our families or in our communities. This is something that white women often fail to understand— that for us, unifying the community is of paramount importance. Our struggle is not just with the black male "patriarchy"; it is often more complicated than that. In this society, black men are increasingly powerless and too often believe themselves to be powerless. Too many of them take their anger out on the only people they feel are within their domain—"their" women and children. It is wrong. It is unfair. And it is frightening. But it is also pitiful.

I have seen the look in my father's eyes after he has been pulled over by the police for driving what they deemed a "pimp-mobile," a Lincoln Continental. I have watched my brother be transformed from a kid who loved cartoons and video games to a boy 'n the hood, a so-called menace to society. But I have also watched him come home and hang his head in shame because he has no money, he has no high school diploma and he has a police record. He is twenty-one years old and he already acts like a broken man. I have looked into the eyes of lovers and friends and seen fear, disappointment and weakness. I have sat on the subway and watched old black men, my grandfather's age, sing and dance, cup in hand, like Sambo or a modern-day minstrel show. I've watched white people clap and smile and oblige with spare change, seemingly unaware of how degrading it is for a seventy-year-old black man to sing 1920s ditties for his supper. I believe in the African traditions of ancestral worship and elder-run societies. Every time I see an old black man beg, my heart is heavy with pain. These are my brothers and my father figures—any feminism that I embrace must be humanist enough to recognize that they have also been wronged.

Seven years ago I went to Simon's Rock College, a good liberal arts, liberal politics school in western Massachusetts. Like many young women of all colors and ethnic backgrounds, I had my first feminist awakening at college. Through books and classes and a dynamic women's studies teacher, Dr. Patricia Sharpe, I found Simone de Beauvoir and Gloria Steinem, Alice Walker and Paula Gunn Allen. My first year, Barbara Smith gave a lecture, and for me, she was like a silver-screen apparition. Black *and* feminist—a rare bird that I'd only read about and never actually seen.

I come from a family of strong black women, but to my mother, feminism was a four-letter word. To the people in my neighborhood, feminists were man-haters. Feminists were also referred to as lesbians—a stigmatized status, given the rampant homophobia in the black community. To be strong, smart, independent and *unashamed* were necessary elements for survival in the Brooklyn of my youth. The black women I knew growing up embodied these qualities with the wiles and grace of Amazon warriors. They were, in other words, sisters who didn't take no shit. I knew strength, and I was taught from birth, "Don't allow no man to walk all over you." My mother, once a battered wife, had lived many years in fear and gave me strength as my most valuable inheritance. She had a small but potent circle of women friends who could count on each other for sustenance, both physical and emotional; who encouraged each other to keep on keepin' on; who were good for advice and for actual physical help—if you needed to move, if you needed someone to watch the kids, if you needed to know how to deal with your creep of a boss at work.

When I bought Barbara Smith's *Home Girls: A Black Feminist Anthology*, I carried it like a prayer book. It was in this book that I first read Audre Lorde, Michelle Cliff, June Jordan and Luisah Teish. When I read Michelle Cliff's "If I Could Write This in Fire, I Would Write This in Fire," the title alone reverberated in my head like a drumbeat. As I continued my readings, I realized that in all incarnations of the women's movement, black women were there. At the turn of the century, there were black women who were both abolitionists and suffragists. There were black women in the sixties and seventies giving their time and effort to the struggle, demanding that white men and white women take them seriously. When white women talked about equality, we insisted that they mean black women too. But as it was, at any table of discussion our specific issues were—and still often are—low on the list of priorities. Even among feminists, we are "minorities." That simply isn't good enough.

White feminists of earlier generations have passed these values onto their daughters. The young women I went to school with, for all their notions of feminism, still basked in the glory and privilege of their whiteness. I remember being very upset during a first-year English class because on the day when we were supposed to have read a Toni Cade Bambara story, no one in the class had read it except me. The white boys I dismissed more readily—I knew they didn't care. But the white girls, the same ones who would proclaim their sisterhood time after time, had simply been too lazy or too uninterested to read the only story by a black woman on our syllabus. Was it racist? No, of course not. But it was insensitive and myopic, and I was furious. Hadn't I read Willa Cather? Hadn't

I dived right into Margaret Atwood? Hadn't I explored worlds foreign to my own? I guess that was why I had been so excited to read the Toni Cade Bambara story. I wanted the class to know what my world was like, what our parties were like, what my people were like. It seemed nobody, including the white women, cared.

My junior year, I was awarded a women's studies scholarship to complement the "minority" scholarship that had enabled me to attend this expensive college in the first place. Outside of class, I became active in both "minority" student groups and the wimmin's center. Often at the wimmin's center, I'd be one of only a handful of women of color. I tried to persuade my black friends to come, but they just weren't interested. Little by little, I became frustrated with being the token black at the women's activities. Like many black women before me, I learned the hard way that some people, including many white feminists, like having blacks at their meetings and social gatherings. Whether you were happy there, whether you were taken seriously there, was beside the point. To have a black presence was and is trendy. It is politically correct. But when it came down to it, I could not trust most white women to have my back.

Every couple of months, one or another of the glossy women's magazines runs an article about shoplifting. Take, for example, an article entitled "The Thrill of the Steal" by Kathryn Harrison that appeared in *Mademoiselle* in October of 1993. Like many of these pieces, this one suggests that a lot of women shoplift as an act of female aggression against the big, bad male system of capitalism. "The stores from which women steal," Harrison writes, "together with the apparatus for detection and apprehension, are often experienced as masculine and patriarchal worlds."

What Harrison doesn't say is that those are essentially white patriarchal worlds. If shoplifting can be construed as a feminist act, then whose feminist act is it? My black female friends could never take such a "feminist" stand because *we* would be caught.

We are tailed in every store we enter, from Kmart to Blooming-dales to Saks Fifth Avenue. We are harassed and assumed to be "browsing"/"shoplifting" wherever we go. My friends Sarah and Renée, on the other hand, card-carrying feminists that they are, are habitual shoplifters. It is "getting even," Sarah says with glee, mailing me a copy of the *Mademoiselle* article. No wonder black women sometimes feel that they have no time for white women. Sisterhood, sometimes, is simply trifling.

Another major obstacle among feminists of my generation is how black women are still expected to fit white standards of beauty and how little white women acknowledge or understand this. While white women are also held to unreasonable beauty stan-dards, it is frustrating how often many women try to skirt around the reality that racism adds another potent strain to the standards of beauty that black women are held to. To say simply, "I don't look like Cindy Crawford either," or "I think Whitney Houston is *really* beautiful," doesn't address the real pain that many black women have experienced. We are still acculturated to hate our dark skin, our kinky hair, our full figures. "What are you going to do? You can't dye your skin," African American model Veronica Webb said in a recent interview. What are you gonna do? You're not gonna talk to your white sisters because they're so busy being defensive, so busy assuring you that they aren't racist, that they rarely hear what you're saying at all.

It was with this feeling of disappointment and betrayal that I read Naomi Wolf's *The Beauty Myth*. Surely, Wolf would address how the tyranny of the beauty myth had scarred so many women of color—not only black women, but Asian, Latina and American Indian women as well. She did not. And as far as I could tell, in all of the media hoopla that surrounded her, neither the white press nor the black press called her on it. Furthermore, Wolf made the classic mistake of positing blacks versus women as if six percent of the population—millions of women—were not both. "A black employee can now charge, sympathetically, that he doesn't *want* to look more white, and should not have to look more white in order to keep his job," writes Wolf. "Though the professional beauty qualification ranks women in a similar biological caste system, female identity is not yet recognized to be remotely as legitimate as racial identity (faintly though that is recognized)."[1] Notice that Wolf uses the generic "he" when she refers to a black employee. Moreover, by implying that blacks are somehow ahead of women in terms of cultural legitimacy, Wolf fails to recognize that for black women, by the very nature of their womanhood, this cannot be true. As for the rigidity of corporate society, Wolf does not even give voice to the many ways that black women *are* instructed to look as "white" as possible, especially with regard to their hair. She doesn't mention the African American flight attendant who brought a famous suit against her employers, who had fired her because she wore braids. She doesn't mention how often braids, dreads and even Afros are strictly prohibited in many workplaces, forcing many black women to straighten their hair and wear styles that are more "mainstream." In a book full of figures and facts and well-documented research, Wolf committed a classic act of betrayal feminism. Maybe she did not know about the issues that face black women and other women of color. But she should have made it her business to find out.

It is this sense of invisibility and betrayal that makes many young feminists of color think that the idea of a women's movement may not necessarily serve their best interests. Better, some contend, to work within your cultural and multicultural frameworks to infuse the men with a broader ideology. I stand on the shoulders of women like Barbara Smith, Audre Lorde and Luisah Teish, but I suffer as they did from a numbing isolation. I cannot change the mind of every white feminist that I encounter. That is not my interest or my job. Unfortunately, within white women's organizations, what little female solidarity I feel is overshadowed by a much greater sense of tokenism, racism, ignorance and condescension. I continue with my work because I know that eventually something must give. But looking at how far we have come since the sixties and seventies shows that among women, racism remains too big a beast for black women to conquer alone. White women must look within themselves and their organizations and address the issue of why more women of color do not stand by their side. Only then will we be any closer to truly being sisters.

1. Naomi Wolf, *The Beauty Myth* (New York: Anchor Books, 1992), p. 55.

Imagine My Surprise

Ellen Neuborne

When my editor called me into his office and told me to shut the door, I was braced to argue. I made a mental note to stand my ground.

It was behind the closed door of his office that I realized I'd been programmed by the sexists.

We argued about the handling of one of my stories. He told me not to criticize him. I continued to disagree. That's when it happened.

He stood up, walked to where I was sitting. He completely filled my field of vision. He said, "Lower your voice when you speak to me."

And I did.

I still can't believe it.

This was not supposed to happen to me. I am the child of professional feminists. My father is a civil rights lawyer. My mother heads the NOW Legal Defense and Education Fund. She sues sexists for a living. I was raised on a pure, unadulterated feminist ethic.

That didn't help.

Looking back on the moment, I should have said, "Step back out of my face and we'll continue this discussion like humans."

I didn't.

I said, "Sorry."

Sorry!

I had no idea twenty-some years of feminist upbringing would fail me at that moment. Understand, it is not his actions I am criticizing; it is mine. He was a bully. But the response was my own. A man confronted me. My sexist programming kicked in. I backed off. I said, "Sorry."

I don't understand where the programming began. I had been taught that girls could do anything boys could do. Equality of the sexes was an unimpeachable truth. Before that day in the editor's office, if you'd asked me how I might handle such a confrontation, I never would have said, "I'd apologize."

I'm a good feminist. I would never apologize for having a different opinion.

But I did.

Programming. It is the subtle work of an unequal world that even the best of feminist parenting couldn't overcome. It is the force that sneaks up on us even as we think that we are getting ahead with the best of the guys. I would never have believed in its existence. But having heard it, amazingly, escape from my own mouth, I am starting to recognize its pattern.

When you are told you are causing trouble, and you regret having raised conflict, that's your programming.

When you keep silent, though you know the answer—programming.

When you do not take credit for your success, or you suggest that your part in it was really minimal—programming.

When a man tells you to lower your voice, and you do, and you apologize—programming.

The message of this programming is unrelentingly clear: Keep quiet.

I am a daughter of the movement. How did I fall for this?

I thought the battle had been won. I thought that sexism was a remote experience, like the Depression. Gloria had taken care of all that in the seventies.

Imagine my surprise.

And while I was blissfully unaware, the perpetrators were getting smarter.

What my mother taught me to look for—pats on the butt, honey, sweetie, cupcake, make me some coffee—are not the methods of choice for today's sexists. Those were just the fringes of what they were really up to. Sadly, enough of them have figured out how to mouth the words of equality while still behaving like pigs. They're harder to spot.

At my first newspaper job in Vermont, I covered my city's effort to collect food and money to help a southern town ravaged by a hurricane. I covered the story from the early fund-raising efforts right up to the day before I was to ride with the aid caravan down South. At that point I was taken off the story and it was reassigned to a male reporter. (It wasn't even his beat; he covered education.) It would be too long a drive for me, I was told. I wouldn't get enough sleep to do the story.

He may as well have said "beauty rest." But I didn't get it. At least not right away. He seemed, in voice and manner, to be concerned about me. It worked. A man got the big story. And I got to stay home. It was a classic example of a woman being kept out of a plum project "for her own good," yet while in the newsroom, hearing this explanation about sleep and long drives, I sat there nodding.

Do you think you would do better? Do you think you would recognize sexism at work immediately?

Are you sure?

Programming is a powerful thing. It makes you lazy. It makes you vulnerable. And until you can recognize that it's there, it works for the opposition. It makes you lower your voice.

It is a dangerous thing to assume that just because we were raised in a feminist era, we are safe. We are not. They are still after us.

And it is equally dangerous for our mothers to assume that

because we are children of the movement, we are equipped to stand our ground. In many cases, we are unarmed.

The old battle strategies aren't enough, largely because the opposition is using new weaponry. The man in my office who made a nuisance of himself by asking me out repeatedly did so through the computer messaging system. Discreet. Subtle. No one to see him being a pig. Following me around would have been obvious. This way, he looked perfectly normal, and I constantly had to delete his overtures from my E-mail files. Mom couldn't have warned me about E-mail.

Then there is the danger from other women. Those at the top who don't mentor other women because if they made it on their own, so should subsequent generations. Women who say there is just one "woman's slot" at the top power level, and to get there you must kill off your female competition. Women who maintain a conspiracy of silence, refusing to speak up when they witness or even experience sexism, for fear of reprisals. These are dangers from within our ranks. When I went to work, I assumed other women were my allies.

Again, imagine my surprise.

I once warned a newly hired secretary that her boss had a history of discrimination against young women. She seemed intensely interested in the conversation at the time. Apparently as soon as I walked away, she repeated the entire conversation to her boss. My heart was in the right place. But my brain was not. Because, as I learned that day, sisterhood does not pay the bills. For younger women who think they do not need the feminist movement to get ahead, sisterhood is the first sentiment to fall by the wayside. In a world that looks safe, where men say all the right things and office policies have all the right words, who needs sisterhood?

We do. More than we ever have. Because they are smooth, because they are our bosses and control our careers, because they are hoping we will kill each other off so they won't have to bother. Because of all the subtle sexism that you hardly notice until it has already hit you. That is why you need the movement.

On days when you think the battle is over, the cause has been won, look around you to see what women today still face. The examples are out there.

On college campuses, there is a new game called rodeo. A man takes a woman back to his room, initiates sexual intercourse, and then a group of his friends barges in. The object of this game is for the man to keep his date pinned as long as possible.

Men are still afraid of smart women. When Ruth Bader Ginsburg was nominated to the Supreme Court, the *New York Times* described her as "a woman who handled her intelligence gracefully." The message: If you're smarter than the men around you, be sure to keep your voice down. Wouldn't want to be considered ungraceful.

A friend from high school calls to tell me he's getting married. He's found the perfect girl. She's bright, she's funny and she's willing to take his last name. That makes them less likely to get divorced, he maintains. "She's showing me she's not holding out."

In offices, women with babies are easy targets. I've seen the pattern played out over and over. One woman I know put in ten years with the company, but once she returned from maternity leave, she was marked. Every attempt to leave on time to pick up her baby at day care was chalked up as a "productivity problem." Every request to work part-time was deemed troublemaking. I sat just a few desks away. I witnessed her arguments. I heard the editors gossip when she was absent. One Monday we came into work and her desk had been cleaned out.

Another woman closer to my age also wanted to work part-time after the birth of her son. She was told that was unacceptable. She quit. There was no announcement. No good-bye party. No card for everyone in the office to sign. The week she disappeared from the office, we had a party for a man who was leaving to take a new job. We also were asked to contribute to a gift fund for another man who had already quit for a job in the Clinton administration.

But for the women with babies who were disappeared, nothing happened. And when I talked about the fact that women with babies tended to vanish, I was hauled into my boss' office for a re-education session. He spent twenty minutes telling me what a great feminist he was and that if I ever thought differently, I should leave the company. No question about the message there: Shut up.

I used to believe that my feminist politics would make me strong. I thought strong thoughts. I held strong beliefs. I thought that would protect me. But all it did was make me aware of how badly I slipped when I lowered my voice and apologized for having a divergent opinion. For all my right thinking, I did not fight back. But I have learned something. I've learned it takes practice to be a strong feminist. It's not an instinct you can draw on at will—no matter how equality-minded your upbringing. It needs exercise. You have to think to know your own mind. You have to battle to work in today's workplace. It was nice to grow up thinking this was an equal world. But it's not.

I have learned to listen for the sound of my programming. I listen carefully for the *Sorry*s, the *You're right*s. Are they deserved? Or did I offer them up without thinking, as though I had been programmed? Have you? Are you sure?

I have changed my ways. I am louder and quicker to point out sexism when I see it. And it's amazing what you can see when you are not hiding behind the warm, fuzzy glow of past feminist victories. It does not make me popular in the office. It does not even make me popular with women. Plenty of my female colleagues would prefer I quit rocking the boat. One read a draft of this essay and suggested I change the phrase "fight back" to "stand my ground" in order to "send a better message."

But after falling for the smooth talk and after hearing programmed acquiescence spew from my mouth, I know what message I am trying to send: Raise your voice. And I am sending it as much to myself as to anyone else.

I've changed what I want from the women's movement. I used to think it was for political theory, for bigger goals that didn't include my daily life. When I was growing up, the rhetoric we heard involved the theory of equality: Were men and women really equal?

Were there biological differences that made men superior? Could women overcome their stigma as "the weaker sex"? Was a woman's place really in the home?

These were ideas. Important, ground-breaking, mind-changing debates. But the feminism I was raised on was very cerebral. It forced a world full of people to change the way they think about women. I want more than their minds. I want to see them do it.

The theory of equality has been well fought for by our mothers. Now let's talk about how to talk, how to work, how to fight sexism here on the ground, in our lives. All the offices I have worked in have lovely, right-thinking policy statements. But the theory doesn't necessarily translate into action. I'm ready to take up that part of the battle.

I know that sitting on the sidelines will not get me what I want from my movement. And it is mine. Younger feminists have long felt we needed to be invited to our mothers' party. But don't be fooled into thinking that feminism is old-fashioned. The movement is ours and we need it.

I am one of the oldest of my generation, so lovingly dubbed "X" by a disdainful media. To my peers, and to the women who follow after me, I warn you that your programming is intact. Your politics may be staunchly feminist, but they will not protect you if you are passive.

Listen for the attacks. They are quiet. They are subtle.

And listen for the jerk who will tell you to lower your voice. Tell him to get used to the noise. The next generation is coming.

Your Life As a Girl

Curtis Sittenfeld

In fifth grade, you can run faster than any other girl in your class. One day in the spring, the gym teacher has all of you do a timed mile, and by the third lap, half the girls are walking. You come in seventh, and the boys who are already finished stick up their hands, and you high-five them. When you play kickball you're the first girl to be picked, and when you play capture the flag you're the one who races across the other team's side to free the prisoners. At recess, you're the foursquare queen. You slam the red rubber ball onto your three opponents' patches of pavement, and you gloat when they get disqualified. Sometimes your teacher supervises, standing in a raincoat by the door to the school building. Once, after she's rung the bell to call you inside, you pass her, your body still tense and excited, your face flushed. She says in a low voice, a voice that sounds more like the one she uses with adults and not with the other children in your class, "Anna, aren't you being just a bit vicious?" The next time you're playing, you fumble and let the ball slide beyond the thin white lines that serve as boundaries.

By sixth grade, your friends no longer like foursquare. Neither, really, do you, though you teach the game to your younger sister and sometimes play it with her in your driveway, in the evenings. At school, you sit with the other girls on top of the jungle gym by the swing set, and you argue about how often you're sup-posed to shave your legs. Your friend Nell says every two days. You probably talk about other things, but later, you can't remem-ber what they are.

When Nell spends a Saturday night at your house, her boy-friend Steve calls seven times. At eleven o'clock, you grab the phone from Nell and say: "Steve, we have to go. My parents will be home soon, and they'll be mad if we're still talking to you." He protests but then relents and asks to say good-bye to Nell. You pass her the phone. After she's hung up, she says that he told her to tell you that you're a bitch.

You can't learn how to play football. Early in the winter of seventh grade, you stand with your junior high gym class on the field behind the cafeteria. The gym teacher, whose name is Ted and who has a mustache, goes over various kinds of passes. They all seem alike to you though, and mid-game, when someone tosses you the ball, you just stand there with no idea what to do. "Throw it," bellow the boys on your team, so you do, but you don't want to watch where it lands or who catches it. After that, for the re-maining weeks of football and even on into basketball and volley-ball season, you're careful to station yourself in the back, or at the edges, wherever you're least likely to be accountable.

In the spring, you get moved from the higher to the lower math class, because you have a C-plus average. At first, you don't mind because in lower math you have the best grade in your class. Your teacher, Mr. Willet, asks for the answers to problems he's working out on the chalkboard, and he's pleased when you respond. But sometimes he doesn't call on you, even when you're the only one raising your hand, and he says in a humorless voice: "Well, we all know Anna has the answer. Let's see if anyone else does." On the comments sent home to your parents, Mr. Willet writes that though he appreciates your hard work, he wishes you'd give other stu-dents a chance to speak. He says that you're intimidating them.

At the Halloween dance in eighth grade, when you and Nell are standing by the buffet table, Jimmy Wrightson appears from nowhere and says, "Hey, Anna, can I suck your tits?" At first you don't understand what he's said, but he's coming closer, and Nell is giggling, and then Jimmy is pawing you. You press your fists into his stomach, pushing him away. He smirks at you before he saunters back to where his friends are waiting. You still don't know what he's said, and you have to ask Nell.

You don't tell any teachers, of course. You're not a snitch, and besides, you can take care of yourself. In social studies class the following Monday, you're sitting next to Nate, one of Jimmy's friends. You ask why Jimmy tried to feel you up, and Nate shrugs and says, "Probably someone dared him to." You say, "Yeah, well it was kind of obnoxious." Nate gives you a scornful expression. "It was a joke," he says. "Take it easy."

You hear that Jimmy got ten dollars.

In the summers, you swim for the team at the country club near your house. Before your races you wander around in a huge T-shirt, and you never eat. You and your friends go on a thousand diets, and you don't say anything else as often as you say that you're fat. In June, your father keeps the air-conditioning blasting through your house. You always wear sweatpants, even though it's ninety degrees outside. You spend the mornings making elaborate desserts: lemon tarts, puddings, pies. You allow yourself to eat the batter but not the finished product. You jog in place, or you do jumping jacks, leaping around your kitchen like a crazy lady. Two or three years later, you find photographs of yourself from that summer when you were fourteen. The girl you see looks grim, pale and so thin her collarbone sticks out like a rod.

In ninth grade, you go away to boarding school, where you begin to practice making ashamed facial expressions in the mirror. You embarrass yourself on a daily basis, so you want to make sure you're acting appropriately. Everything about you is horrifying: your voice, body, hair, inability to be witty and panicky desires for approval and companionship. In classes you speak as infrequently as possible and walk around with your head lowered. You play on the soccer team, but if boys ever watch, you make only halfhearted attempts to kick the ball.

To your mother's dismay, you begin reading romance novels. The covers show chesty, lusty heroines in torn clothing and men with long hair and fierce stares. The premises of the stories are identical, though the specifics change: The man and woman are attracted to each other, they quarrel, they end up alone together, they have wild sex. The women always say they don't want it, but they really do. The characters live in eighteenth-century France or on the Scottish moors or in Hawaii. You start to think that you were born at the wrong time. You would have done better a hundred years ago, when a girl knew that she'd be protected, that she wouldn't have to find a man because one would come to claim her.

When you're in tenth grade the students who write for your high school yearbook compile a list of people's nicknames and what they're known for. You hear that for your roommate they're going to write "doesn't like cherries." This is supposed to be a subtly amusing reference to the fact that at a party in the fall, she had sex with a guy she barely knew. You go to the yearbook editor and say, looking at the floor, that you think your roommate would be very upset if that particular line were printed. Afterward you blush, which is something you've just begun to do. You're glad that you got the hang of it because there certainly is a lot for you to be ashamed of. When you walk away from the editor, you hear him murmur, "What a weirdo."

On your grandmother's bed, she has a small pillow that says in needlepoint, "Women are such expensive things." When you and your sister go to your grandmother's house for brunch, your grandmother gives the two of you advice about men. First off, she says, learn to dance. And be a good conversationalist. Read book reviews, and even read the newspaper from time to time, in case he's an intellectual. Never turn down a date, because he might have a handsome brother. Once when your mother cannot open a jam jar, she passes it to your father, and your grandmother says chirpily, "The women admit their natural inferiority." "I think I'm going to throw up," says your sister. You laugh as if you agree, but for a minute you're not even sure what she's referring to.

Every day during the summer after your junior year in high school, you run two miles to the country club, then you climb 250 flights on the StairMaster. You wear spandex shorts that make you feel like your legs are pieces of sausage, and you pant the whole time. Men stick their heads out the windows of their cars and hoot at you as you run past. At first you take their yells as compliments, but you realize how hideous you look, and then you realize that they aren't seeing you, not as a person. They are seeing you as long hair and bare legs, and you are frightened. Recently, you have found yourself wishing that you'd get raped now, and then it would be done with. It will happen sooner or later; you've read the news reports, and you'd rather just get it out of the way.

Senior year, you develop a schedule: Sunday mornings you burn your skin. Not in glory, though, not you: What you do is rub hot wax onto your calves, and then for half a day, your legs are as smooth as pebbles. Or you use rotating silver coils that rip out hair from the root, or you use bleaching cream. You stand in front of the mirror, bleeding and stinging and knowing full well that the boys in your class will never think you're beautiful anyway.

Sometimes the boys are just so rich and handsome and indifferent. They get drunk on Saturday nights, and after they've seen a movie with an attractive woman in it, they say, "Hell yeah, I'd do her." It is hard to explain how your insides collapse when they say those words, how far apart from them you start to feel. Maybe they don't know that you want terribly to like them, or maybe they know that you'll like them anyway, however they act. When you protest, even mildly, the boys have words for you: cunt, ho, bitch. They say feminist like it's a nasty insult.

You've changed a little. You've read magazine articles that discuss other teenage girls who get eating disorders and flunk math, and now you know that you're a statistic, not a freak. Somewhere inside, you start to feel a little pissed off. You think of the fairy tales your mother read to you when you were small: Cinderella and Snow White and Rapunzel and the rest of their dippy, flaxen-haired sisters. You think of the songs you chanted with the neighborhood kids, tapping each other to see who had to be "it" when you were playing tag or hide-and-seek: "Inka-binka-bottle-of-ink/The cork falls off and you stink/Not because you're dirty/Not because you're clean/Just because you kissed the boy behind the magazine." Or, "My mother and your mother were hanging up clothes/My mother punched your mother in the nose/What color blood came out?" The world has given you two options: You can be a slut or a matron.

Late at night a kind of sadness descends and grips the girls in your dorm. You watch television shows about men and women who go to work in the morning, who experience amusing mishaps like getting stuck in elevators with their bosses or having their mother's parakeet die, and then they go on, to sleep or home or to more places where equally witty encounters are had by the handful. The characters' lives unfold in front of you, brisk and brightly colored, and you are sitting on the common room floor or on lumpy, worn couches, you're eating pork-flavored noodles and raw cookie dough, and you have four papers to write before Tuesday. You're waiting for your life to start.

And maybe the boys can save you. Maybe if you do sit-ups before you go to bed at night your stomach will be flat, and they'll love you well. Not that you actually believe that, not that you haven't been told a million times about just waiting until college where dozens of guys will treat you nicely. But you want love now, you want to have a boy standing there after you've failed a French test or fought with your roommate. The boy can hold you up with his strong arms and his common sense. You'll start to cry, and he'll get embarrassed and shuffle around and say, "Come on, Anna, don't worry like this." You'll worship his incoherence. You'll wish that you could stay up all night like he does. At two in the morning, guys watch the Home Shopping Network with the younger kids in the dorm, or they set up hockey games with bottles of ketchup, or they play complex tricks involving vacuum cleaners on each other, and the next morning they snore through math class.

Friday night the boy next to you is feeling playful. No one has more than three classes the following morning, so you stay at dinner an hour and a half. The boy keeps saying he's in love with you. He rubs your shoulders and says, "Your hair is magnificently soft," and everyone at the table cracks up. You say, "I forgot to wish you Happy Birthday yesterday," so he says, "Do it now," and he sticks out his cheek for you to kiss. You say, "No way!" You're grinning ferociously, you're practically hyper from the attention, and you think that if he offers you the option of kissing him, you couldn't be that gross after all. And then on Saturday morning, when you pass in the hall, he looks at you exhaustedly and says not a word.

Girls like you are well-fed and well-clothed and are loved by parents who send checks and say that you don't call home enough. Alumni return to tell you that when God was creating the world, He smiled just a little longer on your campus. On sunny days you believe this. But in the middle of the term, when the sky is gray and your notebooks are shabby and your skin is dry, it gets harder. The weather grows so cold it reminds you of cruelty.

You and your friends get sick with fevers, and you are hungry for something immense. You say, "Let's buy hamburgers, let's order pizza," and you walk to town blowing your noses on your parkas. At the grocery store you are so overwhelmed by the variety of food that you don't buy anything but Pepsi.

In the morning, after the heater has roared all night, your skin is so dehydrated you tell your roommate you're starting the Roasted Nostrils Club, only boarding school students need apply. You find yourself deliciously witty over toothpaste and Ivory soap, and then at breakfast you start slipping. It's the boys' tiredness. They kill you with their tiredness. You just wish they were more interested. You wish you knew the thing to say to make them stop shoveling oatmeal in their mouths. You want to shout, "Look at me! Dammit!" But you murmur, "I'm worried about the physics quiz/I heard it's supposed to rain tomorrow."

Once when it snows, you and your friends go to the lower

fields and make angels. Other eighteen-year-olds are enlisting in the army or getting married, but at boarding school, you still open Advent calendars. When a group of boys in your class comes over the hill and down toward where you are standing, you pack the snow into balls and throw them. The boys fly forward, retaliating, smothering you. The air is filled with powdery flakes and everyone is yelling and laughing. One of the boys grabs you around the waist and knocks you down, and he's on top of you, stuffing snow in your mouth. At first you are giggling, and then you are choking and spitting, and you say, "Stop, come on." Your hat has fallen off, and the boy is pressing his arm on your hair so that your head is pulled backward. "Please," you gasp. "Come on." For an instant, your eyes meet his. Your faces are only about three inches apart, and his stare is like a robot's. You think he is breaking your neck, you're going to die or be paralyzed. But then the other boys are wanting to leave, and the boy pulls away and towers over you.

"What the hell is wrong with you?" you ask. You're still lying on the ground shaking, but you're furious, which is something you haven't been for a long time. Your fury gives you power. "Why did you just do that?"

The boy grins sickeningly and says, "Suck it up, Anna." Then he turns and walks away.

You never tell your friends because you yourself can hardly believe it happened. Later, it seems like a nightmare—rapid, violent, vague. When you were a first-year student, there was a beautiful senior girl in your dorm, and her boyfriend was president of the student council. You heard that they'd go for walks off campus and get in fights. He'd beat her and leave her there, and later, bearing roses or pieces of jewelry, he'd apologize tearfully. It sounded glamorous to you, at the time.

When the sun is out, the boys tease you again. From across the quadrangle, they shout your name in an enthusiastic voice, then they walk over, thrilled to see you, and the golden sky shines down, lighting their hair from behind, and they are wonderfully good-looking and clever, and you think how absolutely happy they sometimes make you.

After class, you are feeling so good that you boldly announce they'd better do their parts of the lab that's due on Monday, and they give you a phony smile and turn away. They are walking with a boy you know less well than the other boys, and they gesture toward you and mutter something to him. You cannot hear everything they say, but you make out your name and the word "nagging." You have overstepped your boundaries, and they have put you in your place.

You've had trouble sleeping lately. You can fall asleep easily enough, but you awaken during the night as many as nine times. Often, your heart is pounding, and you have the sensation that you've narrowly missed something disastrous, but you never can identify what it was. The dark hours pass slowly, and when it's finally light outside, you start to relax. Your bones loosen, your head feels large and soft. You fall asleep again around dawn, and dreams from a long time ago come to you: across all the distance of your life so far, you go back to elementary school, to the afternoon when you ran a timed mile. The air was warm and green, your lungs were burning, and clear, pure lines of sweat fell down the sides of your face. You crossed the finish line, and your eyes met the eyes of the six boys who were already cooling down. For a minute, in the sunlight, they smiled at you, and you smiled back as if you all had something in common.

Better in the Bahamas? Not If You're a Feminist

Lisa Bowleg

"Be careful Lisa, most of those girls are lesbians, you know." This was my mother's rejoinder when, during a telephone call to her my sophomore year of college, I announced that I was a feminist. I remember a wry smile crossing my lips as her words echoed through my head. Her warning was a bit late: Unbeknownst to her, I had already come out as a lesbian. I found her prescience amusing, but I was more intrigued by the fact that even though she lived in the Bahamas, miles away from any organized feminist movement, my mother had fallen prey to that popular myth: All feminists are lesbians.

Bahamians hold no monopoly on misconceptions about feminism. The current U.S. sociopolitical climate is rife with rhetoric about man-hating feminists and feminists who prey on other women. Who can forget that during the 1992 presidential campaign, Pat Robertson wrote a fanatical fund-raising letter opposing the insertion of the word "women" into the Iowa state constitution? Robertson claimed there was a "secret feminist agenda" that was "not about equal rights for women [but rather about] a socialist, anti-family political movement that encourages women to leave their husbands, kill their children, practice witchcraft, destroy capitalism and become lesbians."

My mother's misunderstanding about feminism was worrisome. Though incipient, my feminist identity was certainly becoming important to me, and I wanted her to know and understand this wonderful development. My hopes were quite unrealistic: Feminism was a novel concept to most Bahamians (after all, I have no memory of ever hearing the word "feminism" or any speech that could be construed as explicitly feminist during my childhood). I did not know it at the time, but that conversation was a harbinger of the conflict I would soon encounter as my friends and family, coming from our patriarchal Bahamian culture, struggled to understand my identity as a feminist.

Nassau, Bahamas has been my home for most of my life. I was born there in 1965 to a family that, by Bahamian standards, was solidly middle-class. My mother worked, as she still does, as a medical technologist, and my father taught biology at the high school level. My status as my parents' first child and the first grandchild of my maternal and paternal grandparents conferred a bounty of privileges such as love, attention and, of course, dreams and aspirations for my future. As in many middle-class families, education was prized. Both of my parents were college-educated, and the fact that I would attend college in the U.S. was unquestioned.

In 1986, I headed to Connecticut to attend the University of Hartford. My Aunt Coralee, not a blood relative but a dear and lifelong friend of my mother's, had called Hartford home for almost twenty years. Her presence made attending the university there especially appealing.

My mother and sister, Janelle, who was six years old at the time, traveled with me to Hartford for my college send-off. Although I shared most of the anxieties and fears of my fellow first-year students, mine were compounded by being a foreign student and far away from my home, family and friends. I spent much of my first year longing to be in Nassau with my loved ones. My homesickness was second only to my culture shock. Life at the

University of Hartford was a far cry from life in Nassau. Students at the university were predominantly white, very wealthy (I was astonished to discover that most of the luxury sports cars on campus belonged to students) and chose to socialize rather differently from folks in Nassau (a room with a keg of beer, no dancing, and food for which eating utensils were not required was not my idea of a party). My transition to university life and life away from home was soon eased by the friendships that I formed with the women who lived in my dormitory suite.

My sophomore year of college brought dramatic changes. Within the first few weeks of school I met Kim, a beautiful African American woman from Delaware who was also in her second year of college. Our friendship jelled quickly. We were middle-class black women in an environment where there were few, and we shared a passion for music, books and psychology. We soon assumed our position on the lesbian continuum. Feminist poet and writer Adrienne Rich has described the continuum as "a range— through each woman's life and throughout history—of woman-identified experience, not simply the fact that a woman has had or consciously desired genital sexual experience with another woman." Rich believes that her definition can be expanded "to embrace many more forms of primary intensity between and among women, including the sharing of a rich inner life, the bonding against male tyranny, the giving and receiving of practical and political support . . ."[1]

My bond with Kim inspired me to experience my femaleness in relation to myself and other women in a way that I had never before conceived or encountered. Life on the continuum was powerful, giddily overwhelming and liberating: I no longer felt compelled to wear makeup and marveled at the ease with which I came to appreciate my cosmetics-free face; I abruptly ended a series of unsatisfactory sexual dalliances with men on campus after discerning that what I had perceived as sexual freedom was neither liberating nor fun; and I eventually realized that I was romantically and sexually attracted to Kim. Shortly after discovering that Kim identified as lesbian, I professed my attraction to her and we became lovers. That summer, after I decided to transfer to Georgetown University, we decided to end the relationship rather than trying to make it work long-distance. I had no regrets about my decision to transfer. I was madly in love with Kim, but I desperately needed a more culturally diverse environment. Washington, D.C., nicknamed "Chocolate City," beckoned.

My first women's studies class at Georgetown further kindled my identity as a feminist. Margaret Stetz, a graceful and gentle-spoken white, middle-class woman with British mannerisms, was my professor. Margaret introduced me to the writings of feminists of color such as Cheryl Clarke, bell hooks, Audre Lorde, Barbara Smith and Beverly Smith. The thoughts and words of black lesbian feminists such as Lorde and the Smith sisters resonated deeply within me. We were black, female and lesbian in a culture that, when it recognized us at all, treated us with disdain and disrespect.

If alliances between women symbolize feminism in its broadest sense, then my entire girlhood was a lesson in feminist training. Although none of the women in my family has ever identified as feminist, these confident, independent career women were, in a sense, my earliest feminist role models. These fiercely loyal, intimate and keenly funny women introduced me to the wonderful world of womanhood and female bonding. The home of Mommie Rosie, my maternal grandmother, was the meeting place for impromptu and lively women's gatherings. Almost every day after school, my mother would take my younger brother, Jay, and me to visit Mommie Rosie. Within hours, Karen and Myo, my mother's two younger sisters who lived with my grandmother, would wander in from work and the fun would begin. Mommie Rosie's delicious Bahamian food provided the perfect backdrop for idle evenings filled with chat, gossip, teasing and laughter.

My childhood in the Bahamas was enjoyable, but when I returned to Nassau later as a feminist, I discovered that my Bahamian and feminist cultures clashed. In Nassau, my identity as a feminist and my predilection for vocalizing and defending the rights and concerns of women garnered me reactions of demeaning curiosity, hostility and rejection as "too American."

There was the time, for example, when I attended a party in Nassau during my summer vacation after my sophomore year of college. I was talking with a man and mentioned, although I cannot recall how or why, that I was a feminist. I might as well have told him that I had five retractable heads, because within seconds he had called his friends over to meet "a feminist." His friends seemed to take a perverse delight in bombarding me with derisive questions and comments such as "Oh, so you think men and women should have equal pay?" and "You know, the Bible says that men are superior to women."

On another occasion, Stephen, my "friend" from fourth grade, who was living in Washington, called me a feminist as an explative. We were returning to my office after a lunch date. I do not remember what we discussed during this stroll, but I do recall that after I made some pro-women statement, Stephen snorted, "You feminist! You feminist!" While I knew that feminism was an explative in many circles, I had never been the target of such anger. Stephen uttered his misogynist curse with the same tone of revulsion that Marc Lépine must have used when he exclaimed, "You're all a bunch of fucking feminists," before gunning down fourteen women in a University of Montreal classroom in 1989.

My most potent memory of my two worlds colliding is an interaction with Celeste, my closest girlhood friend. Although she was a school year ahead of me, Celeste and I were inseparable during our high school years and after. Five years ago, Celeste and her boyfriend, Peter, stayed at my apartment during a visit to Washington. On their last day in Washington, Celeste, in a gesture of gratitude, announced that she would cook a traditional Sunday Bahamian meal (peas and rice, baked macaroni, potato salad and chicken) and invite another Bahamian couple to join us. My mouth watered in anticipation of the meal (it had been ages since I had last tasted a real Bahamian dish) spiced with the company of fellow Bahamians. But my nostalgia and hopes for an enjoyable dining experience were soon soundly squelched.

The men cornered their turf: the living room TV set. Celeste and her friend retreated to theirs: the kitchen. I settled for the dining room table, where I observed Celeste and her friend obsequiously tending to the men and their requests for food and drink. Relax, Lisa, I assured myself. Surely the men will clean after we've finished eating. The food must have made me delirious because soon I was watching Celeste leave her unfinished plate to serve Peter seconds. Peter's request for dessert was the final straw. In full earshot of Peter and his friend, who by this time had returned to the television set, I told Celeste how disgusted I was about what I had just witnessed. Surprisingly, Celeste was not defensive. She calmly whispered, "Girl, you don't understand Bahamian men, girl. You been in America too long." I asked what being in America had to do with demanding social equity between men and women and an acknowledgment that women were not placed on earth to serve men. But my protests were dismissed as militant feminist rantings, and I was transformed from fellow native to antagonistic outsider. It was official: I was now an American.

The question at the core of these painful experiences is: How do we as women begin to integrate the traditions of our families and cultures within the cultures and lives that we have created for ourselves? One way is to create new families that affirm those parts of ourselves that we hold most dear. My chosen family in Washington now consists of a wonderfully diverse group of feminists such as my friends from academia, Cynthia and Kathy; social buddies such as Michelle, Patty and Sheila; and my home girls, Lori and Cindy.

Another is to search for ways to incorporate some of the traditions and cultures of the families into which we were born into the traditions and cultures that we have come to treasure. I was pleasantly surprised to learn that I could do this last year while visiting my family in Nassau. On our way home from the airport, Phyllis, my best friend from Washington, and I paid Mommie Rosie a visit (it also helps to take members of our chosen families with us when we visit our families of origin). As my dear grandmother and I got re-acquainted, I found myself embracing our relationship as women in a way that I had never consciously experienced. Several hours later, my aunts walked through the door and I was transported back to my childhood after-school days. As we chattered wildly and laughed loudly, it dawned on me that I was partaking in one of my chosen family's favorite activities. But these were not the women in my chosen family; this was my biological family—my mother, my grandmother, my aunts. Even though our lives had diverged over the years, there was still a bridge over which we could come together and connect intimately as women. In that moment, I had accomplished what I had struggled to do for the past six years. I had successfully integrated my feminist and Bahamian cultures. I was elated.

This ability to blend different aspects of our personal lives is not unlike the work that feminists seek to do in our political lives when we attempt to bridge our different races, ethnicities, nationalities, socioeconomic classes, abilities, ages and sexual preferences and orientations in a manner that is meaningful, noncompromising and productive. I find this the most appealing and promising aspect of feminism as a movement for social change.

The radical feminist quest to eradicate patriarchy has astounding implications for transforming the society that we now dread into one that is better for all women, men and children. However, feminists will not effect this transformation by insulating ourselves from nonfeminists and, as my grandmother would say, "preaching to the choir." If we isolate ourselves from others who do not identify as feminists or who know nothing about our ideology, we lose significant opportunities to inform and educate.

Feminist theorist bell hooks has called for a "door-to-door

movement to educate people about feminism."[2] Our first target in this door-to-door outreach can be those with whom we have the most contact—our open-minded family and friends. By speaking openly and honestly with my family and friends in the Bahamas about my politics, I have initiated a dialogue about feminism and its impact on my life. If my outreach has been successful, I have also challenged my family and friends to examine society from a novel and critical perspective.

Last week, for example, my father surprised me with an afternoon call from Nassau. The purpose of his call: He had been reading and enjoying Clarissa Pinkola Estés' book *Women Who Run With the Wolves: Myths and Stories of the Wild Woman Archetype* and wanted to discuss the book with me. I smiled as I listened to him excitedly recount his attempts to translate what he was reading from his male point of view to a woman's perspective. Estés' masterpiece had prompted him to, if only briefly, consider the world from a woman's point of view—a small but not insignificant victory.

I have also noticed that the nature of my conversations and letters with my mother and grandmother has changed. Whereas our initial letters and talks were predominantly focused on the mundane and perfunctory, our more recent exchanges are more intimate and candid as we share our lives and experiences as women. Often, when I speak to or read a letter from my mother I am reminded of Margaret Stetz' pearl of wisdom: "Feminism makes women appreciate their mothers more."

Upon graduating from Georgetown in 1988, I decided to settle permanently in the U.S. My decision to live in the U.S. was influenced as much by the availability of opportunities for educational and professional advancement as by the importance of creating a home in an environment that is home to other feminists. However, like most difficult decisions, mine carried a heavy price. Choosing to live in the U.S. meant being away from my family and friends and missing my sister Janelle's transformation into womanhood.

I often fantasize about returning to Nassau in the future to teach women's studies at my high school and the College of the

Bahamas—a more systematic door-to-door approach to feminism. Perhaps the Bahamas will look better for feminists by then.

1. Adrienne Rich, "Compulsory Heterosexuality and Lesbian Existence," *Blood, Bread and Poetry: Selected Prose 1979-1985* (New York: W. W. Norton & Company, 1986), p. 51.

2. "Let's Get Real about Feminism: The Backlash, the Myths, the Movement," *Ms.*, September/October 1993, p. 37.

Word Warrior

Jennifer DiMarco

When I was three years old, my father was killed. His body was never found. I learned very quickly that living is harder than dying. Two years later, my mother married a woman and taught me what the word *survivor* meant.

Mama says, *My daughter was born during an incredible thunder storm. She was energized at birth by the Goddess' electrical light show.*

I remember the studio apartment. The wallpaper had tiny flowers beneath the dark stains. The carpet was worn thin and scratchy on bare feet. There were four of us: Mama, Mumu, baby Angel and me. Life was overalls from the Salvation Army, parents who worked more for less pay, and an elder daughter with long, wild hair and eyes full of dreams. Full of pride.

Mumu says, *Remember: As a woman, nothing is ever handed to you. You have to fight for everything. And a fighter faces the world head on.*

We had nothing, so we took nothing for granted. I never expected more, didn't know what more was, but was taught to always reach for it. To always demand better. And we did have love. I knew what love was: the power behind holding hands as readily as you could make a fist. Strength through protection.

Mama says, *My daughter told me something today. She said,*

"Mama, only a coward hates, so I'm going to be brave." And I told her, *"You don't ever hate anyone, except a bigot."*

I never knew what school-shopping was, and new clothes meant Mumu's old ones. Everything was shared, from toys to tea to time. Even working double shifts, one of my parents always seemed to be home to tuck me in, kiss me good night. And when exhaustion found them asleep on the couch, I would be the one to bring in the blanket and wish them sweet dreams.

True, at dinnertime there wasn't always food on the table, but we still gathered together.

Mumu says, *Dear Goddess, thank you for this time together and for our strong girls. Bless and guide them with courage, strength, faith and love. Walk with them as they grow and face the world.*

Courage, strength, faith and *love.* These are the things that made my soul. These are the things that my parents gave me. I knew they were important. I felt them and lived them. But I never knew that they could be weapons and armor as well, until I was ten years old.

I went away for the summer. I had always dreamed of traveling. My parents wanted the world for me. The trip seemed perfect. I would stay with family, and family meant safety. I felt perfect. I stood an inch over four feet, my eyes perpetually wide, taking in everything about me—a young owl, ready to try out her wings for the first time. I flew from Seattle in a huge plane to the huger New York City, and into the arms of my great-uncle, who had offered and paid for it all.

She'll learn culture, he had told my parents with a wide grin that showed his teeth. But his idea of culture had nothing to do with Broadway plays or art galleries. *She'll see all of New York.* But all I saw were the three rooms of his house, drawn blinds, locked doors, hard walls and harder floors.

He never had any intention of showing me New York. No intention of showing me anything outside the darkness of his home. He had lied to my parents. They had no idea the danger their daughter was in. He was the first person I ever knew who lied.

Mama says, *God lets bad things happen to good people to test their faith, but the Goddess knows the faithful and knows that bad things make people stronger. And there's nothing wrong with stronger.*

And so it was with *courage* that I held my head high, even when my chin trembled. With *courage* that I kept breathing, living, even when I was terrified.

You feel free to call your parents whenever you want. The phone is right here. He sneers as he speaks. His eyes gleam shadows. He stands so close to the phone that his shoulder touches it. He watches me. He is always, forever watching me. Whenever my parents call me, he stands with his hands on my neck, locking our eyes. He knows I'm too afraid to even touch the phone. With his sneer he pounds a slice of beef for dinner.

Blood splatters on the phone . . .

the wall . . .

the floor . . .

the sheets . . .

all summer long.

Once more, there is a shadow blocking the doorway, sucking the safety from my borrowed room. The shadow says, *I pray to God every day and light candles, so that I'll never do this again.* But every night "again" happened, and so it was with *strength* that I lived, even when I was too scared to open my mouth and scream, *no. . . .*

During the night, my blue eyes would stare into the darkness for hours. I would measure my breathing, slow it down so it made barely a whisper. My body ached, but I did not move from my tight, curled position. I worried that my thundering heart was making too much noise. I knew I mustn't make a sound. Never must the blankets rustle or the headboard creak, because that would tell him I was awake. That would bring him to my room, to me.

And then it would begin again . . .

his hard hands . . .

his crushing weight . . .

his thick breath . . .

all night long.

During the day, his deep-set eyes watched me. To say he watched me constantly would be an understatement. He was never more than one or two feet away. I was always where he could reach me. Eating, bathing, walking aimlessly from room to room, using the toilet: I was never without his stare.

Never without his presence . . .

his snarls . . .

his glare . . .

his ugliness . . .

all day long.

I was not allowed out of his house. I was not allowed to open the blinds or unlock the doors. Day was not safe. Night was not safe. I was not safe. But I fought despair and fear to stay alive. I fought the living, breathing horrors my life was suddenly made of. I fought by living. By opening my eyes each morning. By continuing to breathe.

And it was *faith* and *love* that brought me, scrambling, sobbing with joy, to the phone, after he finally went out, finally left me alone, nearly sixty days after it all began. *Faith* that even after so long, the sun still shone beyond those dark shutters, and that beyond the locked doors, the world still existed. *Love* that told me I would have enough time before he returned with his threats and violence, that there would be enough time for Mama and Mumu to answer my phone call, to hear in my voice everything, to believe me, and bring me home.

And they did.

Mumu says, *Everyday heroes go unnoticed. They look darkness in the eye and still shine their light. Everyday someone goes without recognition. My daughter will never be overlooked.*

There were long nights after that summer. Too much fear to explain and a lot of denial. I questioned life, *Why?* and death, *Why not?* There were night-terrors instead of nightmares, skin-memories instead of safe memories. I wondered if there would ever be an end to the hurt, to the haunting darkness. I wondered if I would ever find myself again, if I still knew who I was.

Mama says, *This is for you. A real book, but with blank pages, for you to fill with anything you want. And you can keep it all to yourself . . . or you can share it with the world. Because I love you.*

Words. Words had become more and more sparse for me. Words were truth, and the truth was hard. So hard. There are a lot of ways to deal with darkness: Ignore it, lie about it, scream at it, cry . . . or talk about it. I wanted so badly to tell my story, to tell my parents everything that had happened, everything I had thought, felt, seen. I knew that if I could just speak, just say the words, then the three of us would share the horror, face it, kill it. But I couldn't. My own voice terrified me. My own life had become my worst fear. I loved my parents, but I hated the darkness in my past. I was scared that if I spoke about it, it would return. I was still very afraid.

But when Mama gave me that special book with the clean, ready pages, she gave me a safe place. A place where the truth could be my own. My parents did not ask me to forget my experience or stop me from realizing that others felt pain as well. They let me see the world as it really was. No, it wasn't all safe, but safety still existed. They didn't ask me to pour out the pain and wash it away, they simply asked me to show it, to reveal the darkness, perhaps make room for some light. They knew healing would come at its own pace, in its own space. And it did. My space was that book, my pace was the turning of the pages that I wrote upon.

So, it was words. My parents had taught me with their own lives: the way they stood strong but knew how to cry, the way their pride shone even when they were afraid. And their principles: the never-ending courage to live, strength to face fear and faith in love. Their understanding of themselves, of women, of me, had been the reason for my survival. They gave me, from the day I first saw them, the skills to survive. And now, surrounded by all this that they were, words became my healing. Words became my expression, my voice, my activism, joy, rage and release. Mama and Mumu said to me, *Write, share it all.* And I did.

By the time I was eighteen, I had filled up dozens of journals and notebooks. I had written twelve novels and four stage plays. First I would write, face my emotions on paper, and then I could share them, talk about them. I reclaimed my power, my energy and my life with a passion. I wrote until I cried, until I laughed out loud. I wrote about dispelling pain, darkness, hate. I was suddenly looking at the world, looking at fear and prejudice with an overwhelming need for justice. *Without fear,* I decided, *there could be no hate.* And hate was what I had found in my great-uncle, hate was the root I wanted to destroy.

So I wrote. I wrote books about strong women, and men, facing the world head on, demanding that it do better. I created characters from real people, and told their stories of battling darkness, their stories of triumph. I wrote stories that never got told, the true ones. Stories that reflected life, that weren't always safe, because life wasn't always safe. I wrote for me. I wrote for others. I wrote to make a difference.

With words I battled abuse, challenged bigotry. Issues that so many people brushed aside or refused to see. People chose to be blind to struggle. I chose to open their eyes. The more open eyes we have, the less darkness will be allowed to exist. If you ignore abuse and bigotry, they do not go away. They grow. I wanted to stunt that growth. I wrote so others wouldn't be swallowed by horror as I was. Words allowed me to deal with the world around me, to make sense of it all, to put it in perspective. I wrote to continue living my life, instead of reliving my past. I told my parents, *I write to bring light to the shadows and voice to the silence. To shed light on misconceptions, bring light into the darkness. To speak for those not spoken for, to speak the truth.* They held me tight. They told me I was brave and bold, that I was their warrior.

I said, *I'm not afraid.* And my truth was bright.

Mumu says, *Healing comes from inside. From within. Healing is a constant, shining, powerful process.*

And when my written words became spoken words, when chapters became speeches, my parents stood with me, encouraged me. They continued to light my path of verse and phrase. I went on to speak at high schools, conferences and community centers. I spoke about crossing over the boundaries of prejudice to embrace each other, about the power of challenging the world, reaching for your dreams and accepting only the best. In a strong, steady voice I talked about hate and how it is a force that must be stopped, here, now. I made the connections that so many turned away from: Prejudice is fear of the unknown, child abuse is the fear of innocence, and fear creates hatred. I shared with everyone the courage and faith I had grown up with, the fear I had fought with strength and love, and the words I had used, and still use, to reach out and touch the world.

I said, *Open your eyes. By doing nothing to stop hate, we are condoning it. Stand up against the horrors. Segregation is wrong. Battery is wrong. Oppression is wrong. Abuse is wrong. There is no time to choose blindness. Do not run, do not hide. Stop it from happening again.*

Mama says, *From the fires my daughter has risen. She was born in lightning, she fought with lightning, and now she will live like lightning: bright and brilliant.*

And when I fell in love, I fell with all my heart and soul. Unconditionally, loyally, completely. Just like I had been surrounded with, just like I felt inside my whole life.

My Love, she turned to me with pride in her eyes, beneath her silver curls, and told me she was dying of cancer. She waited for me to run away. She said, *It's a risk to love me.* I took her hands in my own and returned, *It's a bigger risk not to.* And I ran nowhere.

In my twenty years, I have learned that there are forces in the world that can take away women's rights. They can invalidate our love, beat us down, rape us, make up our minds for us. These forces insist that all strong women only undermine men, and that all lesbians hate men altogether. They insist if we're beautiful, we must be stupid, and if we don't take extreme measures to stop their rape, then we are to blame.

A lot can be taken away from a woman. A lot can be done to break her. Fear is a disease, and hatred and violence are the symptoms. There are those who wish to crush us, defeat us. But we must not, we will not, grant their wishes. Together, all women must rise up. We must take our stand in unity and power. Raise our voices against the darkness. Then, instead of being crushed, we will stand strong. Instead of being defeated, we will be victorious. We will conquer hate. I will never forget these facts. I will never for an instant doubt. Because through the fear, the hatred and the violence, we are indeed standing strong in our victory. We are surviving.

I was raised by two women. I was raised in a feminist household. I am very proud of my family and my herstory. My parents taught me more than I could ever tell in one story, perhaps more than I could tell in one hundred. But my soul is still made of courage, strength, faith and love, even as it is tested by fire, by pain and by struggle. My parents gave me these tools of survival, and someday I will pass them on to a child of my own. I will continue the fight.

Even if I could, I would never change anything about my life. My life has made me who I am today.

I was raised to survive. And I will.

Ghosts and Goddesses

Bhargavi C. Mandava

I remember walking into my dorm room at New York University on March 15, 1985. I had just been swaying to the gloomy music of Depeche Mode at the Beacon Theater. I saw the note on the floor from a roommate and even before reading it, I felt my stomach take a dive. It read, *Bhargavi, Your father is very sick. Call home.* I reached for the phone before I knew what I was doing and was met with what sounded like the cry of a wounded animal. It was my mother, and I knew before she uttered a coherent word that my father had died. She kept saying, "My life is over," in Telugu, our native tongue. I commanded her to stop talking such nonsense and assured her that I was on my way home. Everything was going to be fine. In truth, I felt the same way she did at that moment, but on instinct, I had taken over the reins my father once held so tightly. I hung up the phone and crumbled. I could never have known at the time how much my father's death would serve as a catalyst for my personal growth. My father's death accelerated my independence as a woman, my discovery of my cultural roots and my reconnection with my mother, whom I had rejected. I guess in a way my mother was right when she said that her life was over. In a way it was, and a new life had begun for both of us.

The acrid white filled me with dizziness as I sleepwalked into the room where my father lay. I kept thinking he looked so real, so alive. He was just sleeping, wasn't he? As I walked closer, I saw his face. It was pulled taut on one side, and there was some dried blood near his lips. Quivering, I kissed my father on the cheek. There. Nothing. I kissed him some more. "Dad, I'm home now. It was wrong of me to move away from home and go to college. I knew it made you unhappy, but I did it anyway. Well, now I'm home. Okay? Dad? Dad, remember all those times you wanted me to kiss you good night and I ran away? And all those times I wouldn't sit on your lap because I felt funny? Well, here. See, I'm covering your face with kisses like I used to when I was a little girl. Why is nothing happening? You told me I was a princess, and princess kisses are magic, aren't they? Dad? Nana? I am so sorry."

The chain of events that followed was especially intense because no one wanted to talk about what he or she was feeling. My brother continued his studies in India, and I went back to NYU. My mother returned to working at the state mental hospital where she was a psychiatrist, but she resigned after a few months. My sister, unable to commute to the city because she didn't know how to drive, had to leave her job. It didn't help that my mother had inherited thousands of dollars in debts my father had racked up through his numerous failed business ventures. My sister defended my father as my mother bitterly denounced his deceptions. She had fully trusted my father and handed him all financial responsibilities. By telling my sister it was okay not to have a driver's license because he'd drive her everywhere, and by relieving my mother of such nuisances as balancing her checkbook, my father paved a path of dependence for both of them. At the end of that path, of course, was isolation.

Prior to my father's death, I had already had a taste of feeling trapped. I often found myself struggling to keep the peace between my siblings and my father, who would erupt in fits of violence. As the youngest, I was hit only twice in my life. I didn't understand why I was favored so much over my brother and sister, but I felt guilty about it. All three of us were pressured to become doctors.

My brother and sister tried but failed to fulfill my parents' dream in this regard because their hearts were elsewhere. I exclaimed about my dislike of blood ever since I could talk. In the twelfth grade, when I announced I wanted to be a writer, they insisted I pursue broadcast journalism because "that's where the money is." I explored the option and decided I was much too shy for that field. Writing was what truly interested me.

My feelings of alienation were heightened by the fact that I wasn't allowed to date or even have male friends. My father made me account for all my time, including my social activities, which consisted of one weekly trip to the movies. My parents pressured my sister into an arranged marriage, which failed miserably, and talked about arranging one for me as well. Witnessing the horrible injustice of my sister's marriage in silence, I felt like an accomplice in burying my sister alive. I secretly vowed to run away if I was going to be forced into a marriage. Although at the time I had no idea what feminism encompassed, instinct prompted me to protect my rights: I was a woman, not a commodity to be bartered. I resisted the notion that female offspring were burdensome because parents had to "pay off" a groom and his family with an attractive dowry.

During high school, I saw the halls of my life lined with a lot of closed doors. By the time I decided on a college, I was lusting to break free from my isolation. Before I moved out, my sister had already filed for an annulment and my father had mellowed quite a bit—evidenced by the fact that he permitted me to go to NYU. Neither of my parents was happy that I was living in the city, but something made them respect my decision. Perhaps because of the failure of my sister's marriage, they realized that ruling with an iron fist was not working.

I was nonchalant about living on my own in the big city, which my parents dubbed a "jungle." Though I appeared to be confident and quite calm about leaving home, inside I was anxious and frightened. But I wanted to dive into the sea of the city's vast opportunities, to make mistakes, to survive on my own. I turned up the music in my room and created worst-case scenarios: What if I wanted to date a white guy? What if I dropped out of college and was happy being manager of the local Burger King? What if I got pregnant? What if I got pregnant by a black guy? What if I wanted to have the baby? What if I wanted to have an abortion? What if I was a lesbian? Then what? I started to think about what my rights were not only as an individual, but as a woman. I started to forget about how my parents would react and started to think about how *I* would react. I was tired of adopting my parents' prejudices and judgments. Wanting to identify my struggle and fight my own battles steered me toward feminism. I was ready for another type of education.

My father took my moving out of the house pretty hard. He called me a lot and insisted I come home every weekend. I didn't mind doing so at first, but eventually the heavy loads of studying and club-hopping cut down my visits. By the winter of my first year, I had bopped down to Astor Place Haircutters and had my long hair cut into a tomboyish crop. I had never been allowed to cut my hair because long hair is very desirable in Indian culture. In my struggle to loosen the grip of a culture I could not comprehend at the time, I created a new persona. I was meeting people who knew nothing about me. I was in charge of telling my story, and I chose to forget all about my precollege life. This allowed me to distance myself from my family, its problems and my culture.

As a child, I was always embarrassed about the fact that I was Indian. I dreamed of having hair like the Breck girl—the *white* girl. Panic would flutter in my chest whenever a friend asked me over to her house, which wasn't often. I knew I'd have to reciprocate by extending an invitation to my house. In the event a friend was coming over, I would start brainwashing my mother and father into adapting their behavior for the occasion. "Please, please don't eat with your hands. And don't burp. Just say 'hello' and leave. Don't ask questions, and whatever you do, Dad, please don't walk around in your *lunghee*. It looks like a skirt." They'd always agree and nod their heads, and then something would happen. My mother would saunter into the living room wearing a sari and eating some curry with her hand or offer us her Indian version of an American food, such as curried meatballs. My friends would just stare and say something like, "Ewww! What is that?" Yes, meatballs. By then, my mother was convinced that in order to get a sufficient amount of protein in our diets, we had to start eating meat. We were doing our part to fit in to U.S. pop culture—my mom donned pantsuits, my father played the stock market and we kids became Big Mac-Coke-Twinkies junkies. This did not mean we converted to Christianity, although I will admit that, in my desperation to fit in, I wouldn't have thought it such a bad idea. Whenever my friends caught a glimpse of the clay statues of Hindu gods and goddesses sitting on the bureau in my parents' bedroom, I would pretend not to hear their questions. The fact is, I didn't fully understand myself what these bizarre-looking figurines were all about, but I was too embarrassed to admit I cared at that age.

I looked in the mirror at myself with short hair and didn't recognize the person I saw. I had begun to disappear. Without my father—the object of my defiance—my rebellion turned to confusion. Shortly after my father's death, my sister and mother both called me at college. They said that they needed me at home, that it was crucial for the family to stay together. They pleaded with me to come home. Before I had even fully processed their stunning request, I answered matter-of-factly: "No. I can't drop out of school. I'm sorry." That was the end of the conversation. From that day on, I was on my own. I knew I had to put myself through college. I was shocked at them for backing me into a wall like that, for being so selfish. I understand now that they were acting out of sheer fear. We were always taught to put familial welfare above our individual concerns. But family, which I was raised to depend on and trust, had fallen through. My father had left us all to fend for ourselves with little concern for our financial well-being. After his death, through a veneer of anger and disappointment, I began to question the motives of all family members more carefully. This is not to say they were ill-intentioned, but each of us was playing with a different rule book. What was good for the family was not necessarily good for each of its members. After feeling guilty for so long about the unhappiness in my family, I finally refused to be suffocated under the weight of its seemingly endless catastrophes. The pinch of courage that had propelled me to leave home had grown considerably. With each passing day, I became stronger, more independent, and walked farther from home.

Healing was hindered by my hectic schedule, which I packed with classes, waitressing, campus work, studying and freelance music writing. I believed that strength meant forging ahead no matter what. I kept busy enough so I wouldn't have time to feel the pain. In a state of denial, I embarked on a rampage of drinking, shoplifting, staying out till all hours with other lost souls, listening to angry music and making myself unapproachable. This vexatious behavior stemmed from a variety of things: wanting to make the world pay for my father's death, a here-today-gone-tomorrow mindset, hypersensitivity to any inkling of racism, and my own insecurity. I was angry with my father not only for abandoning me, but also for promising me that he would always be around to take care of me. I felt cheated that he had been ripped away at such a young age—an age when he seemed to be relaxing his tyranny and allowing his benevolent side, which I had been privy to as a child, to blossom again.

Shortly after I was nabbed for shoplifting (I received only a warning), I began to realize that my anger was really self-directed. I started to let my buzzed hair grow long again. It suddenly clicked that I had cut my hair to defy the cultural preference for long hair in India—to strip away my Indian identity—and not because I really liked the way I looked with short hair. When I arrived in the U.S. at the age of five, I almost immediately began a campaign to change my hair. I begged my mother to make my pin-straight hair curly. She reluctantly complied by slopping on the Dippity-Do. She laughed when I ended up looking like Shirley Temple with a wicked tan. Now, we laugh together at the incident. She is so happy that, at last, I no longer want to be the Breck girl.

A major impetus in my healing was the class "Hinduism, Buddhism, Taoism," in which I was enrolled at the time of my father's death. Originally, I took the class because I felt I could never honestly and properly respond when someone asked me what Hinduism is all about. Religion was never forced on me, although bits of divine mythology crept into my daily life. "Do you know why the goddesses are shown sitting on lotuses?" my mother might say. "No, Mom." "Because the lotus is a symbol of purity." I didn't understand the meanings of her stories because I had no context for them.

Seeing her children devour cheeseburgers, my mother would always demand to know, "Are you Indian or American?" None of us could ever answer. I had hidden my fear behind a veil of arrogance. Now, *I* wanted to know. I finally discovered that pinning down this beast of a cultural identity whirling inside of me was a key part of my struggle.

Although I was not yet openly communicating with my mother, I started to flash back to times when she would start off her "when I was growing up" stories and I would tune her out with a quick nod. I began to realize that although we seemed worlds apart, filaments joined our warrior souls. Indian or American? I was becoming strong enough to handle the answer, and more important, to fight to hold on to and take pride in all that made me so different.

At the time of my father's death, our class was smack in the middle of the *Bhagavad-Gita* (*The Song of God* or *Celestial Song*), a Hindu scripture that addresses death, reincarnation and loyalty to family. I read and reread the small book. I cannot say I fully grasped the text at the time, but I found the answers to some of my questions. Explains the divine Sri Krishna to Arjuna, who was resisting going to war because he couldn't bear to kill family and friends in the process, "The truly wise mourn neither for the living nor for the dead. There was never a time when I did not exist, nor you, nor any of these kings. Nor is there any future where we shall cease to be. . . . That which is nonexistent can never come into being, and that which is, can never cease to be." The *Bhagavad-Gita* soothed me with its tranquil simplicity. I finally managed to smile, and by the end of that year I had begun on a labyrinthine path to solace.

Minoring in religion and delving into religious philosophy, I started to take pride in my Indian heritage during my final years in college. However, I never truly embraced the idea of being Hindu, perhaps because I also found truth in Buddhism, Zen Buddhism, mysticism and Taoism. Rather than labeling this a state of confusion, I now choose to see it as being in a state of quest. In order to understand the soul, I had to locate it first, and mine was floating like a broken jigsaw puzzle in an ocean. I still hadn't determined what being an Indian American woman was all about. I was disjointed, loose, homeless. At the time, I couldn't even entertain the thought of worship, because it involved a degree of submission. After my father's death, I had just gotten a grasp of my life—or so I thought—and started seeing myself as an individual. I was wary of prematurely melting into the masses.

It wasn't until I journeyed back to India with my mother in 1991 that I really began to understand who I was and whence I sprang, culturally and religiously. Gradually, our relationship had become more fluid and natural. By the time I graduated we had learned to talk as peers—as women with common struggles. We shared stories about our disappointments, our victories and our unfulfilled dreams. It was the first time since elementary school that I showed my mother my writing. This trip, which was my mother's idea, revealed to me the palette of colors with which I am painting.

Traveling all over India, I was bombarded with images of goddesses, the stomach-turning plight of the poor, and the rich mythology of my people. I devoured it all ravenously, and my mother kept my plate piled high. I stared into the eyes of Parvati, the fierce goddess of courage after whom I was named, and felt an inextinguishable connection. Who was this woman who through numerous incarnations slayed demon after demon? Who was this woman who was as ravishing and gentle as she was brutal? "Parvati is the goddess of courage, creation and destruction; she is whom I named you after," explained my mother for the nth time. But this time it was different. This time I was really listening.

As I stretched across the bed in a dank hotel room in Nasik, where my mother had taken me to be blessed by the spirit of the saint Shri Sai Baba of Shirdi, I remembered my first battle. Two sixth-graders pushed me down, snatched my Scotch-plaid lunch pail and books and threw them all over the street. Sobbing, I met my mother after a few blocks. She said she had gotten caught up watching *General Hospital* and had practically run to the school when she noticed what time it was. After a sweet treat, I hid any outward signs of injury. Inwardly, I felt that I had been attacked because I was dark and ugly. I guess my mother knew the effects such an incident could have on a child; she refused to keep quiet. The next day, she asked me to point out the two boys who had attacked me. I did, and she approached them. They ran in different directions. My mother ran after one, part of her sari trailing behind her in the wind, and caught him by the collar. She again asked me if this was one of the bullies. I nodded. Finger wagging in his face, she said with utter lucidity, "If you touch my daughter again, I'll kill you." I knew my mother wasn't capable of actually killing anyone, but at that moment, even I believed her. So much for Indian passivity. I was so proud to be her daughter. That day, my mother was as cool as Bugs Bunny (whom I idolized and mimicked as a child). Today, I know she was much cooler than that cartoon rabbit. She was a woman warrior in the image of Parvati. She was my defender and my life force. In those ten seconds, she gave me a taste of courage. She showed me what a woman was capable of doing—standing up for herself and for what she believed to be just. Remembering this, I began to understand my connection to Parvati and to my mother.

I gazed across the hotel room at my mother, who was sleeping peacefully. Who was this woman? What made her wait an entire day in the rain to be blessed by a dead saint? What made her smile so broadly when our turn had finally arrived and we were shuffled past the white marble statue of Sai Baba of Shirdi? A disciple took the blanket my mother held out and draped it around Sai Baba's shoulders. He handed back the blanket and took our offering of flowers. And we were on our way. Outside, my mother gave me the blanket almost ecstatically and told me to take care of it. I promised her I would. Watching her, I realized a little more clearly what I had been striving for these past few years. I wanted something to believe in. I wanted the faith my mother had in God, in doing good deeds, and most important, the ability to believe in herself and her independence. I had been rejecting her because I perceived her as weak, helpless and trapped. On the contrary, my mother is a woman who made many sacrifices in order to become a doctor. She encountered discrimination and sexism in her predominantly male field. Some of her superiors gave her an especially heavy workload so she could "prove" her abilities. My mother held steadfastly to her dreams.

I started asking her a lot of questions about her childhood, and what I learned amazed me. My mother was a fiercely independent woman who got married to my father because of duty, not because she was spineless. She was sad to leave her successful medical practice and start from scratch in America. She cried when she had to temporarily leave behind my brother and sister, eleven and twelve. Deep down in her soul, she knew the idea that there was something wrong with an unmarried woman was false. She was never thrilled with the idea of getting married herself because she felt it would interfere with her career plans. I believe the seeds of feminism were sown by her mother, as my mother was taught to persevere, excel, respect herself and demand equality not only between nationalities but also between the sexes. So, my mother's decision to honor some of her parents' wishes was a sign not of weakness, but of incredible courage and strength. She was going to stand by her husband and children even if that meant leaving her own dreams unfulfilled.

Almost seven years after my father died, I realized how much my mother and I were running from similar cultural expectations. We learned not to blame ourselves and somehow found our own answers. My mother realized that old beliefs had to change with the times after my sister's disastrous arranged marriage. Naturally, it is still somewhat difficult for her to accept certain things, such as the fact that at the age of twenty-eight, I'm still not married. She is all too familiar with the echoes of lost dreams, and she encourages me to pursue my hopes. I didn't want to be a doctor, and I wasn't going to major in broadcast journalism because "that's where the money is." I just wanted to be a writer. She grew to tolerate my decision because she recognized the spark in my eyes. It's the same spark that was in her eyes when as an adolescent she announced that she wanted to be an artist. Her father growled, and she soon set her sights on medicine, an equally unusual career choice for a woman in her day. She knows now that my career choice is my decision. Whom my sister married should have been solely her decision. And it should have been my mother's decision when she married my father back in 1949, a year after India gained its independence.

My mother doesn't blame her parents. She knows that her individual strength was never discouraged, but rather misdirected. Her mother and father were devout Gandhians and fought to free the Indian people from British subjugation. She beams when she tells how her mother was pregnant with her when she was incarcerated for a peaceful protest against British rule. She stands proudly next to her mother, the warrior. And I stand proudly next to my mother, the warrior. Our mutual enemies of sexism and racism may have been different in appearance, but our sights were always fixed on freedom.

All along, I think my mother was unknowingly preparing me to fight for, explore and relish the freedoms that she was denied as a young woman who was quite ahead of her time. My mother raised me as her mother raised her—without a label for the progressive philosophy she lived. I have the advantage of viewing a "map" of feminism revealing where women have been, how far we have come and where we are going. I can link arms with other women and join feminist organizations that were not available to my mother. When my rights are violated, I can seek the support of sisters who will understand and give me strength when I feel weak. I have plenty of women to lean on.

Four years ago I became a vegetarian again. I am constantly pestering my mother for recipes of my favorite Indian dishes. Eating the food of my native land sits well with me. My body seems to digest more efficiently, and I have more energy. Interwoven with the recipes, my mother occasionally throws in a myth describing a battle fought by one of the Hindu goddesses. I find these goddesses—multihanded warriors who are loving, beautiful, revered and feared—inspirational. I marvel at the thought that at one time women embodied such power. I know that our fight is perpetual and that like the demons in Indian mythology, our oppressors are serpentine, slippery, faceless. Preparation for the battle is as crucial as the battle itself. There is no doubt in my mind that my mother prepared me well. Following her example, I could not be anything but a feminist, which, to me, means that I must do everything in my power to work with other women to abolish gender inequality.

My mother has dealt with her own conflicts, especially balancing her need for solitude with raising a family. A day before my father died, she expressed to him her desire to once again be alone as she had been before they married. She craved her freedom. As painful as it was for her to say and for him to hear, she stayed true to herself. Maybe it was the permission my father was waiting to hear to release him from this life. My mother is alone now, and she is rediscovering the fiery spirit that had been caged for decades—the goddess that had been silenced by a ghost. The woman who wanted to paint is finally painting. She is free to travel and garden. She is free to live. I thank her for kindling my spirit to seek out those freedoms.

My mother and I silently acknowledge that my father's death marked the beginning of our lives independent of family. As

Hinduism asserts, death is not an ending, but a beginning. Currently, I am living the farthest I have ever lived from my mother, yet I feel the strongest, closest bond with her. Eager to live and learn, we are teaching each other about our individual cultures and perspectives. We don't always agree, but we listen. Oddly enough, the cultural void that blew us apart is the same entity that reunited us. Every time I hear another story, I understand a little more about the choices she made. Increasingly, I see that we are much more alike than different. As a surgeon who delivered babies, my mother spent much of her time handing out birth control and pregnancy prevention information to women in poverty-stricken areas of India. She had a thirst to educate other women, as I do. When I moved to Los Angeles, I became a counselor for a rape and battering hotline run by the L.A. Commission on Assaults Against Women. My mother and I discussed how important it is to answer the desire to connect with our sisters—to take action, participate and educate. I know now that before we are Indian, we are women—we are mother and daughter. That is our paramount bond, and all else strengthens that union. Finally, I can say that I am proud to be a woman, a warrior, myself.

The Body Politic

Abra Fortune Chernik

My body possesses solidness and curve, like the ocean. My weight mingles with Earth's pull, drawing me onto the sand. I have not always sent waves into the world. I flew off once, for five years, and swirled madly like a cracking brown leaf in the salty autumn wind. I wafted, dried out, apathetic.

I had no weight in the world during my years of anorexia. Curled up inside my thinness, a refugee in a cocoon of hunger, I lost the capacity to care about myself or others. I starved my body and twitched in place as those around me danced in the energy of shared existence and progressed in their lives. When I graduated from college crowned with academic honors, professors praised my potential. I wanted only to vanish.

It took three months of hospitalization and two years of outpatient psychotherapy for me to learn to nourish myself and to live in a body that expresses strength and honesty in its shape. I accepted my right and my obligation to take up room with my figure, voice and spirit. I remembered how to tumble forward and touch the world that holds me. I chose the ocean as my guide.

Who disputes the ocean's fullness?

≈

Growing up in New York City, I did not care about the feminist movement. Although I attended an all-girls high school, we read mostly male authors and studied the history of men. Embracing mainstream culture without question, I learned about womanhood from fashion magazines, Madison Avenue and Hollywood. I dismissed feminist alternatives as foreign and offensive, swathed as they were in stereotypes that threatened my adolescent need for conformity.

Puberty hit late; I did not complain. I enjoyed living in the lanky body of a tall child and insisted on the title of "girl." If anyone referred to me as a "young woman," I would cry out, horrified, "Do not call me the *W* word!" But at sixteen years old, I could no longer deny my fate. My stomach and breasts rounded. Curly black hair sprouted in the most embarrassing places. Hips swelled from a once-flat plane. Interpreting maturation as an unacceptable lapse into fleshiness, I resolved to eradicate the physical symptoms of my impending womanhood.

Magazine articles, television commercials, lunchroom conversation, gymnastics coaches and write-ups on models had saturated me with diet savvy. Once I decided to lose weight, I quickly turned expert. I dropped hot chocolate from my regular breakfast order at the Skyline Diner. I replaced lunches of peanut butter and Marshmallow Fluff sandwiches with small platters of cottage cheese and cantaloupe. I eliminated dinner altogether and blunted my appetite with Tab, Camel Lights, and Carefree bubble gum. When furious craving overwhelmed my resolve and I swallowed an extra something, I would flee to the nearest bathroom to purge my mistake.

Within three months, I had returned my body to its preadolescent proportions and had manipulated my monthly period into drying up. Over the next five years, I devoted my life to losing my weight. I came to resent the body in which I lived, the body that threatened to develop, the body whose hunger I despised but could not extinguish. If I neglected a workout or added a pound or ate a bite too many, I would stare in the mirror and drown myself in a tidal wave of criticism. Hatred of my body generalized to hatred of myself as a person, and self-referential labels such as "pig," "failure" and "glutton" allowed me to believe that I deserved punishment. My self-hatred became fuel for the self-mutilating behaviors of the eating disorder.

As my body shrank, so did my world. I starved away my power and vision, my energy and inclinations. Obsessed with dieting, I allowed relationships, passions and identity to wither. I pulled back from the world, off of the beach, out of the sand. The waves of my existence ceased to roll beyond the inside of my skin.

And society applauded my shrinking. Pound after pound the applause continued, like the pounding ocean outside the door of my beach house.

The word "anorexia" literally means "loss of appetite." But as an anorexic, I felt hunger thrashing inside my body. I denied my appetite, ignored it, but never lost it. Sometimes the pangs twisted so sharply, I feared they would consume the meat of my heart. On desperate nights I rose in a flannel nightgown and allowed myself to eat an unplanned something.

No matter how much I ate, I could not soothe the pangs. Standing in the kitchen at midnight, spotlighted by the blue-white light of the open refrigerator, I would frantically feed my neglected appetite: the Chinese food I had not touched at dinner; ice cream and whipped cream; microwaved bread; cereal and chocolate milk; doughnuts and bananas. Then, solid sadness inside my gut, swelling agitation, a too-big meal I would not digest. In the bathroom I would rip off my shirt, tie up my hair, and prepare to execute the desperate ritual, again. I would ram the back of my throat with a toothbrush handle, crying, impatient, until the food rushed up. I would vomit until the toilet filled and I emptied, until I forgave myself, until I felt ready to try my life again. Standing up from my position over the toilet, wiping my mouth, I would believe that I was safe. Looking in the mirror through puffy eyes in a tumescent face, I would promise to take care of myself. Kept awake by the fast, confused beating of my heart and the ache in my chest, I would swear I did not miss the world outside. Lost within myself, I almost died.

By the time I entered the hospital, a mess of protruding bones defined my body, and the bones of my emaciated life rattled me crazy. I carried a pillow around because it hurt to sit down, and I shivered with cold in sultry July. Clumps of brittle hair clogged the drain when I showered, and blackened eyes appeared to sink into my head. My vision of reality wrinkled and my disposition turned mercurial as I slipped into starvation psychosis, a condition associated with severe malnutrition. People told me that I resembled a concentration camp prisoner, a chemotherapy patient, a famine victim or a fashion model.

In the hospital, I examined my eating disorder under the lenses of various therapies. I dissected my childhood, my family structure, my intimate relationships, my belief systems. I participated in experiential therapies of movement, art and psychodrama. I learned to use words instead of eating patterns to communicate my feelings. And still I refused to gain more than a minimal amount of weight.

I felt powerful as an anorexic. Controlling my body yielded an illusion of control over my life; I received incessant praise for my figure despite my sickly mien, and my frailty manipulated family and friends into protecting me from conflict. I had reduced my world to a plate of steamed carrots, and over this tiny kingdom I proudly crowned myself queen.

I sat cross-legged on my hospital bed for nearly two months before I earned an afternoon pass to go to the mall with my mother. The privilege came just in time; I felt unbearably large and desperately wanted a new outfit under which to hide gained weight. At the mall, I searched for two hours before finally discovering, in the maternity section at Macy's, a shirt large enough to cover what I perceived as my enormous body.

With an hour left on my pass, I spotted a sign on a shop window: "Body Fat Testing, $3.00." I suggested to my mother that we split up for ten minutes; she headed to Barnes & Noble, and I snuck into the fitness store.

I sat down in front of a machine hooked up to a computer, and a burly young body builder fired questions at me:

"Age?"

"Twenty-one."

"Height?"

"Five nine."

"Weight?"

"Ninety-nine."

The young man punched my statistics into his keyboard and pinched my arm with clippers wired to the testing machine. In a moment, the computer spit out my results. "Only ten percent body fat! Unbelievably healthy. The average for a woman your age is twenty-five percent. Fantastic! You're this week's blue ribbon winner."

I stared at him in disbelief. *Winner? Healthy? Fantastic?* I glanced around at the other customers in the store, some of whom had congregated to watch my testing, and I felt embarrassed by his praise. And then I felt furious. Furious at this man and at the society that programmed him for their ignorant approbation of my illness and my suffering.

"I am dying of anorexia," I whispered. "Don't congratulate me."

I spent my remaining month in the hospital supplementing psychotherapy with an independent examination of eating disorders from a social and political point of view. I needed to understand why society would reward my starvation and encourage my vanishing. In the bathroom, a mirror on the open door behind me reflected my backside in a mirror over the sink. Vertebrae poked at my skin, ribs hung like wings over chiseled hip bones, the two sides of my buttocks did not touch. I had not seen this view of myself before.

In writing, I recorded instances in which my eating disorder had tangled the progress of my life and thwarted my relationships. I filled three and a half Mead marble notebooks. Five years' worth of: *I wouldn't sit with Daddy when he was alone in the hospital because I needed to go jogging; I told Derek not to visit me because I couldn't throw up when he was there; I almost failed my comprehensive exams because I was so hungry; I spent my year at Oxford with my head in the toilet bowl; I wouldn't eat the dinner my friends cooked me for my nineteenth birthday because I knew they had used oil in the recipe; I told my family not to come to my college graduation because I didn't want to miss a day at the gym or have to eat a restaurant meal.* And on and on for hundreds of pages.

This honest account of my life dissolved the illusion of anorexic power. I saw myself naked in the truth of my pain, my loneliness, my obsessions, my craziness, my selfishness, my defeat. I also recognized the social and political implications of consuming myself with the trivialities of calories and weight. At college, I had watched as classmates involved themselves in extracurricular clubs, volunteer work, politics and applications for jobs and graduate schools. Obsessed with exercising and exhausted by starvation, I did not even consider joining in such pursuits. Despite my love of writing and painting and literature, despite ranking at the top of my class, I wanted only to teach aerobics. Despite my adolescent days as a loud-mouthed, rambunctious class leader, I had grown into a silent, hungry young woman.

And society preferred me this way: hungry, fragile, crazy. *Winner! Healthy! Fantastic!* I began reading feminist literature to further understand the disempowerment of women in our culture. I digested the connection between a nation of starving, self-obsessed women and the continued success of the patriarchy. I also cultivated an awareness of alternative models of womanhood. In the stillness of the hospital library, new voices in my life rose from printed pages to echo my rage and provide the conception of my feminist consciousness.

I had been willing to accept self-sabotage, but now I refused to sacrifice myself to a society that profited from my pain. I finally understood that my eating disorder symbolized more than "personal psychodynamic trauma." Gazing in the mirror at my emaciated body, I observed a woman held up by her culture as the physical ideal because she was starving, self-obsessed and powerless, a woman called beautiful because she threatened no one except herself. Despite my intelligence, my education, and my supposed Manhattan sophistication, I had believed all of the lies; I had almost given my life in order to achieve the sickly impotence that this culture aggressively links with female happiness, love and success. And everything I had to offer to the world, every tumbling wave, every thought and every passion, nearly died inside me.

As long as society resists female power, fashion will call healthy women physically flawed. As long as society accepts the physical, sexual and economic abuse of women, popular culture will prefer women who resemble little girls. Sitting in the hospital the summer after my college graduation, I grasped the absurdity of a nation of adult women dying to grow small.

Armed with this insight, I loosened the grip of the starvation disease on my body. I determined to recreate myself based on an image of a woman warrior. I remembered my ocean, and I took my first bite.

Gaining weight and getting my head out of the toilet bowl was the most political act I have ever committed.

I left the hospital and returned home to Fire Island. Living at the shore in those wintry days of my new life, I wrapped myself in feminism as I hunted sea shells and role models. I wanted to feel proud of my womanhood. I longed to accept and honor my body's fullness.

During the process of my healing, I had hoped that I would be able to skip the memory of anorexia like a cold pebble into the dark winter sea. I had dreamed that in relinquishing my obsessive chase after a smaller body, I would be able to come home to rejoin those whom I had left in order to starve, rejoin them to live together as healthy, powerful women. But as my body has grown full, I have sensed a hollowness in the lives of women all around me that I had not noticed when I myself stood hollow. I have made it home only to find myself alone.

Out in the world again, I hear the furious thumping dance of body hatred echoing every place I go. Friends who once appeared wonderfully carefree in ordering late-night french fries turn out not to eat breakfast or lunch. Smart, talented, creative women talk about dieting and overeating and hating the beach because they look terrible in bathing suits. Famous women give interviews insulting their bodies and bragging about bicycling twenty-four miles the day they gave birth.

I had looked forward to rejoining society after my years of anorexic exile. Ironically, in order to preserve my health, my recovery has included the development of a consciousness that actively challenges the images and ideas that define this culture. Walking down Madison Avenue and passing emaciated women, I say to myself, *those women are sick.* When smacked with a diet commercial, I remind myself, *I don't do that anymore.* I decline invitations to movies that feature anorexic actors, I will not participate in discussions about dieting, and I refuse to shop in stores that cater to women with eating-disordered figures.

Though I am critical of diet culture, I find it nearly impossible to escape. Eating disorders have woven their way into the fabric of my society. On television, in print, on food packaging, in casual conversation and in windows of clothing stores populated by ridiculously gaunt mannequins, messages to lose my weight and control my appetite challenge my recovered fullness. Finally at home in my body, I recognize myself as an island in a sea of eating disorder, a sea populated predominantly by young women.

~

A perversion of nature by society has resulted in a phenomenon whereby women feel safer when starving than when eating. Losing our weight boosts self-esteem, while nourishing our bodies evokes feelings of self-doubt and self-loathing.

When our bodies take up more space than a size eight (as most of our bodies do), we say, *too big*. When our appetites demand more than a Lean Cuisine, we say, *too much*. When we want a piece of a friend's birthday cake, we say, *too bad*. Don't eat too much, don't talk too loudly, don't take up too much space, don't take from the world. Be pleasant or crazy, but don't seem hungry. Remember, a new study shows that men prefer women who eat salad for dinner over women who eat burgers and fries.

So we keep on shrinking, starving away our wildness, our power, our truth.

Hiding our curves under long T-shirts at the beach, sitting silently and fidgeting while others eat dessert, sneaking back into the kitchen late at night to binge and hating ourselves the next day, skipping breakfast, existing on diet soda and cigarettes, adding up calories and subtracting everything else. We accept what is horribly wrong in our lives and fight what is beautiful and right.

Over the past three years, feminism has taught me to honor the fullness of my womanhood and the solidness of the body that hosts my life. In feminist circles I have found mentors, strong women who live with power, passion and purpose. And yet, even in groups of feminists, my love and acceptance of my body remains unusual.

Eating disorders affect us all on both a personal and a political level. The majority of my peers—including my feminist peers—still measure their beauty against anorexic ideals. Even among feminists, body hatred and chronic dieting continue to consume lives. Friends of anorexics beg them to please start eating; then these friends go home and continue their own diets. Who can deny that the millions of young women caught in the net of disordered eating will frustrate the potential of the next wave of feminism?

Sometimes my empathy dissolves into frustration and rage at our situation. For the first time in history, young women have the opportunity to create a world in our image. But many of us concentrate instead on recreating the shape of our thighs.

As young feminists, we must place unconditional acceptance of our bodies at the top of our political agenda. We must claim our bodies as our own to love and honor in their infinite shapes and sizes. Fat, thin, soft, hard, puckered, smooth, our bodies are our homes. By nourishing our bodies, we care for and love ourselves on the most basic level. When we deny ourselves physical food, we go hungry emotionally, psychologically, spiritually and politically. We must challenge ourselves to eat and digest, and allow society to call us too big. We will understand their message to mean too powerful.

Time goes by quickly. One day we will blink and open our eyes as old women. If we spend all our energy keeping our bodies small, what will we have to show for our lives when we reach the end? I hope we have more than a group of fashionably skinny figures.

It's a Big Fat Revolution

Nomy Lamm

I am going to write an essay describing my experiences with fat oppression and the ways in which feminism and punk have affected my work. It will be clear, concise and well thought-out, and will be laid out in the basic thesis paper, college essay format. I will deal with these issues in a mature and intellectual manner. I will cash in on as many fifty-cent words as possible.

I lied. (You probably already picked up on that, huh?) I can't do that. This is my life, and my words are the most effective tool I have for challenging Whiteboyworld (that's my punk-rock cutesy but oh-so-revolutionary way of saying "patriarchy"). If there's one thing that feminism has taught me, it's that the revolution is gonna be on my terms. The revolution will be incited through my voice, my words, not the words of the universe of male intellect that already exists. And I know that a hell of a lot of what I say is totally contradictory. My contradictions can coexist, cuz they exist inside of me, and I'm not gonna simplify them so that they fit into the linear, analytical pattern that I know they're supposed to. I think it's important to recognize that all this stuff does contribute to the revolution, for real. The fact that I write like this cuz it's the way I want to write makes this world just that much safer for me.

I wanna explain what I mean when I say "the revolution," but

I'm not sure whether I'll be able to. Cuz at the same time that I'm being totally serious, I also see my use of the term as a mockery of itself. Part of the reason for this is that I'm fully aware that I still fit into dominant culture in many ways. The revolution could very well be enacted against me, instead of for me. I don't want to make myself sound like I think I'm the most oppressed, most punk-rock, most revolutionary person in the world. But at the same time I do think that revolution is a word I should use as often as I can, because it's a concept that we need to be aware of. And I don't just mean it in an abstract, intellectualized way, either. I really do think that the revolution has begun. Maybe that's not apparent to mainstream culture yet, but I see that as a good sign. As soon as mainstream culture picks up on it, they'll try to co-opt it.

For now the revolution takes place when I stay up all night talking with my best friends about feminism and marginalization and privilege and oppression and power and sex and money and real-life rebellion. For now the revolution takes place when I watch a girl stand up in front of a crowd of people and talk about her sexual abuse. For now the revolution takes place when I get a letter from a girl I've never met who says that the zine I wrote changed her life. For now the revolution takes place when the homeless people in my town camp out for a week in the middle of downtown. For now the revolution takes place when I am confronted by a friend about something racist that I have said. For now the revolution takes place in my head when I know how fucking brilliant my girlfriends and I are.

And I'm living the revolution through my memories and through my pain and through my triumphs. When I think about all the marks I have against me in this society, I am amazed that I haven't turned into some worthless lump of shit. Fatkike-cripplecuntqueer. In a nutshell. But then I have to take into account the fact that I'm an articulate, white, middle-class college kid, and that provides me with a hell of a lot of privilege and opportunity for dealing with my oppression that may not be available to other oppressed people. And since my personality/being isn't divided up into a privileged part and an oppressed part, I have to deal with the ways that these things interact, counterbalance and sometimes even overshadow each other. For example, I was born with one leg. I guess it's a big deal, but it's never worked into my body image in the same way that being fat has. And what does it mean to be a white woman as opposed to a woman of color? A middle-class fat girl as opposed to a poor fat girl? What does it mean to be fat, physically disabled and bisexual? (Or fat, disabled and *sexual at all*?)

See, of course, I'm still a real person, and I don't always feel up to playing the role of the revolutionary. Sometimes it's hard enough for me to just get out of bed in the morning. Sometimes it's hard enough to just talk to people at all, without having to deal with the political nuances of everything that comes out of their mouths. Despite the fact that I do tons of work that deals with fat oppression, and that I've been working so so hard on my own body image, there are times when I really hate my body and don't want to deal with being strong all the time. Because I am strong and have thought all of this through in so many different ways, and I do have naturally high self-esteem, I've come to a place where I can honestly say that I love my body and I'm happy with being fat. But occasionally, when I look in the mirror and I see this body that is so different from my friends', so different from what I'm told it should be, I just want to hide away and not deal with it anymore. At these times it doesn't seem fair to me that I have to always be fighting to be happy. Would it be easier for me to just give in and go on another diet so that I can stop this perpetual struggle? Then I could still support the fat grrrl revolution without having it affect me personally in every way. And I know I know I know that's not the answer and I could never do that to myself, but I can't say that the thought never crosses my mind.

And it doesn't help much when my friends and family, who all know how I feel about this, continue to make anti-fat statements and bitch about how fat they feel and mention new diets they've heard about and are just dying to try. "I'm shaped like a watermelon." "Wow, I'm so happy, I now wear a size seven instead of a size nine." "I like this mirror because it makes me look thinner."

I can't understand how they could still think these things when I'm constantly talking about these issues, and I can't believe that they would think that these are okay things to talk about in front of me. And it's not like I want them to censor their conversation around me. . . . I just want them to not think it. I know that most of this is just a reflection of how they feel about themselves and isn't intended as an attack on me or an invalidation of my work, but it makes it that much harder for me. It puts all those thoughts inside me. Today I was standing outside of work and I caught a glimpse of myself in the window and thought, "Hey, I don't look that fat!" And I immediately realized how fucked up that was, but that didn't stop me from feeling more attractive because of it.

I want this out of me. This is not a part of me, and theoretically I can separate it all out and throw away the shit, but it's never really gone. When will this finally be over? When can I move on to other issues? It will never be over, and that's really fucking hard to accept.

I am living out this system of oppression through my memories, and even when I'm not thinking about them they are there, affecting everything I do. Five years old, my first diet. Seven years old, being declared officially "overweight" because I weigh ten pounds over what a "normal" seven-year-old should weigh. Ten years old, learning to starve myself and be happy feeling constantly dizzy. Thirteen years old, crossing the border from being bigger than my friends to actually being "fat." Fifteen years old, hearing the boys in the next room talk about how fat (and hence unattractive) I am. Whenever I perform, I remember the time when my dad said he didn't like the dance I choreographed because I looked fat while I was doing it. Every time I dye my hair I remember when my mom wouldn't let me dye my hair in seventh grade because seeing fat people with dyed hair made her think they were just trying to cover up the fact that they're fat, trying to look attractive despite it (when of course it's obvious what they should really do if they want to look attractive, right?). And these are big memorable occurrences that I can put my finger on and say, "This hurt me." But what about the lifetime of media I've been exposed to that tells me that only thin people are lovable, healthy, beautiful, talented, fun? I know that those messages are all packed in there with the rest of my memories, but I just can't label them and their effects on my psyche. They are elusive and don't necessarily feel painful at the time. They are well disguised and often even appear alluring and romantic. (I will never fall in love because I cannot be picked up and swung around in circles. . . .)

All my life the media and everyone around me have told me that fat is ugly. Which of course is just a cultural standard that has many, many medical lies to fall back upon. Studies have shown that fat people are unhealthy and have short life expectancies. Studies have also shown that starving people have these same peculiarities. These health risks to fat people have been proven to be a result of continuous starvation—dieting—and not of fat itself. I am not fat due to lack of willpower. I've been a vegetarian since I was ten years old. Controlling what I eat is easy for me. Starving myself is not (though for most of my life I wished it was). My body is supposed to be like this, and I've been on plenty of diets where I've kept off some weight for a period of several months and then gained it all back. Two years ago I finally ended the cycle. I am not dieting anymore because I know that this is how my body is supposed to be, and this is how I want it to be. Being fat does not make me less healthy or less active. Being fat does not make me less attractive.

On TV I see a thin woman dancing with a fabulously handsome man, and over that I hear, "I was never happy until I went on [fill in the blank] diet program, but now I'm getting attention from men, and I feel so good! I don't have to worry about what people are saying about me behind my back, because I know I look good. You owe it to yourself to give yourself the life you deserve. Call [fill in the blank] diet program today, and start taking off the pounds right away!" TV shows me a close-up of a teary-eyed fat girl who says, "I've tried everything, but nothing works. I lose twenty pounds, and I gain back twenty-five. I feel so ashamed. What can I do?" The first time I saw that commercial I started crying and memorized the number on the screen. I know that feeling of shame. I know that feeling of having nowhere left to turn, of feeling like I'm useless because I can't lose all that "unwanted fat." But I know that the unhappiness is not a result of my fat. It's a result of a society that tells me I'm bad.

Where's the revolution? My body is fucking beautiful, and every time I look in the mirror and acknowledge that, I am contributing to the revolution.

I feel like at this point I'm expected to try to prove to you that fat can be beautiful by going into descriptions of "rippling thighs and full smooth buttocks." I won't. It's not up to me to convince you that fat can be attractive. I refuse to be the self-appointed full-figured porno queen. Figure it out on your own.

It's not good enough for you to tell me that you "don't judge by appearances"—so fat doesn't bother you. Ignoring our bodies and "judging only by what's on the inside" is not the answer. This seems to be along the same line of thinking as that brilliant school of thought called "humanism": "We are all just people, so let's ignore trivialities such as race, class, gender, sexual preference, body type and so on." Bullshit! The more we ignore these aspects of ourselves, the more shameful they become and the more we are expected to be what is generally implied when these qualifiers are not given—white, straight, thin, rich, male. It's unrealistic to try to overlook these exterior (and hence meaningless, right?) differences, because we're still being brainwashed with the same shit as everyone else. This way we're just not talking about it. And I don't want to be told, "Yes you're fat, but you're beautiful on the inside." That's just another way of telling me that I'm ugly, that there's no way that I'm beautiful on the outside. Fat does not equal ugly, don't give me that. My body *is* me. I want you to see my body, acknowledge my body. True revolution comes not when we learn to ignore our fat and pretend we're no different, but when we learn to use it to our advantage, when we learn to deconstruct all the myths that propagate fat-hate.

My thin friends are constantly being validated by mainstream feminism, while I am ignored. The most widespread mentality regarding body image at this point is something along these lines: Women look in the mirror and think, "I'm fat," but really they're not. Really they're thin.

Really they're thin. But really I'm fat. According to mainstream feminist theory, I don't even exist. I know that women do often look in the mirror and think that they are fatter than they are. And yes, this is a problem. But the analysis can't stop there. There are women who *are* fat, and that needs to be dealt with. Rather than just reassuring people, "No, you're not fat, you're just curvy," maybe we should be demystifying fat and dealing with fat politics as a whole. And I don't mean maybe, I mean it's a necessity. Once we realize that fat is not "inherently bad" (and I can't even believe I'm writing that—"inherently bad"—it sounds so ridiculous), then we can work out the problem as a whole instead of dealing only with this very minute part of it. All forms of oppression work together, and so they have to be fought together.

I think that a lot of the mainstream feminist authors who claim to be dealing with this issue are doing it in a very wrong way. Susie Orbach, for example, with *Fat Is a Feminist Issue*. She tells us: Don't diet, don't try to lose weight, don't feed the diet industry. But she then goes on to say: But if you eat right and exercise, you will lose weight! And I feel like, great, nice, it's so very wonderful that that worked for her, but she's totally missing the point. She is trying to help women, but really she is hurting us. She is hurting us because she's saying that there's still only one body that's okay for us (and she's the one to help us get it!). It's almost like that *Stop the Insanity* woman, Susan Powter. One of my friends read her book and said that the first half of it is all about fat oppression and talks about how hard it is to be fat in our society, but then it says: So use my great new diet plan! This kind of thing totally plays on our emotions so that we think, Wow, this person really understands me. They know where I'm coming from, so they must know what's best for me.

And there are so many "liberal" reasons for perpetuating fat-hate. Yes, we're finally figuring out that dieting never works. How, then, shall we explain this horrible monstrosity? And how can we get rid of it? The new "liberal" view on fat is that it is caused by deep psychological disturbances. Her childhood was bad, she was sexually abused, so she eats and gets fat in order to hide herself away. She uses her fat as a security blanket. Or maybe when she was young her parents caused her to associate food with comfort and love, so she eats to console herself. Or maybe, like with me, her parents were always on diets and always nagging her about what she was eating, so food became something shameful that must be hoarded and kept secret. And for a long, long time I really believed that if my parents hadn't instilled in me all these fucked-up attitudes about food, I wouldn't be fat. But then I realized that my brother and sister both grew up in exactly the same environment, and they are both thin. Obviously this is not the reason that I am fat. Therapy won't help, because there's nothing to cure. When will we stop grasping for reasons to hate fat people and start realizing that fat is a totally normal and natural thing that cannot and should not be gotten rid of?

Despite what I said earlier about my friends saying things that are really hurtful to me, I realize that they are actually pretty exceptional. I don't want to make them seem like uncaring, ignorant people. I'm constantly talking about these issues, and I feel like I'm usually able to confront my friends when they're being insensitive, and they'll understand or at least try to. Sometimes when I leave my insular circle of friends I'm shocked at what the "real world" is like. Hearing boys on the bus refer to their girlfriends as their "bitches," seeing fat women being targeted for harassment on the street, watching TV and seeing how every fat person is depicted as a food-obsessed slob, seeing women treated as property by men who see masculinity as a right to power. . . . I leave these situations feeling like the punk scene, within which most of my interactions take place, is so sheltered. I cannot imagine living in a community where I had nowhere to go for support. I cannot imagine living in the "real world."

But then I have to remember that it's still there in my community—these same fucked-up attitudes are perpetuated within the punk scene as well; they just take on more subtle forms. I feel like these issues are finally starting to be recognized and dealt with, but fat hating is still pretty standard. Of course everyone agrees that we shouldn't diet and that eating disorders are a result of our oppressive society, but it's not usually taken much further than that. It seems like people have this idea that punk is disconnected from the media. That because we are this cool underground subculture, we are immune to systems of oppression. But the punkest, coolest kids are still the skinny kids. And the same cool kids who are so into defying mainstream capitalist "Amerika" are the ones who say that fat is a symbol of capitalist wealth and greed. Yeah, that's a really new and different way of thinking: Blame the victim. Perpetuate institutionalized oppression. Fat people are not the ones who are oppressing these poor, skinny emo boys.

This essay is supposed to be about fat oppression. I feel like that's all I ever talk about. Sometimes I feel my whole identity is wrapped up in my fat. When I am fully conscious of my fat, it can't be used against me. Outside my secluded group of friends, in hostile situations, I am constantly aware that at any moment I could be harassed. Any slight altercation with another person could lead to a barrage of insults thrown at my body. I am always ready for it. I've found it doesn't happen nearly as often as I expect it, but still I always remain aware of the possibility. I am "the Fat Girl." I am "the Girl Who Talks About Fat Oppression." Within the punk scene, that's my security blanket. People know about me and know about my work, so I assume that they're not gonna be laughing behind my back about my fat. And if they are, then I know I have support from other people around me. The punk scene gives me tons of support that I know I wouldn't get elsewhere. Within the punk scene, I am able to put out zines, play music, do spoken-word performances that are intensely personal to me. I feel really strongly about keeping nothing secret. I can go back to the old cliché about the personal being political, and no matter how trite it may sound, it's true. I went for so long never talking about being fat, never talking about how that affects my self-esteem, never talking about the ways that I'm oppressed by this society. Now I'm talking. Now I'm talking, I'm talking all the time, and people listen to me. I have support.

And at the same time I know that I have to be wary of the support that I receive. Because I think to some people this is just seen as the cool thing, that by supporting me they're somehow receiving a certain amount of validation from the punk scene. Even though I am totally open and don't keep secrets, I have to protect myself.

This is the revolution. I don't understand the revolution. I can't lay it all out in black and white and tell you what is revolutionary and what is not. The punk scene is a revolution, but not in and of itself. Feminism is a revolution; it is solidarity as well as critique and confrontation. This is the fat grrrl revolution. It's mine, but it doesn't belong to me. Fuckin' yeah.

Lusting for Freedom

Rebecca Walker

I had sex young and, after the initial awkwardness, loved it. For days and nights, I rolled around in a big bed with my first boyfriend, trying out every possible way to feel good body to body. I was able to carry that pleasure and confidence into my everyday life working at the hair salon, raising my hand in English class, hanging out with my best girlfriend, and flirting with boys. I never felt any great loss of innocence, only great rushes of the kind of power that comes with self-knowledge and shared intimacy.

But experiences like mine are all too rare. There are forces that subvert girls' access to freeing and empowering sex—forces like AIDS, limited access to health care, and parental notification laws that force thousands of young women to seek out illegal and sometimes fatal abortions. The way we experience, speak about and envision sex and sexuality can either kill us or help us to know and protect ourselves better. The responsibility is enormous. Unfortunately, moral codes and legal demarcations complicate rather than regulate desire. And judgments like "right" and "wrong" only build barriers between people and encourage shame within individuals. I personally have learned much more from examining my own life for signs of what was empowering for me and what was not, and from listening to and asking questions of my friends: What did you feel then, what did you learn from that?

When I look back at having sex during my teenage years, I find myself asking: What was it in my own life that created the impulse and the safety; the wanting that led me and the knowing that kept me from harm?

If you are a girl, sex marks you, and I was marked young. I am ashamed to tell people how young I was, but I am too proud to lie. Eleven. I was eleven, and my mother was away working. One autumn night Kevin, a boy I had met in the neighborhood, called and said he had a sore throat. I told him I would make him some tea if he wanted to come over. He said he was on his way. I had told him that I was sixteen, so I ran around for a few minutes, panicking about what to wear. I settled on a satin leopard-print camisole from my mother's bureau and hid it beneath a big red terry-cloth robe.

I have a few vivid memories of that night: I remember being cold and my teeth chattering. I remember his black Nike high tops and red-and-gray football jersey, and the smell of him, male and musky, as he passed me coming through the front door. I remember sitting on our green sofa and telling him rather indignantly that I was not a virgin. I remember faking a fear that I might get pregnant (I didn't have my period yet). I remember his dry penis, both of us looking elsewhere as he pushed it inside of me. I remember that I wanted him to stay with me through the night, but that instead he had to rush home to make a curfew imposed upon him by his football coach.

Shocking, right? Not really. Sex begins much earlier than most people think, and it is far more extensive. It is more than the act of intercourse, much more than penis and vagina. Sex can look like love if you don't know what love looks like. It gives you someone to hold on to when you can't feel yourself. It is heat on your body when the coldness is inside of you. It is trying out trusting and being trusted. Sex can also be power because knowledge is power, and because yeah, as a girl, you can make it do different things: I can give it to you, and I can take it away. This sex is me, you can say. It is mine, take it. Take me. Please keep me.

By the time I was eighteen I was fluent in the language of sex and found myself in restaurants with men twice my age, drinking red wine and artfully playing Woman. By then I had learned about the limitations of male tenderness, men's expectations about black female desire, the taboo of loving other women, the violence of rape. And, like women all over the world, I had mastered the art of transforming myself into what I thought each man would fall in love with. Not at all in control of each affair, but very much in control of the mask I put on for each man, I tried on a dozen personas, played out a dozen roles, decided not to be a dozen people. When Bryan said I was too black, I straightened my hair. When Ray said I was too young, I added four years. For Miles I was a young virgin, nervous and giggly. For Jacob I was a self-assured student of modern art. For Robbie I was a club girl. I was Kevin's steady.

When I think of what determined my chameleonlike identity then, I think of the movie *Grease*, with the dolled-up Olivia Newton-John getting the guy and popularity too after she put on pumps and a push-up bra and became "sexy." I also think about my best girlfriend in the fourth grade who stopped speaking to me and "stole" my boyfriend over Christmas break. It was a tricky world of alliances in those younger years. You could never be sure of who was going to like you and why, so I tried my best to control what parts I could. That explains my attempts to be cool and sexy, my pretending to know everything, my smoking cigarettes, and of course, my doing it with boys. I did what I thought had to be done.

But there were also other elements, other factors. Like curiosity, desire and my body. These are the urges that account for the wet, tonguey ten-minute kiss outside the laundry room that I remembered with a quivering belly for weeks afterwards. Ditto for my desire to bury my face in my boyfriend's armpits in order to learn his smell well enough to recognize it anywhere. This very same desire to know also made me reach down and feel a penis for the first time, checking almost methodically for shape, sensitivity and any strange aberrations on the skin. My quest was not simply a search for popularity, but a definite assertion of my own nascent erotic power. This strange force, not always pleasurable but always mine, nudged me toward physical exploration and self-definition, risk taking and intimacy building, twisting each element into an inextricable whole.

Because my mother was often away, leaving me with a safe and private space to bring my boyfriends, and because my common sense and experience of nonabusive love led me to decent men, my relationships consisted of relatively safe explorations of sex that were, at the time, fulfilling physically and emotionally. I also began to play with different kinds of strength. While I learned about my partners' bodies, I learned that I had the power to make them need me. While I learned how much of myself to reveal, I learned how to draw them out. While I learned that they were not "right" for me, I learned that I was more than what they saw.

Did I know then that I was learning to negotiate the world around me and answering important questions about the woman I would become? Probably not, but looking back, it seems obvious: I peeled back endless layers of contorted faces, checking out fully the possibilities of the roles I took on. I left them again and again when I felt I could not bring all of myself to the script. I couldn't just be the football player's cheerleader girlfriend, or the club girl friend of a bartender. I wasn't happy faking orgasm (self-deceit for male ego) or worrying about getting pregnant (unprotected ignorance) or having urinary tract infections (victim of pleasure) or sneaking around (living in fear). Instinctively I knew I wanted more pleasure and more freedom, and I intuitively knew I deserved and could get both.

When I think back, it is that impulse I am most proud of. The impulse that told me that I deserve to live free of shame, that my body is not my enemy and that pleasure is my friend and my right. Without this core, not even fully jelled in my teenage mind but powerful nonetheless, how else would I have learned to follow and cultivate my own desire? How else would I have learned to listen to and develop the language of my own body? How else would I have learned to initiate, sustain and develop healthy intimacy, that most valuable of human essences? I am proud that I did not stay in relationships when I couldn't grow. I moved on when the rest of me would emerge physically or intellectually and say, Enough! There isn't enough room in this outfit for all of us.

It is important to consider what happens when this kind of self-exploration is blocked by cultural taboo, government control or religious mandate. What happens when we are not allowed to know our own bodies, when we cannot safely respond to and explore our own desire? As evinced by the worldwide rape epidemic, the incredible number of teenage pregnancies, and the ever-increasing number of sexually transmitted diseases, sex can be an instrument of torture, the usher of unwanted responsibility or the carrier of fatal illness.

It is obvious that the suppression of sexual agency and exploration, from within or from without, is often used as a method of social control and domination. Witness widespread genital mutilation and the homophobia that dictatorially mandates heterosexuality; imagine the stolen power of the millions affected by just these two global murderers of self-authorization and determination. Without being able to respond to and honor the desires of our bodies and our selves, we become cut off from our instincts for pleasure, dissatisfied living under rules and thoughts that are not our own. When we deny ourselves safe and shameless exploration and access to reliable information, we damage our ability to even know what sexual pleasure feels or looks like.

Sex in silence and filled with shame is sex where our agency is denied. This is sex where we, young women, are powerless and at the mercy of our own desires. For giving our bodies what they want and crave, for exploring ourselves and others, we are punished like Eve reaching for more knowledge. We are called sluts and whores. We are considered impure or psychotic. Information about birth control is kept from us. Laws denying our right to control our bodies are enacted. We learn much of what we know from television, which debases sex and humiliates women.

We must decide that this is no longer acceptable, for sex is one of the places where we do our learning solo. Pried away from our parents and other authority figures, we look for answers about ourselves and how the world relates to us. We search for proper boundaries and create our very own slippery moral codes. We can begin to take control of this process and show responsibility only if we are encouraged to own our right to have a safe and self-created sexuality. The question is not whether young women are going to have sex, for this is far beyond any parental or societal control. The question is rather, what do young women need to make sex a dynamic, affirming, safe and pleasurable part of our lives? How do we build the bridge between sex and sexuality, between the isolated act and the powerful element that, when honed, can be an important tool for self-actualization?

Fortunately, there is no magic recipe for a healthy sexuality; each person comes into her or his own sexual power through a different route and at her or his own pace. There are, however, some basic requirements for sexual awareness and safe sexual practice. To begin with, young women need a safe space in which to explore our own bodies. A woman needs to be able to feel the soft smoothness of her belly, the exquisite softness of her inner thigh, the full roundness of her breasts. We need to learn that bodily pleasure belongs to us; it is our birthright.

Sex could also stand to be liberated from pussy and dick and fucking, as well as from marriage and procreation. It can be more: more sensual, more spiritual, more about communication and healing. Women and men both must learn to explore sexuality by making love in ways that are different from what we see on television and in the movies. If sex is about communicating, let us think about what we want to say and how will we say it. We need more words, images, ideas.

Finally, young women are more than inexperienced minors,

more than property of the state or of legal guardians. We are growing, thinking, inquisitive, self-possessed beings who need information about sex and access to birth control and abortion. We deserve to have our self-esteem nurtured and our personal agency encouraged. We need "protection" only from poverty and violence.

And even beyond all of the many things that will have to change in the outside world to help people in general and young women in particular grow more in touch with their sexual power, we also need to have the courage to look closely and lovingly at our sexual history and practice. Where is the meaning? What dynamics have we created or participated in? Why did we do that? How did we feel? How much of the way we think about ourselves is based in someone else's perception or label of our sexual experiences?

It has meant a lot to me to affirm and acknowledge my experiences and to integrate them into an empowering understanding of where I have been and where I am going. Hiding in shame or running fast to keep from looking is a waste of what is most precious about life: its infinite ability to expand and give us more knowledge, more insight and more complexity.

You're Not the Type

Laurel Gilbert

I had a baby at sixteen. Perhaps I should say that first, surprise you
with that statement up front. Because usually I don't. There are
people I've known for years who would be shocked or not believe
me if I were to casually mention that I am a mother.

You're too young!

I'm almost twenty-five. I have a daughter in the second grade.

You're so busy!

I'm a student. Teacher. Writer. I ride horses, bake banana bread
(on slow weekends), follow the underground riot grrrl movement.
I read *Ms.* and listen to Nine Inch Nails and the Violent Femmes. I
spend an extraordinary amount of time on the Net. I'm a
twentysomething, thirteenth-generation "slacker" with an attitude:
apathetic, angry, cynical, creative. I'm a young mother with alternative body piercings that attract questions in the mall.

You're not the type.

What type?

You know . . . the type to get pregnant.

Well. I can take that lots of ways. Does that mean I'm too smart? Or
too sophisticated? Too talented, perhaps? I have too much going

for me? Maybe I'm too "knowing." I can't think of myself as quite innocent, nor exactly stupid, though I guess I could be naive. I guess if I'm not the type, I'm either too much of something or not enough of something else. I wish I knew what.

Define, please, *the type.*

My teenage "crush" was a woman named Kris. While I was a fifteen-year-old junior, Kris was an older and wiser seventeen-year-old senior. I was a virgin when we met; she was experienced. My only encounters with alcohol were glasses of watered-down wine at family parties, my only drug use the second-hand smoke of my hippie-parents' joints. Kris had been transplanted by her mother and stepfather to my small, southern Utah town from the (I imagined) endless prairies of Kansas. I romantically indulged in private thoughts of Kris' short, curvy body against the lines of stark wheat that continued from horizon to horizon. Her dirty-blonde hair was indistinguishable (in my imagination) from the rippling grain. Years later—not having seen Kris for almost a decade—I can still formulate the curve of her upper lip over teeth that barely touched her full bottom lip; I can close my eyes and see the blue in hers. Kris and I were inseparable; we hijacked my mother's Volvo wagon late one night months before either of us could legally drive. We climbed out her basement window after her parents were asleep and returned before they awoke. We both eventually slept with the same high school senior and told ourselves and each other he was the only link between us, that if we could (and no one in southern Utah had words for what we might have been, then), we would erase his presence between us and love only each other.

"Someday, girl," Kris whispered, on our tired walk back to her bedroom window with the early morning moon as witness, "we'll be old and gray, two mean old ladies on our front porch, and we'll tell our kids about the night we snuck out of my stepdad's house and went skinny-dipping in the Comfort Inn pool."

I accepted this at face value. *Of course* we'd sit on our porch, rocking together on identical chairs. This was the natural outcome of a relationship like ours, wasn't it? Somehow, we could stay outside that life where men eventually come in, to fill in our spaces with their stories, their bodies. I didn't know that we weren't the first to verbalize our dream of being alone together. I don't know if Kris knew what we were, what we might have been.

What I do know: The night we swam at the Comfort Inn (my friend Michael had given us a key to a room and threatened us with death if we woke up any of the vacationing seniors), I rubbed lotion into the thick skin of Kris' back. After our illicit swim, I was breathless with the comfort of being and belonging with her. I was at home. The ridges were still on her back; my fingers pushed rivers of lotion through those tight canyons of scars from when her father had beaten her, years before. I felt cheated by the culture of our fathers, the culture that promised to take care of us, keep us safe, somehow, from the other men who might "ruin" us. Instead, that culture ruined our sense of our selves. I squeezed tears back into my eyes because the thought of anyone, any man, Kris' incestuous father, lashing those crevices into the back of the woman I might have (romantically) claimed I would die for caused my insides to grind and my hands to gently draw the knobs of her spine.

I knew I loved her.

I didn't know, however, that the next year, we would both be mothers: her eighteen, me sixteen.

Where is a group of women that I belong with, could be a part of? I've spent years fighting various educational, governmental, family and religious systems for my right to be a mother within those systems. I became a statistic when I got pregnant, another when I gave birth and yet another when I kept my daughter to raise. I got to be another statistic when I graduated from high school with my class (not with the "alternative" school I refused to attend), sweating in the June heat under my cap and gown. I got to be another when I completed my B.A. five years later, and another when I began my quest for the intellectual pot of gold, the Ph.D. at the end of the educational rainbow. The statistics change wherever I look for numbers to reassure me that I'm "normal," that my experiences somehow reflect the reality of a group of women who are "disadvantaged." I've grown tired, confused, hearing number on top of number, statistic after statistic. No statistics I've found, no numbers on a chart, express my experiences or reflect my stories. The *expectations* for teenage mothers are low; I've exceeded almost every one.

But if I'm so lucky and intelligent and talented, how did I get pregnant in the first place? I am not the stereotypical teen mother, who is thought of as dim-witted, weak, below average—a failure. I am one of those intellectual types. I have friends with whom I drink wine and discuss literature, philosophy and MTV. I haven't yet buckled under the weight of graduate school politics. I refuse to think of myself as a failure. And that's the problem. My words, my stories don't reflect any other words or stories being spoken about my kind. And I can't find any other words or stories being spoken *by* my kind; it seems other women like me are keeping their secret too, keeping quiet about their history. We're all silenced by expectations, perhaps because we've exceeded them.

Tonight, I wash dishes. I cook chili and my lover bakes brownies, and we—my lover, my daughter and I—eat dinner. Then, I pile the dishes around the sink and my lover vacuums the rugs; the "illegitimate" daughter of a teen mother rides her bike around the block. As I run the hot water over the slick surfaces of plates, bowls, knife edges, my sense of myself can split two ways. On one hand, I might be the exact image of Kris, or any other woman in her mid-twenties with a daughter in grade school. Washing dishes on a sweaty evening. But on the other, I have class in the morning. I have papers to write, conferences to attend. Things I was told no teenage mother would ever get to do—though everyone told me to expect to wash dishes on hot nights.

∾

Okay. So I slept with a man. Did IT. Got caught. Knocked up. Stuck. Screwed.

After I found out, I couldn't decide if I wanted to stay in school. I mean, I knew I wanted to *go* to school, but the prospect of waking up and actually walking through the doors seven months pregnant wearing my dad's flannel shirts terrified me. I was fighting off the looks—both real and imagined—of others who had (I supposed) been smarter. Wiser. No one reassured me that my "difference" was, in fact, normal. Not one of my friends on the college-bound track confided her own fears of missed periods or broken condoms, and I wasn't part of the other crowd who seemed blasé about their sexual escapades and contraceptive disasters. I wasn't even the only one wearing maternity clothes, but I felt like the only "different" one alive. The only one not "normal." The others in my extended group may have been different, but they weren't wearing their difference. Homosexuality, abusive parents, suicidal depression, even drug and alcohol use (or abuse) could be invisible in classrooms, unlike my rounding figure. Other students may have had problems, living some secret life after the sun went down and they left our shared life of teen angst and first cars. But if they did, I didn't know about it. They, however, did know about my difference—my swelling middle made it obvious. I couldn't hide it, keep it secret.

I finished high school because of the subtle pressure of friends and teachers. I kept my head up, eyes straight forward, over the eyes of those who would stare. I spent lunch hours hidden in the catwalks of the auditorium, curled up in a fetal position in the dust and cobwebs, like a child inside a child's belly. At one o'clock, I crawled out of my den, my eyes blinking like an animal coming out of hibernation, and joined everyone else for afternoon classes.

I slept a lot when I came home.

What seemed a lifetime, but was actually only a few years after a pregnant Kris followed her abusive, drug-using husband to Kansas, I discovered Adrienne Rich's "Compulsory Heterosexuality and Lesbian Existence." I'd been so ignorant! I didn't go through childhood aware of my so-called abnormality, able to put a name to my feelings. I wasn't terrified when I was young that someone might call me "queer" or "dyke," for those words literally never entered the sphere of my teenage life. I was progressive; open-minded; active in theatre, debate, radical politics (as much as a teen in a small town knows of radical politics). I had "crushes" on boys, told my friends that so-and-so was attractive. This was normal: I had friends who were boys and with whom I occasionally had sex; thus, they were obviously "boyfriends." It wasn't abnormal, exactly, for Kris and me to adore each other; we were friends, and we had boyfriends (sometimes the same one) so we weren't "queer" or "sick." It's only looking back that I realize that our love (like gravity before the apple fell) had no name, not even a secret, evil, unable-to-be-spoken name; therefore, it couldn't possibly exist.

And here's the biggest paradox: Had I been able to love Kris—and had that kind of difference been my reality—I might never have become a teenage mother in the first place. I had sex with my first male lover because I was fascinated with the sexual relationship he had with Kris. What he did, I wanted to do, though at the time that desire was vague and without definition. What I *wanted*, apparently, was to sleep with Kris. Since women were unavailable to women sexually, what I *did* was sleep with the man who could—and did—sleep with Kris. Unfortunately, I got, in a phrase, "knocked up."

Getting pregnant at sixteen in a southern Utah high school is incredibly easy. I assume—though I hope I'm wrong—that any small town, in fact, maybe any high school, is comparable. Of the one hundred and fifty girls in my graduating class, two were wearing maternity dresses under their graduation gowns. Three (myself included) had children in tow at the ceremony. Two married a month after graduation and produced babies within nine months. Between eighth and twelfth grades, countless numbers of girls dropped out, attended a year of "alternative" school, and then disappeared. I knew of two abortions, but there were rumors of many more. Abortions were difficult; if the girl's parents knew and consented, they traveled to Salt Lake City. In a city settled by Catholics in a Mormon state, however, the chances of a girl having pro-choice parents were slim. If the boy-father had money, a trip could be arranged to Colorado, where abortions were possible but still expensive. No doctor in town would prescribe the Pill to an unmarried teen, and the only Planned Parenthood—located conspicuously on the busiest street—was anything but anonymous. I'm not trying to put down my own time or place. The eighties may have been no different from the sixties—or today. A small Utah town may be no different from Chicago. But in my town in my time, no obvious difference, no deviation from the norm, was—or could be—visible. Or available. Girls were heterosexual virgins, or else they got "in trouble" and "dropped out." There was no way to be different, and no way to name any kind of difference.

I had no words.

I've since found words and phrases others use to name me and others like me. Words that classify difference in a patriarchal world, define me and other women in terms of relationships—or lack of them—with men. These are the words given to me by the establishment to categorize what they think I am:

Single mother. I have no man, but have had one. I'm ruined. Slut. Whore.

Lesbian. I have no man, and obviously can't get one. Pervert. Sick.

Feminist. I will never have a man. Man-hater.

Lesbian-feminist-single-mother. Whoa, here!

What I want are words to define myself without the connotations of absence.

About a week before purchasing a pregnancy test for myself (from the farthest drugstore I could drive to), I went to Planned Parenthood with a friend who thought that *she* might be pregnant. Strangely, Heather and I were not close; we had one or two classes together and were both members of the Drama Club. I was depressed; everything was either razor-sharp or under water, but both sensations were painful. I talked to no one about my own suspicions, but for some reason agreed to accompany a girl I barely knew to an anonymous clinic for her own pregnancy test.

Heather babbled continuously from the moment we got in her car until the lab assistant gave her the negative result and set up an appointment for her to get birth control pills. I watched my hands in my lap and the muted sunshine glinting the hairs on my wrist gold. I sat detached from myself in the brown-and-yellow waiting room and scanned the fronts of pamphlets titled "What to do if you're pregnant," "Help! I think I'm pregnant!" and "Options: Abortion, Adoption, and Parenthood." I didn't read them. I didn't even stash them in the bottom of my backpack for later reading. I only looked back and forth from my golden arms to the pamphlet rack. Heather's voice trickled in and out of my ears, as if the examining room next to the waiting room were also underwater. I listened to Heather's stilted droning to the nurse about her Mexican American boyfriend, her fear of telling her mother, her terror at being seen leaving Planned Parenthood.

I can only assume I seemed pleased and relieved when Heather tearfully told me she was not pregnant.

As we drove back to school, back into the lives we'd deviated from for an afternoon to fix her big mistake, I imagined all the words that might be in the pamphlets. Questions loomed. How many fail? What have I done? How do I fix this? I'm supposed to be smart. How did this happen to me?

I carried my pregnancy test with me to school—when I finally got brave enough to mix it. In the bottom of my backpack was a small vial of my own pee, turning the bottom of the test tube pink. The pinkness seemed so benign, harmless, such a sweet color, the color of babies. Pink can be lethal for those who don't want sweetness.

A couple of weeks after my escapade with Heather, my friend Chrysalyne casually mentioned that her mom had seen me leaving

Planned Parenthood. She congratulated me on getting birth control and commended my bravery to use the option the clinic provided and to ignore any criticism or ridicule. I'm sure I knew by then I was pregnant. I probably even told Chrysalyne.

When the reality finally hit me, I went into a thick fog. I remember stark moments of my junior year, nothing from the summer before my last year in high school. I scribbled things in my journal from time to time.

I told only two of my teachers before school let out for the summer. My art teacher shrugged and said, "Well, your future's changed, but it's not over." He then gave me a sheet of paper and told me to get back to work. My drama teacher only said, "I knew that," and began a subtle campaign to keep me from losing my sense of self, from giving up before I'd begun. He hired me as yearbook staff photographer. He gave me a scene to prepare for the state drama competition. He put me in charge of coaching sophomore actors for auditions and monologues. He encouraged my writing. He made me work as hard for him as I had before I confessed my "mistake" to him.

In contrast, the guidance counselor who was supposed to help me with college applications said she was helping me more by encouraging me to consider the one-year beauty or secretarial programs at the junior college—careers I had little interest in to begin with. My status as single mother, she pointed out, made it important that I quickly put myself in the position of buck-getting, cash-making, self-supporting head of household. My interest in the humanities—reading and writing—would be fine as a hobby but would not pay the rent. She said it was for my own good and congratulated me for graduating from high school in the first place. It's such a struggle, she said, to balance a family and school. It's so nice, she crooned, to see one young girl who has overcome her "handicap."

I never considered myself a handicapped person. And I firmly believe it's the status of "handicapped" that leads teen mothers into fulfilling the expectations of the stereotypes and failing their own expectations. Many people told me "you can do it," but very few believed it. "You can do it" has to have a slight challenge to it, a bit of expectation to make it work. My drama teacher said "you can do it" when he gave me the job of capturing my senior year on film. His "you can do it" was a statement, however, and not a plea. *You can do it, so don't expect me to relax my expectations of you because you've made what you think is a mistake. You can do it, so don't come back to me and tell me you've failed, because I know your potential, I know what you're capable of and I expect you to succeed.*

The "you can do it" of my guidance counselor, however, was a plea. She didn't really believe it. *Oh, you're so brave and strong, I know you can do just a little bit more than the other young women who are "crippled" like you. You've gone beyond the expectations I had for you as a failure, a burden on society, so if you could just finish one more year of secretarial school and perhaps meet a nice man and get married, you will have succeeded beyond my wildest dreams for you. You can do it.*

I was no longer expected to succeed; I was expected to settle. Whatever it might have been that I wanted to do—planned to do— could no longer be an option after my "mistake." I would have to admit that I had failed and settle for whatever society considered me capable of. I no longer had to prove my worth; I had none.

In order to fulfill my own expectations after my daughter was born, I made myself strong. I kept my motherhood a secret from my "successful" life in school, writing, teaching, and each time I took my daughter to a doctor for an ear infection, I bristled at being condescended to because of my young age.

I became a real enigma.

Here is the connection between my motherhood and my sexual identity: I was convinced I couldn't be a college-bound, writing, reading, pregnant teen, just as I couldn't be a lesbian/bisexual woman. I was sure that an intelligent, strong, educated, willful young mother couldn't possibly exist, in the same way I was convinced I could not love Kris the way I wished in that small desert town. Neither my brand of motherhood nor my sexual identity were ever presented as options to me. When I read Rich's "Compulsory Heterosexuality," a space opened up for me to speak as a lesbian/bisexual woman. Suddenly there were other lesbian/bisexual feminists around, women who welcomed me, supported me, maybe even loved me. I'm still looking for others like me who are "out" as successful, young, single mothers—women who haven't given up their hopes or plans after the teenage birth of their first child. Women—myself included—are often firmly convinced there is only one position open to them and can therefore strive only to fill that position.

The possibility of loving women as well as men (when it finally occurred to me) was so clear, so normal that I felt foolish for not having thought of it before. I became angry with the society that hadn't given me the option—my right—to be a lesbian/bisexual woman. In the same way, the guidance counselor hadn't given me the option—again, my right—to be successful in my own right, by my own terms, in whatever capacity I felt drawn to. Adrienne Rich, Audre Lorde, Susie Bright and other "out" lesbian/feminist activists have opened spaces for women to create their own sensual and sexual choices. It might have been much easier for me to achieve what I have if someone had offered me the freedom to plan my future and set my own goals as a young mother. And I might have struggled less to find out who I was if my guidance counselor hadn't told me who I was to begin with.

I am doing things with my life I didn't know were possible. I'm a student. Teacher. Writer. I ride horses and bake banana bread. I read *Ms.* and listen to Nine Inch Nails and the Violent Femmes. I'm a twentysomething, thirteenth-generation "slacker" with an attitude. I am a young mother with alternative body piercings that attract questions in the mall.

I'm just the type.

Tight Jeans and Chania Chorris

Sonia Shah

I had already been away at college for a few years when my little sister unleashed her budding sexuality onto my unsuspecting suburban Indian family. When I came home to Connecticut from Oberlin on breaks, I would find her furtively posing for the mirror. At dinner, she sat opposite the window, and her eyes darted from the conversation to her reflection, trying to catch a "candid" glimpse of herself. She wore tight, tight stirrup pants and off-the-shoulder blouses and dark lipstick. In the beginning, my parents and I were merely chagrined.

I had just gathered enough resolve, egged on by my feminist boyfriend of the time, to stop shaving my legs and armpits. It felt good, but in a shaky kind of way, like if anyone asked me why I did it I might just get enraged and teary and not be able to explain. That was usually how I got when I tried to explain my new "college ideas" to my parents. I remember confessing to my mother, shyly but slightly self-righteously, that I had applied for a job at a women's newspaper. "You want to work with just women?" she asked. "That's not right. You shouldn't separate yourself from half of humanity. Men and women together, boys and girls together, that's how it should be. I'd get bored with just one or the other," she went on. Defeated, but secretly condemning her for her lack of consciousness, I didn't say more.

I was having even less luck testing out my new ideas on Dad. He seemed to think my insistence on using gender-neutral language, for instance, was a symptom of weak logic. We actually got into some fights over it. He'd argue that I was losing the forest for the trees: "What, we're supposed to say 'snowperson' instead of 'snowman'? How does that help anything?" I'd get flustered and high-strung.

So at the time when my sister started parading and preening about the house, I wasn't feeling too secure as a feminist in the family setting. It seemed I could rant against MTV images of disembodied women, discuss the efficacy of affirmative action for women and debate the philosophy of Simone de Beauvoir only with my friends at college. But I knew, from the building tension in the house and my sister's growing narcissism and self-objectification, that a feminist intervention was necessary; my class-privileged, sheltered life had actually provided me with a situation in which I needed to *act*.

What to do? I worried, privately, that she was exploiting herself and setting herself up for the kinds of exploitation and abuse I had suffered at the hands of the white boys of our local public high school when I sexualized my dress and manner in high school. I wanted them to notice me, and they did—when they couldn't get the attention of any of the pretty girls from "nice" (that is, white) families. And then they wanted action, fast. And if they didn't get it, they got mad. They spread ugly rumors, harassed me, orchestrated humiliating pranks.

I had just gotten over all that, purging it as a time of insecurity and naiveté in a sexist, racist high school, when my sister seemed to be starting it all over again. Only she was getting better results: Boys were calling her on the phone; when I picked her up from the mall with her friends, she was surrounded by adoring white boys (their brothers had called me names); she was charming, lovely, flirtatious, everyone wanted to be near her.

So I was a little jealous, hating myself for feeling jealous, and trying to use the blunt tools of my college-learned feminism to understand why and what to do. My friends advised me. "She's objectifying herself. If she sets herself up as a sexualized Other, she will never centralize herself, she'll never be truly Subject," they said. "Tell her to throw away her tight jeans!"

One morning, we were both combing our hair in front of the big bathroom mirror. She was done up in typical regalia: scant, restrictive clothes with straps and belts and chains. "Aren't you kind of uncomfortable in that?" I asked. "Nooooo," she cooed, "why should I be?" "Well, don't you wish that boys would like you even if you didn't wear things like that?" I couldn't help feeling like I was coming off as jealous or something. "They would," she said resolutely, as if I were crazy for thinking things could be otherwise. "Sonia, you wear your clothes because you like them and you like how you look in them—not just because they are comfortable," she shot at me. "So don't give me this thing like you don't care how you look." She paused. "I like these clothes for me."

Fair enough, I guessed.

She's not going to throw away the tight jeans.

Vaguely displeased with the results of my intervention, but quelled, I turned my attention elsewhere.

A year passed. I graduated from college and moved to Boston. The challenges presented me were overwhelming; home and family life seemed dreamily effortless in contrast. So I was disturbed when my mother confided in me that she was having trouble with my sister.

"She doesn't listen, she's stubborn, she's wayward, she talks on the phone all the time, she always wants to go out, she's boy-crazy!" Pause. "I bet she's having sex," she whispered.

It was brave for my mother to say this last thing. She seemed a little scared when she said it, almost as if it was profane to even think this, but what could she do? My mother grew up in a small town in southern India, the smartest girl in the family, the one they all saved for to send to medical school. But not everyone in her family was so supported. My mother's oldest sister was abruptly taken out of school at the age of fourteen for writing a scandalous secret love letter to a local boy. Afterwards, she slit her wrists. This situation was never spoken of again. She never went back to school. She stayed in the kitchen with my grandmother and got married young, to a sensible and kind man of limited possibilities. Her sisters and brothers all live in a big world, speak many languages, are upwardly mobile. This oldest aunt stays at home all day in a dusty, exploited village and prays. She seems much older than she is.

In contrast, my mother emigrated to New York City when she was twenty-five years old, shortly after graduating from medical school and marrying my father by arrangement. He settled here first, and she followed six months later, arriving in a wintry JFK airport in her thickest sari, a woolen shawl and chappals. On her first day, while my dad was at work, she took two trains and a bus to Macy's and rode the escalators up and down, up and down, for hours, enthralled by the glitter and lights. She hadn't been on an escalator before, nor had she heard the delicate rhythmic ticking of a car's turn indicator, both of which signified the great advances and ingenuity of the New World to her. Now, perhaps, with her daughter at the brink of one of women's oldest tragedies, U.S. society did not seem so rich.

I didn't know whether my sister was having sex or not, but beyond the fact that I didn't like how she chose to express her sexuality (still those tight jeans!), I thought she should be supported if she were having sex. It's her sexuality, and any attempt on our part to rein it in would be disingenuous and oppressive, I reasoned. Sure, she's young, but with the proper guidance and support, she can gain from the wisdom of others. Knowing my mother's attitude—that is, absolute terror that her daughter may be having sex before marriage—I knew my sister would be getting no guidance from her.

Intervention Number Two. I invited her up to Boston, and we

talked about it. I told her she shouldn't do anything she doesn't want to do, she should practice safe sex, she should know what she does and does not want, and in general tried to instill a healthy mistrust of the boy's so-called expertise. She seemed prepared.

I don't know how it went with the boy, but soon afterwards, in a flurry of family disgruntlement, my sister was sent on a three-month visit to India with our extended family. Exile.

She came back changed. More introspective, less self-conscious. She had brought back presents. When I came home, my parents prodded her excitedly to show me the new *chania chorri* she had bought in India. Chania chorris are sets of midriff-baring blouses and long full skirts worn under saris. Young girls get colorful brocaded ones to wear without the sari. She put it on. It was beautiful: all covered up in the front, regal, royal looking. When she turned around, I saw that it was backless, with just two little bows holding the front part on.

I was shocked at this taboo display of flesh in full parental view. Apparently unlike my sister, I remembered my dad's stern command to us not to wear nightgowns around the house. I remembered her having to conceal her tiny outfits with big flannel shirts.

But my parents loved the backless chania chorri. Both Mom and Dad oohed and ahhed, telling her to turn around again, to wear it to an upcoming festival. She pirouetted about flirtatiously. They beamed and clapped.

I was dumbfounded, the family friction over my sister's sexuality suddenly and miraculously dissipated. Gone! No problem! Feeling suckered and resentful of my obvious misunderstanding, I gave up: We lived in different families, she and I.

It was years before I felt I finally understood the rollercoaster conflict over my sister's budding sexuality. By flaunting her tight jeans and red lipstick outfits and by insistently making boys her first priority, she was demanding parental approval for her sexuality, obviously, as many young people do. But for us, Indian daughters isolated from India, parental approval means cultural approval. And my sister picked the wrong culture. She wore "Western" sexiness and asked her parents to say: sexy is okay, Western is okay.

Like me, she had to deal with her sexuality in the context of both white patriarchy and Indian patriarchy. When she played to white patriarchy, my parents didn't like it. They were scared of its possibilities, that she would lose her "Indian" female self, which is obedient, never talks back and doesn't have sex before marriage. I was scared too, of the possibility of violence. But when she played to Indian patriarchy, when she played the Indian coquette, all covered up but safely naughty on the side, like one of Krishna's cow-girls, they felt safe again. And so did she.

Though it didn't make sense in my cultural setting, I had tried to force my intellectualized, white feminist ideas on my family. Tell my father to use gender-neutral language! This is a man for whom English is a second, less evocative language. Tell my mother to give my sister condoms for safe sex! This is a woman who knows firsthand the tragedy that can occur when patriarchal systems are challenged. Tell my sister not to wear tight jeans and to stop shaving! She'll just revert to revealing saris, and that's no better.

I was analyzing the situation on white feminism's terms, which don't recognize cultural duality. So I thought my sister was buying into sexist myths about beauty and female sexuality, when she was seeking an appropriate cultural expression of her sexuality in a society that doesn't recognize anything outside the monoculture of "Americanism." Telling her to throw away her tight jeans was never the answer. The answer was to establish that an Indian American feminist girl doesn't have to choose between American patriarchy and Indian patriarchy. She also doesn't have to lose her culture, whatever it may be.

I could have shown her how Asian American feminists incorporate feminism into their Asian lives and their American lives, and thus create new spaces for action. That far from needing approval from the cultural guardians (either white boys or parents in this case), we can subvert both. If instead of criticizing her for wearing tight jeans I had perhaps encouraged her to wear a chorri with them, knowing what I know now, she would have been amenable, maybe even interested in doing so. And doing so at once marks her as outside of the cultural arena controlled by white patriarchy and the one controlled by Indian patriarchy. It is uniquely hers. And it gives her so much more: the ability to envision new realities.

As I realized that I couldn't simply graft white feminist ideas onto my life, things started to work out better. I explained to my dad about how feminism was also about spiritual liberation, about subverting both the internal and external cages that keep women down. I explained to my mom about how sexual experimentation, in the context of a supporting, loving environment, is useful in preparing kids for the responsibilities of adult relationships and families. A simple concern for the spirit and for the family is vitally important to them and to me; reinterpreting feminist ideas in this context lets the ideas actually get heard.

What Is Mine

Sharon Lennon

Once upon a time there was Me. Oh, there were others, I guess, but if they existed they would have to go through Me first. It was Me that made it possible for me to speak my mind without apology, laugh as loud as I wanted, think and feel freely, assume respect from others and most of all, play baseball. After all, I had decided that I would grow up to replace the catcher for the Yankees. It was beside the point that there were no women in Major League Baseball, because I was not a girl, I was just Me. And that was that.

However, the endlessly fabulous Me was completely clueless when it came to the realities of gender roles. I tried out for Little League in 1975, without realizing that girls had been officially allowed to play for the first time just a year earlier. The Little League world was no more comfortable with this concept than the majority of people in the suburban New Jersey town where I lived. But I made the team and received my first official baseball cap, which I promptly placed on my head and refused to take off for any reason other than a bath. So, at the age of eight, while still safe from the adolescent categorizing that determines who is "popular" and who is not, my hat and mitt, along with my favorite Fonzie T-shirt, were staples in my wardrobe. But as I approached the wise old age of ten, the concept of Me started being challenged by Sergio Valentes and tube tops. Suddenly, Fonzie began to seem like a rather inappropriate role model, and my hat and mitt attachment became a dilemma, as did most of my natural inclinations.

The rise and reign of *Charlie's Angels* brought in feathered-back hair and a commitment to the style that required a large plastic comb to be stored in one's snug back pocket during those rare moments when it was not being used. I had never really given much thought to combing my hair at all, and the idea of trading in my baseball cap for a Farrah Fawcett look completely confounded me. But the girls in school whose bangs were getting wispier and whose jeans were getting snugger were making it clear to me that I was an oddball. So I entered fifth grade with the harsh realization that tight jeans were a wise alternative to Toughskins with patches on the knees if I was to have any hope of avoiding geek status. What I didn't realize was that my ability to fit these requirements would shape not only how I was known to others as a girl, but the size and shape of the box that I would eventually have to break out of as a woman.

My mother, who had the power to control my social destiny with a few simple decisions, thought designer jeans were just a ridiculous waste of money, and I was given two choices for my bimonthly haircut: "You can have a short shag or a long shag. That's what you can have." My younger sister later eased away from this routine by talking my mother into a pixie, which led to a begging session that resulted in a Dorothy Hamill. My mother loved it: "Ohhh, that's *cute!*" If I was going to do this, the last thing I was going to be was cute. I decided that I would make the shag my ticket to fitting in. I simply bought myself the big plastic comb and flipped all those layered bits over so they faced the back of my head, and I had myself a makeshift feathered-back look. I talked my mother into one pair of Sassoon jeans, which I wore almost daily. However, neither my popularity nor my comfort level had risen.

It became increasingly difficult to keep the friends I thought I had, and while this was partly due to my history of unfortunate fashion choices, I was mostly being ostracized for my sense of individuality, my somewhat strident nature and my big mouth. It was finally sinking in that things like Little League, tackle football, telling people what I thought, threatening boys with physical violence if they messed with me and occasionally acting like Vinnie Barbarino were hurting my chances for having girl friends. For a while I got by socially by continuing one-on-one relationships with some of them. They liked me when we spent time alone. We could act naturally, without the fear of being judged. However, in the clique I was "weird" and often shushed or simply told to shut up because I was detracting from their group statement. They were girls who knew how to fit in, and I was not. Unfortunately, I had no way of knowing that being expected to abandon my actual personality for the sake of a uniform standard of behavior is the perpetual order of patriarchy. So when friends started keeping their distance, I took it hard and very personally.

Being hyper-aware of girls' reactions to me, I made nervous attempts to distract their attention by making jokes and performing impersonations of kids and teachers. I developed an earnest need to entertain, all the while feeling the girls' acute awareness of my nonconformity. I mistakenly thought that I could duck behind a raised voice and more antics, but girls watched and caught everything. This only caused me to lose more friends and spend a lot of hours in detention, with my mother developing such a familiar rapport with the principals and teachers that she knew just about all of them on a first-name basis.

While I was stockpiling hours of detention time, I was gradually losing my fondness for other girls. They were exhausting me. In fact, they were really starting to get on my nerves. So I detached myself from them and stopped setting my sights on school friends. I started hanging out with the boys on my block. They had to let me play with them because I was older and bigger and seemed to have the largest of all the egos in the neighborhood. I was the decision maker. I split up the teams for street hockey and picked who would be "it" when we played Manhunt. I ruled my block after three in the afternoon and during the weekends. My relationships with the neighborhood boys were relatively painless and uncluttered by anxiety. As long as I could throw a football, they didn't notice I was a girl. Both my mother and my father were aware of this and encouraged my assertive behavior for a long time. They almost got a kick out of it.

Then, as the second baseball season approached, my exclusively female body parts started to develop, and my status as a girl became clearer to me every day. I picked up on a growing discomfort both kids and adults had with my presence on the field, and boys began routinely calling my strength and intelligence into question. This didn't stop me from wanting to try out for catcher, an opportunity that was never awarded me by my second-year coach, Mr. Slank. Afternoon practices were humiliating experiences, and games were two hours of pure, unwavering angst. I used to sweat profusely while sitting on the bench, waiting for Mr. Slank to put me up to bat. I didn't worry about hitting the ball or bruising my hip from sliding into base. The feelings I had simply leaving the dugout were enough to strip me of all sense of self-worth. A meaty index finger pointed at me, then pointed at home plate. I was up and looking at Mr. Slank for the standard "All right, way ta go, let's go" that he would grace the boys with. Instead, he would gaze off into the field, popping his gum and fiddling with his cap, while I tried my hardest not to look at my proud parents who sat grinning in the bleachers.

However, I believed that if given the chance to really play, I would dazzle everyone with my abilities and receive the proper respect from my coach and teammates. "Mr. Slank," I found myself saying one day after practice, "Umm, do you think, maybe, I could possibly catch in a game?" Suddenly, the boys who had been horsing around among themselves were now riveted to our conversation, which I had tried so hard to make discreet. As I looked up into Mr. Slank's cool, amused smirk, every pore in my body pleaded with him to just answer the question so I could walk away with a little dignity. He waited a few moments, smiled and said, "All right." For a few beats I felt overwhelming relief and excitement. Then he continued, "But you'll have to wear a cup like everyone else."

The boys who had gathered around snickered, and Mr. Slank looked rather pleased with himself. For me, the chance to prove myself was enough to snicker back at him and say, "Big deal, fine." After spinning around on my heel and walking off proudly, I couldn't help wondering, What is a cup and why is everyone laughing? Later, when I relayed the story to my mother, she gasped and said, "He said *what*?" I promptly told her I didn't care, I'd do it.

"Sharon, honey," she said, "Do you know what a cup is?"

"Yeah," I snapped.

"Honey, a cup holds a man's penis and testicles in and protects them, because that part of their body is vulnerable."

"Oh," I said, and thought about it for a moment. "Really?"

"Yes, really."

"So I don't have to wear one."

"Honey, no, you don't have to wear one."

Finally, after a long silence and some piecing together, I was faced with two undeniable truths: I was being treated badly because I was a girl, and Mr. Slank was nothing more than a big jerk. My mother and I discussed it both then and at other times, but the word "sexism" was never uttered. No one I knew ever said it, so I had no knowledge of it or its widespread existence. I still thought I wasn't good enough.

Rather than divorce myself from my favorite things, I dropped the whole idea of developing friendships with anyone at school or in Little League. Without any support, I was left with an overwhelming sense of isolation and a fear of going on a hunch that there wasn't really anything wrong with me. I simply pressed on with my aspirations and retreated from interactions with my peers.

In a lot of ways I lived a good portion of my youth as a feminist but with no awareness of it. I assumed that I should be treated equally to and taken as seriously as any boy. In fact, I was so convinced of this that the reality of gender inequities took years for me to swallow. Being treated as an individual seemed like an obvious right of birth to me. I had no political or social understanding of what that really meant and no idea that anyone else shared my struggle. It would be another seven years before I started using the term "sexist" to describe misogynistic behavior, an additional three years until I adopted the label "feminist" for myself and two more to realize that feminism was about more than just reclaiming Me.

Alienation is a key ingredient to keeping girls and women performing according to plan. It's the backup system just in case the initial instructions on being female don't sink in. By seventh grade I felt I had been alienated by just about every collective body in school, and my Little League days were numbered. When I sought support from my family to try out for the more advanced Babe Ruth league, my father shocked me with an extreme concern about my "safety."

"The older boys don't play the same. They throw those balls at such a high speed. It's no joke when one of those things comes flyin' at ya."

I was shocked by what he said and that my mother backed him up with equal concern. At first, their intention wasn't to say no to my playing. Instead they took me down to the baseball field one Saturday afternoon to scare me out of it. My father said they wanted me "to see just how strong and big the boys are now. If you want to play, you need to know that. But I think you'll probably change your mind." It had never occurred to me that boys were bigger than me, and I was sure I could match their strength. But on that Saturday morning I found myself leaning over the bleachers considering their capabilities and questioning my own in a way I had never thought to before. Suddenly, I was afraid of getting hurt. I turned to my parents, who sat behind me waiting for the desired reaction, and said, "Wow, they pitch fast."

In the car, on the way home, I tried to push through my fear by making an announcement that I would try out anyway. My father quickly squashed that effort by telling me he wouldn't have the time to drive me to games two nights a week. I felt both relief and disillusionment rip through me. Suddenly, I knew I would never have a career in baseball. I also felt ashamed. I knew I had betrayed myself. It was the first time I felt my sex play a role in how my parents treated me, and I was crushed by the realization that gender would have such an impact on my life choices. There was something terribly wrong and unattractive about my strength and lack of frailty. It had messed up my chances of having an active social life with girls, who would not tolerate it, while the boys refused to see it at all and had stopped including me simply because I was a girl.

Gradually, my repertoire was drastically readjusted to include four pairs of tight jeans, an aloof hair-flipping technique, a lovely shade of Christie-Brinkley-blue eye shadow and a rather highbrow hatred of all sports. I was sick of not having friends, and my relationships with the boys on my block had become obsolete. Although I didn't admit it, I wanted intimacy. Groups of friends and social gatherings were out of the question. They made me insecure and sick to my stomach. So after a while I became skilled in the art of developing one "best" friendship. After two years of changing my entire perspective in order to have more friends and still not acquiring any more than one at a time, I came to understand that I was lucky to have one best friend. I found my best friends weren't spending time with my persona, they were spending time with me. I got into a habit of not wanting it any other way, and chose friends who were also seeking their own tastes, voice, thought process and strengths.

Just before high school graduation, my best friend introduced me to passages she had discovered in a book written by Gloria Steinem. She thought this book was "so cool." I knew vaguely who Gloria Steinem was and that she was a "feminist," but what this meant almost completely eluded me. The "women's movement" was not happening in my world when I was growing up. It was happening on television. Images of women were changing, but where I was no one was budging. Feminism and women's changing views of themselves and society were present in my life in the form of sitcoms like *That Girl* and *The Mary Tyler Moore Show*. I remember network news mentioning the names Gloria Steinem and Bella Abzug, but I had only my mother to translate the meaning of their actions, and she was not pleased with either of them. She yelled expletives at the television set when Gloria Steinem was a guest on *Donahue*. Until I actually read Gloria Steinem's book, feminism and Gloria Steinem were just things that made my mother spray venom through gritted teeth. "That woman is pushy and snooty. She's just obnoxious," she would say. Her vacuuming would become more furious and her dusting more passionate. I thought my mother was just being annoying. I didn't understand just how scared she was of what Gloria Steinem and others like her were saying and how unapologetically they were saying it.

After high school, I decided that additional schooling was appropriate for me only after I figured out just where I wanted to steer my life. I worked and took to educating myself on everything and anything I could get my hands on. I brought home the *New York Times, USA Today* and news magazines, and I collected and read books on every subject imaginable. On Sundays I watched *The McLaughlin Group* and an endless array of news and commentary shows. I filtered everything I learned through feminism because it was one of the first subjects I embraced. My mother, who had allowed and encouraged me to be who I was through most of my youth, viewed this as a major point of contention between us. My father simply stayed out of it. In my quest for individuality through feminism, there were a lot of screaming matches between my mother and me. In my earlier years she validated and supported my determination, ambition, assertiveness, stubbornness—and of course my baseball. All of these things helped lead me to feminism. But when the pressure was on and the struggle to retain these qualities required a more critical approach to the world and a thicker skin, my mother's support gave way to her own internalized fears of feminism. It took me years to forgive her for that.

While learning about how I was just one of many women who struggle with misogyny, I had no desire to link myself to these women or any group effort; connectedness to other women was not on my agenda. I interpreted feminism in isolation and solitude and found strength and validation that had been missing from my life for years. Feminism was too personal to share with others. It was mine. I had tried to share the personal before, with girls in school who called themselves my friends, and at home with my mother. It hadn't worked, and I would not fall prey to that desire again. My emotional need was to get my individuality back and solidly nail it down.

While I was establishing the power and importance of my own voice, I admit I often did so defensively, with blatant condescension. My mother, who did not have a job outside the house, became not only my sounding board but often the target for my anger. I used my mother's choices and the way she lived her life to illustrate how I thought women were oppressed. I thought she personified everything I was fighting against, everything I was determined not to be, and I made her aware of that constantly. In my view, she was just another person who caressed and embraced patriarchy, and women like her were making it harder for me.

I spent a few years stalking my mother in a mode of unwavering pontification, going to great lengths to nail her on everything from shaving her eyebrows to not having a "job." From age eighteen until about twenty-one, I followed my mother around the house, supplying her with an unwelcome editorial on just about everything she did or said. These daily episodes would end in my mother yelling, "Stop all this melodrama and ranting and raving!" Then she would turn on the vacuum cleaner to drown out the sound of my judgmental voice. My words were suffocating her, but I was angry and felt on a very deep level that she had betrayed me over and over. All through my early youth, my mother had been nothing but encouraging, telling me I could do "anything" and "everything" I chose to in my life. But as I became an adult, she did not support the means by which I would achieve success. My anger toward women, including myself, ran deep and my mother bore the brunt of it. I attacked her as a symbol of all the women whom I felt betrayed or shut out by.

It was only later that I began to realize that my mother also had a need to express and understand herself as an individual, and no one was supporting her. I used the rhetoric of feminism without regard to its relevance to all women, including my mother, and without actually calling myself a feminist. Rather than welcome open dialogue and understanding with my mother, I slammed the door on her, shutting out her fears and regrets in order to have a sounding board on which to establish myself and my views. I took my mother to task on the entire structure of her life, criticizing her choice of marriage and a family over college and a career, and the tenacity with which she cleaned our house—the only thing over which she felt a sense of control. As a result of this, my mother's hatred of feminism grew because she thought it hated her. After all, she felt it didn't respect her and neither did her daughter, who was using it to attack her. My mother had no idea of what feminism had to offer her, and as much as I thought I knew what it had to offer me, I kept far away from the most rewarding and empowering part: unity with other women. Feminism was a passage back to myself, to what I thought I had lost. I was unsympathetic to anyone's need for time and growth, except my own. But it was time and growth that taught me that feminism was about more than just Me.

I wish I could say that I aspired to develop the ability to empathize and understand other women's experiences, to embrace a fuller sense of feminism. I'm afraid it was pure exhaustion that relaxed my clenched fists enough to take hold of the term "feminist" for myself. Perhaps it was breaking away from my hometown, thus gradually leaving behind the resentment I felt toward the people I grew up with. Being out of that climate helped to give me perspective to truly become myself. People shape entire characters from the very things that hold them back in their lives. Women have become masters at this highly practiced craft. I have come to understand that those aspects of my personality that made me strong were sometimes the traits that most betrayed me, that magnified my fears. In very recent years I have moved through a gradual and sometimes painful process of letting go of a lot of the guards that were staples in my personality: my furious need for singularity, my egocentrism, the anxiety I felt about aligning myself with other women, my refusal to see my own fears in my mother.

After moving out of the house, I started to call my mother regularly for advice about things that I had taken for granted all through my youth. I believe it was this that helped both of us start to realize just a fraction of the value of my mother's experience and the strong link between us. As I began including her in my ideas about the world, I started having some of the most fulfilling moments I've ever had with another human being. Now she is one of my best friends. We talk about work, relationships, daily and long-term struggles, feminism and the latest guest on Oprah, and she is the only friend in my life who knows how long to boil turnips. After years of throwing temper tantrums, wielding damaging words, stomping around and slamming doors, we have become each other's greatest supporters. We are connected not just by birth, but by experience. I have learned the most amazing truths about real strength from my mother, whom I invalidated so often along my way.

My mother sculpted an entirely self-sacrificing life for herself. It is only now, at the age of fifty, after years of managing family matters, pacifying screaming children, cheering on insecure teenagers and forever sacrificing her time in favor of everyone else's, that she is coming to know who she is. With the room to grow in her own space and on her own time line, I have seen her embrace feminist ideals that have aided her in evaluating her life. Recently, someone asked me if my mother was a feminist and I said yes. When I told my mother of this conversation, she said, "Really, you think I'm a feminist?" I said, "Sure, of course, I just don't think you completely realize it." My mother thought for a while, and I saw something in her that I had never seen before with the mention of feminism. Pride and a sense of accomplishment crept into her expression, and she simply said, "Oh. Well, that's nice." The feminism that pulled us apart in my youth has brought us back together.

As an adult, I have walked with other women—peers, colleagues, friends, lovers, my mother—through a lot of their own self-discovery. In doing this, I've learned the value of relaxing my boundaries, of opening up closed doors, of encouraging women to explore themselves. I have not disappeared or been sucked in yet, and I think perhaps the greatest potential for myself and my development lies in the connections I have and will make with other women. If anything, my character is more solid now than ever, since I learned this. My relationships have been enriched in ways I never before knew were possible.

Now, as a feminist, I have a resource that is like no other: a long line of women who have the beautiful ability to share their experience—their obstacles and triumphs, setbacks and head starts. We can help each other finally be who we are. We walk through life together, as women, in all of our individual ways. This is what makes women so strong, what makes feminism so powerful, what makes an individual. This is what has brought me back to Me. This is mine.

One Bad Hair Day Too Many,
or The Hairstory of an
Androgynous Young Feminist

Jennifer Reid Maxcy Myhre

"Daddy, is that a boy or a girl?" I hear the six-year-old girl whisper the question to her father as I pass by. I smile at her; she articulates aloud what the adults around her are thinking. Her question does not offend me in the way that the "What are you, some kinda monk?" from the burly man in the fast-food restaurant, or the "Hey, is that a fag?" shouted at me from behind as I walk hand in hand with a man down the street, offends me.

I have a crew cut. I also don't shave my leg or armpit hair, but these are surprisingly unimportant details compared to my near-baldness. I have a look that some people call androgynous and others call butch. Daily I face stares, questions and rude comments, and harassment by those who believe that they have the right to pass judgment on my appearance and thus on my person. I am often amazed by the audacity of complete strangers who think it is perfectly acceptable to come up and touch my head. Occasionally, I get looks of envy and plaintive whispered comments from women in elevators: "I wish I had the courage to do that."

When I first began to think about shaving my head, it really wasn't a political statement, or so I thought at the time. I got tired of the blow-drying and curling and hair spraying I had to do to make my hair look presentable. So finally I decided to do it. I was in college and nobody cared what I looked like. I called a salon and asked for someone who would be willing to use the clippers.

When I arrived at the salon (you know, the kind that charges a certain amount to cut men's hair and then charges more if you're a woman, because your hair is inherently more difficult and intractable), I was seated and asked to wait. I was informed that Fifi would be cutting my hair this afternoon. When Fifi wiggled over to me, wearing little slinky gold shorts and tottering on gold high heels, I saw that she had a voluminous mane of hair. I became a bit worried. I tried to make it clear that I wanted my hair cut short, a crew cut. Forty-five minutes later, she still hadn't gotten the clippers out and was exclaiming that she could make me look just like Brigitte Nielsen. No thanks. Had it been now, I would have gotten uppity and insisted on the clippers, but both being assertive and shaving my head was a bit much to ask at the time. In my dorm laundry room, a friend and a pair of clippers finally got the job done.

I got my crew cut about a year and a half after what I call my feminist rebirth. Even as a child, I considered myself a feminist, supported the ERA (even though I knew very little about it) and was quick to react to statements from junior high classmates that women should be barefoot and pregnant. I had a mother who was employed and a father who was as involved as my mother in raising me. In eighth grade, I wrote a paper on the history of the women's suffrage movement in the U.S. In ninth grade, I read *Against Our Will*. But for all this, when I look back now I feel that politically I've traveled light-years from where I was then.

My feminist rebirth came during my college years. One summer, I stuffed the ideas of Millett, Brownmiller and Walker into my eager head. Some of us come to feminism because of abuse, harassment, eating disorders. I came to feminism because I hated shaving my legs. That summer I started to appreciate the amount of time, labor and money women put into their appearance in order to become "women," which in our culture is synonymous with "not-men."

Femininity isn't inherent, natural or biological. It takes work to look like a "woman," and this is evident when one looks at female impersonators and drag queens—men, with the same work, can look just like "women." Put on a pair of high heels and some lipstick and you're halfway there. The disguise is amazingly effective; most people are fooled by good female impersonators. The hullabaloo over the movie *The Crying Game* is testimony to the power of the trappings of femininity—long hair, makeup, dresses, high heels—in shaping our judgments of gender.

So to christen my feminist rebirth, I quit shaving my legs. I threw away my high heels and my tight skirts, my makeup and my jewelry. I grew out my armpit hair, and I talked like a woman with a mission. Why should I have to waste all that time and effort when I looked perfectly fine as I was? Giving up my "femininity" was my first action as a feminist. I didn't consider myself any less of a woman, but not working at looking like a woman meant that most people considered me masculine. I chose to call myself androgynous and hoped to destroy the distinction between masculine and feminine, male and female.

I became a feminist activist after that summer and helped to found a campus organization called Supportive Students Against Sexual Assault. As I became more engaged in working to stop violence against women, my outrage at women's slavery to their appearance subsided somewhat. It became a side issue, a conversation piece. That's about the time when I shaved my head, not really considering it a political statement, only knowing that I had burned my hand on my curling iron once too often. Now I consider it one of the most profound, daily statements of my feminist struggle. I spend less than one minute on my appearance each day, which saves me valuable time that I can choose to fill as I please— keeping myself sane, changing the world. The way I look is a constant slap in the face to those who believe that the boundaries between masculine and feminine are clear and rigid, inherent and right.

My appearance rarely escapes notice. I make people feel extremely uncomfortable. I have been called "butch," I have been called "dyke" and I have been mistaken for a man more times than I can remember. I have been told to wear big earrings and bright red lipstick so that "people can tell." I have been told that someday I will fall in love with a man who will change my mind about shaving my legs. (I can see it now—the romance novel: Rolf, with his commanding presence and masculine charm, shows me the error of my feminist and unfeminine ways. He and I get married; I give up my career and devote myself happily to raising our children. Harlequin would love that plot.)

While these comments often offend me, I find them telling, illustrative of the attitudes people hold about appearance, femininity and masculinity. People are uncomfortable around me because I do not, at first glance, fit easily into a gender category. This is very alarming to homophobic people; after all, if people aren't easily distinguishable as male or female, we run the risk of becoming attracted to a person of the same sex. Homophobic people avoid this risk by avoiding gender blenders like myself. Many people react to me with confused glances and embarrassed stammers; often they avoid eye contact. I am glad they are uncomfortable; it suits my purposes.

Regardless of their possession of X or Y chromosomes, we base judgments of gender on people's appearance—their secondary sex characteristics, their demeanor, their style of dress, their hair. We all hold in our minds a blueprint of our perceptions of femininity and masculinity. In a nutshell, femininity consists of having long-ish hair; wearing makeup, skirts, jewelry and high heels; walking with a wiggle; having little or no observable body hair; and being in general soft, rounded (but not too rounded) and sweet smelling. This nutshell is important because a woman's attractiveness to men is the primary measure of her worth. How often have you heard women actors on talk shows (or any woman, for that matter, in almost any situation) introduced with an adjective about their beauty rather than their talent? How often have you heard both men and women pass judgment on an ugly woman's merits as a person? How often have you heard comments about women sleeping their way to the top, as if sexual attractiveness were the only quality that could earn them such status? A woman's value is gauged according to her appearance, and women are expected to comply with standards set by society.

What is our reward for this constant attention to detail, our ever-vigilant concern with our appearance? The acceptance and approval of those (often men, occasionally women) in power. Those who break too many of the stereotypes are made to pay with social disapproval. A woman can wear her hair short, but not too short. She can forgo makeup as long as she wears earrings. If she doesn't follow the rules, she will be labeled unfeminine, manlike, butch. These are words that provoke an immediate recoil. These are words that antifeminists have used to keep women silent; they are words we must learn not to be afraid of.

I am one of those feminists that are made so much of in the media: a hairy-legged, strident, "masculine" woman, a "manhater" (another word for women who choose to tell the truth about men and patriarchy). I am a feminist with whom even other feminists are sometimes uncomfortable: "She gives the rest of us a bad name."

Rather than shrinking from words like "masculine" and "butch," we should point out why we are called these names and how male supremacy is served if we keep silent in fear of being called these names. We are called masculine when we act as we please, when we take control of our bodies and lives, when we speak out loud and refuse to be silenced, when we assert the dignity of our persons and our right to self-determination, when we are ambitious, courageous, sexy and proud. We are called butch when we decide that an hour in front of the mirror or the closet is better spent helping women, making money, learning, having sex, laughing with friends or raising children. We are called butch when we decide that those eight hours on high heels hobble us and prevent us from fighting back. We are called butch when we become indifferent to the male gaze. We are called masculine and butch in order to keep us in our place, to scare us, to gag and silence us.

So I don't flinch anymore when I am addressed as "Sir." I don't flinch at the pointed fingers and whispers, at the outright harassment. I hold my head up (and swagger, occasionally, when I get carried away). I refuse to live my life in a box labeled "Female." In my more ambitious and perhaps foolishly hopeful moments, I imagine a world in which there is no simple categorization by sex, no gender, but only people. I imagine a world in which I am no longer stared at. I imagine a world in which people are attracted to me not because of what sex I am (or appear to be) but rather because they find me fascinating. I imagine a world in which I am at home.

One Resilient Baby

Cheryl Green

The proud history of the struggles and determination of women and African Americans has shaped who I am today. However, I am not just a woman or just an African American. I am also a person with a visible disability, and I have also been shaped by my awareness that my beliefs and experiences conflict with those of white nondisabled women, nondisabled African Americans and many women and men with disabilities. I identify partially with all these groups, yet at times I feel contempt and exclusion from each of them.

I have spent most of my life feeling isolated and alone. It has taken me years to heal the wounds caused by being rejected by those who should have loved and nurtured me. At the age of twenty-four I have found some peace and a sense of full belonging, with the help of older women mentors who have connected with me across our differences.

I grew up in a working-class neighborhood in Houston, but my parents were from rural Texas, where their families still live. In our family, women were viewed as strong and were expected to be equal to men. In fact, all the African American women in my life adopted the Black Superwoman stereotype. I was taught that African American women have upheld their dignity through centuries of abuse. I learned that African American women are often the only ones keeping the family together. The women in my family talked proudly of enduring the cruel history of growing up on Southern farms, picking cotton, being raped or molested by white men and being cheated in the fields by white men and women. They told us girls to keep a watchful eye on whites because they couldn't be trusted. I heard from black women that feminism was a way for white women to keep power within the white family and away from black people. These women were transmitting more than mere survival tips to their young girls; they were also passing along their legacy of strength, power and self-reliance. However, before I could use this power and strength to buffer me from being maltreated by whites, I first tried to understand why I was mistreated by African Americans, particularly those in my family.

My sense of isolation began while I was quite young; some of my earliest memories center around how my family and others in my culture treated me differently and at times, abusively. With the exception of my parents, the women and men in my family viewed me as cursed by God and a baby of Satan because of my disability. I remember my aunts telling my mother that she must have sinned while carrying me and that's why I came out "cripple." I remember my grandmother calling my "one ugly baby." I remember the neighbors (most of whom were African American) ignoring me, teasing me because I walked "funny" and chastising me for "unrealistically" trying to exert my independence. Because of my disability, I was not thought of as a normal African American girl who would grow up able to uphold the Black Superwoman stereotype. They all told me of the things I couldn't do when I grew up, while they told my sister and our girl cousins of what they could do and, in fact, had to do because they couldn't "depend on no man." When I was ten, my uncle got tired of me being "crippled by the Devil." He beheaded a chicken and collected blood to perform an exorcism ritual on me. I'll never forget that no one came to my rescue even after hours of hearing my constant screams and cries.

Having spent most of my early childhood in the hospital, I was able to attend public school for the first time in the third grade. Because of a desegregation plan, I was bussed into predominantly white schools. I expected to be called "nigger," but no one called me that name to my face. Instead, my memories of early grade school are of little African American boys constantly challenging me to fight. On my first day of public school, I was ridiculed by a bus full of kids from my predominately black neighborhood. A sixth-grade African American boy saw how I "walked funny" and started laughing at me. He then proceeded to curse me and spit on me. Then he started shoving me. When I fell, he laughed. Each time I got up, he tried to push me down again. When I saw that no one was intervening to help me, not even the bus driver, I decided to fight back. I slugged him in the face and kept on swinging until my fists were bloody. Before he could recover from his shock that this "cripple" girl was fighting back, someone stopped me. I won that fight, but because of it, I became a target, the notorious "cripple bitch" who beat up a sixth grader. From then on, school was a combat zone. The boys probably thought that while they may not have been able to beat up every African American girl, they surely could beat me up because I was "cripple." Male ego was on the line. On the bus, in the halls, on the school courtyard and in the cafeteria, I had to fight boys. I won most of the early fights, but as the boys matured, I started coming home with black eyes.

About the time I entered high school, these boys moved away from physical violence and toward sexual violence. When I told my aunt about the abuse she said that I was lying because "what would a boy want with what you got?" My parents had complained once to the principal about the physical assaults because they couldn't dismiss the bodily bruises. When the assaults turned sexual, there were no horrendous marks, so I received no validation or help. I had had so many fights with boys and had been so disappointed with the failure of adults to protect me, that I thought it was going to be my lot in life to fight off physical and sexual abuse by African American males. I kept silent and grew resentful of my family and my culture. I coped with the abuse by burying myself in my studies and dreamed of a better life in the future when people would love me. I became a Christian in high school, and my faith in God buffered me from self-destruction.

By high school, I began to understand that despite all the familial language in my culture, I was never going to be a true "sister." I realized that I appeared to be a weak African American woman. I was bitter. Since I felt that no one wanted me, I chose to protect my self-esteem by distancing myself from my family and my ethnic identity. Trying to be accepted hurt more than just accepting my outcast status and moving on as a loner. My sense of isolation from my family and the African American community was complete. An academic scholarship to Yale University was my ticket out of that horrendous environment.

I didn't consider myself a feminist until after my third year as an undergraduate at Yale. Up until that time, I believed that African American women leaders and celebrities never called themselves feminists and didn't participate in feminist groups. I believed that the reason for this was that the feminist movement's goal was to elevate the position of white women. But early in my junior year, I befriended a young white woman who was a feminist activist. She was different from me—she was so committed to "the cause" and so passionate about her convictions. I asked her: Were feminists out to promote white women's issues? Was feminism full of racism despite the inclusion rhetoric? Was there a litmus test that women must pass in order to be deemed feminist? She didn't have definitive answers, but we talked about the issues. She encouraged me to take women's studies classes and discuss my questions with the professors. I declined because I didn't want to get involved with another group that would find an excuse to exclude me. I was too afraid that feminists were racists and who knew what else. I also felt that I couldn't be a devout Christian and a feminist. My friend told me that no one owns the definition of feminism and that all feminists don't agree on every issue.

During my senior year, I took a sociology class, taught by a black feminist, about marginalization within society. Although I was still too afraid to raise my concerns about feminism and inclusion, the syllabus included a book by bell hooks, *Feminist Theory: From Margin to Center*, which changed my outlook about my place in feminism. hooks gave me crucial words and concepts I needed to describe my feelings as an African American feminist with a disability. She explores the sense of divided loyalties many women of color feel trying to identify with both the women's movement and their own ethnic group. She also describes the pain of being an African American feminist experiencing racism within the feminist movement. Her words helped me find the strength to call myself a feminist—one with experiences and perspectives different from those of nondisabled feminists, including African Americans.

My new ability to call myself a feminist didn't necessarily make me feel accepted by other women. If anything, I became acutely sensitive to how much I differed from nondisabled feminists. I wondered if there were any African American feminists with disabilities. I soon realized that my sense of isolation and alienation was not localized in the feminist community. The conflicts in my life arising from disability, ethnicity and feminism had created in me a sense of isolation from most women.

Although my friend at Yale had told me that no one holds the reins of feminism, I didn't believe her. I struggled with reconciling some so-called "feminist fundamentals" with my beliefs as a person with a disability. The issue of abortion embodies this conflict. I'm certainly a proponent of women's rights, equality and personal choice. However, I am acutely aware that abortion is used as a means to root out those whom society deems imperfect and unworthy of life. Sadly, many women and men believe that having an abortion is the only sensible response to news of carrying a fetus with a disability. I realize that when considering whether to raise a child with a disability, women and their families must weigh economic considerations and emotional, social and logistical demands. A major disincentive to birthing a child with a disability is that their families often have to face society's intolerance without the active support of nondisabled women (including feminists) and their networks. I discussed my concerns with my friend, and I was told that I was challenging a "feminist fundamental." I was made to feel like a traitor. My friend didn't understand that I was questioning not whether a woman should have the right to choose, but whether a woman can make a truly informed choice in light of the discrimination and prejudice against people with disabilities.

My feelings intensified when a bitter national controversy erupted around Bree Walker, a successful television journalist who has a disability that affects the shape of her hands and feet. Walker's decision to conceive a child knowing that she or he would most likely inherit her disability caused a venomous outcry. Some people called her a child abuser. Others said she was cruel and selfish for insisting on giving birth to a child with a disability; many suggested that abortion was more humane than life with a disability. I became particularly distressed that women felt no shame for voicing their prejudices; I was saddened when I heard no national support for Walker from nondisabled feminists. What happened to reproductive rights for *all* women? I began to feel that nondisabled feminists, regardless of color, were fighting for the reproductive rights of only nondisabled women.

Walker's story further solidified my disassociation from political nondisabled women. The movement has come far in acknowledging the diversity of women with respect to ethnicity, sexual preference and economic status. But where the movement still fails miserably is in disability. Women with disabilities are grossly concentrated in the margins. We are women, yet *our* histories and identities are ignored. Our disabilities are accommodated at rallies, conferences and meetings where we mostly hear nondisabled feminists speaking. I believe that all of the accommodations are significant first steps to including us in the movement. However, I can't help being dissatisfied because women with disabilities should routinely be speaking about our own experiences alongside nondisabled feminists.

Disability is a feminist issue. It touches the lives of millions of women—whether because of one's own disability or that of a loved one. The disability could be traumatic brain injury, breast cancer, paralysis, schizophrenia, diabetes, blindness, deafness or numerous other conditions. It may be present at birth or acquired later in life. Women are more at risk for certain disabilities, especially emotional and psychiatric ones. Children are at great risk for disabilities when women have little, no or poor health care. Disability is unjustly neglected by feminists.

To protect myself from the consequences of disagreeing with so-called feminist absolutes, I gave up on trying to find a place within the movement. Sadly, I therefore missed the very real and sincere attempts by some nondisabled feminists to bring women like myself in from the margins. I also cut myself off from opportunities to connect with disabled feminists.

My anger at the African American and feminist communities continued unchecked until my life was forever changed by the mentoring of four very special women. Two of them are nondisabled and two are African American. Brenda Jones is my African American nondisabled mentor. Jeanne Argoff is my white nondisabled mentor. Corbett O'Toole is my white disabled feminist mentor. Diedre Davis, my most important mentor, is African American and has a disability.

A professor and a clinical psychologist, Brenda was exactly whom I needed to enter my life during my junior and senior years in college. I helped her analyze data as part of an independent study. After a short time of talking with her, I sensed that I could trust her and began to reveal the story of the abuse in my past. For two years I called Brenda whenever I was in crisis or just needed to tell her more of my story. She helped me let go of much of the destructive anger toward my family, my culture and myself. We talked about my coping skills as a young child, and she affectionately called me "one resilient baby." Brenda allowed me to vent my anger toward the African American community, but always reminded me that the entire community would not have maltreated me to the degree this subset had. She included me in her family's outings, picnics and dinners so that I could have positive experiences with members of the African American community. Brenda also pumped up my confidence in my future by encouraging me to seek new challenges and pursue a Ph.D. in psychology. She was my first cheerleader and the first nondisabled African American I felt really loved me and saw and affirmed my value. Brenda also strongly encouraged me to pursue an internship in Washington, D.C. She thought it would be good experience for me to get myself grounded in business. However, neither Brenda nor I knew that my internship would change my life.

I was selected to be the scholar/intern for the (Senator Robert) Dole Foundation for the Employment of People with Disabilities. Jeanne, a nondisabled white woman, is the associate director of the foundation. She brought me into the world of disability politics and disabled feminists. When she discovered that I knew nothing of the Americans with Disabilities Act of 1990 (ADA), she used the foundation's discretionary funds to sponsor my training on the ADA. She sent me as the Foundation's sole representative to meetings all over D.C. Jeanne gave me mountains of manuscripts written by disabled feminists. Although I was very happy to read about their experiences, I noted that none of them were African American. Jeanne introduced me to important people in the disability community and the nonprofit sector. She also introduced me to the world of nonprofit organizations run by women. We flew to New York together and spoke to the director of Women and Foundations/Corporate Philanthropy to encourage more grants specific to people with disabilities. We spoke with the women at the Ms. Foundation for Women regarding the grant we awarded to their Take Our Daughters to Work project; we wanted to make sure the Ms. Foundation was adequately accommodating girls with disabilities. Jeanne also encouraged me to continue with my studies, to obtain my Ph.D. and to speak and write about my experiences. Recently she introduced me as her "other daughter" and said she "felt like a proud mother" after I spoke at a conference.

Through her, I found that it was possible to find nondisabled white women who would not discriminate and would love me and women like me.

Jeanne helped me in a most profound way after she heard that I was twenty-three and had never met an African American woman who uses a wheelchair. She introduced me to a business associate of hers—Diedre, a powerful African American woman with a disability, who is a staff attorney in the office of the general counsel at the U.S. Equal Employment Opportunity Commission (E.E.O.C.). Diedre wasted no time assuming the mentor role. She immediately asked me if I wanted to be a part of a massive and prestigious training program on the ADA sponsored by the E.E.O.C. and the Department of Justice for leaders in the disability community. I jumped at the opportunity, and Jeanne immediately agreed that the Foundation would be my sponsor. Diedre and I talked about our experiences growing up with our disabilities. I learned that my family was unusually rejecting of my disability; Diedre's family always accepted her. Although she had negative experiences, she never had the intense trauma I had. I listened to her beautiful stories of how a positive African American family handled raising a child with a disability.

Because of Diedre and Brenda, I felt hope that I could find a sense of belonging in the African American community. Diedre was quick to point out that "brothers don't handle disability well." She wanted me to be prepared for African American men to reject me as a partner for dating or marriage. I loved Diedre's frankness and willingness to bare her own soul while she taught me lessons of life she had learned the hard way. She encouraged me to continue toward the Ph.D. and to speak and write about my experiences. Diedre's powerful position in the E.E.O.C. requires her to travel frequently, so we don't spend much time together. Nonetheless, she is a crucial mentor because she represents the me I have always wanted to be. Diedre gives me hope. Her presence in my life constantly reminds me that my own dreams can come true— my life now and in the future will never be like my early life. Although Diedre has helped me to find the good within my culture, she does not identify herself as a feminist.

Through the ADA training project, I found Corbett—my white disabled feminist mentor who is also my most vocal cheerleader. I met Corbett during the training and we immediately liked each other. When I expressed my dissatisfaction about the invisibility of disabled feminists, Corbett told me of struggling for years to increase the audience for the voices of disabled feminists. She introduced me to a core of highly active disabled feminists; she would tell them that they could relax because she had discovered a powerhouse to whom they could "pass the torch." Although I knew Corbett was joking, I also realized that she saw in me hope that the efforts of disabled feminists in her generation were not in vain. I found in Corbett and my new disabled feminist friends a sense of being needed. Corbett talks about me everywhere she goes, and as a result I receive calls and letters from people across the country who ask me to speak to their group or submit a manuscript regarding my experiences. Corbett encourages me to keep challenging injustice in any social justice movement of which I'm a member. Because of my relationship with Corbett, I am still excited about meeting other African American feminists with disabilities, but I don't feel as if I *have* to meet them in order to get affirmation for my unique experiences.

I wish all girls and women could have loyal mentors like the ones I finally have. I hope that nondisabled women, particularly feminists, will become committed to do more than simply accommodate the disabilities of women and girls at events. My nondisabled mentors continually invite me and other women with disabilities to speak to all kinds of audiences; they also speak about my experiences whenever I am unable to attend, and emphasize the point that one doesn't have to have a disability to be committed fully to justice for those who do. Moreover, they serve as examples to other nondisabled women, showing them that they too can directly mentor girls and women with disabilities.

After twenty-four years of searching, I have now released the anger and pain of my past abuse and sense of isolation. This healing is a direct result of the efforts of my eclectic group of mentors. Together, they provide me not only with a sense of belonging but also with a sense of purpose. Each one encourages me to tell my story to anyone who will listen because it is therapeutic for me and, just as important, it is a means by which other girls and women who are severely marginalized can grasp onto the hope that they too can achieve their dreams—as long as they never give up.

The Immaculate Conception

Amelia Richards

My mother left my father a month before I was born. I have never met this man, and I have never known much about him. Referring to him as "my father" has a strange ring to it, because our only connection is biology—and how much is that really worth? My desire to find this man was never an internal need. It was symbolic. I wanted to fill an external void, to become part of the mythical nuclear family that exists on TV, in the movies and in the minds of Dan Quayle and the Christian Coalition. For many years, I let this external pressure overshadow my internal happiness and wholeness. I fantasized a scene in which I was introduced to my father: He, "tall, dark and handsome," would pull up in his Volvo and take me to his country club, where everyone knew his name and admired his prestigious job. I would walk beside him, hold his hand and smile. This idealized man was not necessarily *my* father, but any male who could play the role. My dreams never took me to the possible reality beyond the facade.

The other side of this "no father" stigma was the "single mother." From Hester Prynne in *The Scarlet Letter* to Murphy Brown in the TV sitcom, single mothers have been characterized and treated as immoral, a threat to society and essentially outcasts. I bought into this stereotype. I believed that my mother must be an inadequate parent and that I was predestined to be a junior high school dropout, serving time for shoplifting and pregnant at the age of fourteen after being "knocked up" in the back of someone's pickup truck. If I had only taken the time to look around me, I would have learned that these consequences have nothing to do with whether you have one parent or two, but with the love and care you receive, regardless of who gives it.

Instead of using my experiences to demystify this stereotype, I accepted it for many years and felt ashamed. It was easier to return to my fantasyland than to deal with the pressures of being "different." As a little girl, and well into high school, I covered up my embarrassment by lying—"I don't see my father that often" or "We just aren't that close" were the usual excuses I gave. Sometimes I even amused myself and others by claiming I was the product of an immaculate conception. Not until college was I honest with myself and then others about my situation. By this time I had encountered other "different" families and realized that my situation was more "normal" than I had ever expected. Eventually, several factors, including exposure to different family types, greater self-esteem, the healthy environment of a women's college and a wonderful extended family of friends, allowed me to be proud of my upbringing and to celebrate being raised by a single mother.

Although I never needed my father, every now and then I experienced a certain curiosity about him and his whereabouts. My maternal grandfather was a father figure to me. He filled a void in a way that allowed me to push my father further out of my mind. I was also able to lessen my father's importance in my life because I did not share his last name. When I was in first grade my mother suggested I take her birth name. This wasn't as easy as it sounds. At the time of my birth, every child was automatically given her or his father's birth name. (It was perceived as "normal" to use the name of a man I didn't even know, yet outrageous to take my mother's name.) Because this had never been done in the state of Pennsylvania, we had to meet with several attorneys before finding one who would take my case. My six-year-old self appeared in court and eventually succeeded in changing my name.

When my grandfather died, my curiosity got the better of me. I asked my mother to tell me everything she knew about my father. She was surprised that it had taken twenty-one years for this conversation to transpire, but as I explained, there was no need for *him*. It was easy to go on with my life without dwelling on his absence. My grandfather's death also came at a time in life when parents begin to play a different role. I was becoming more my mother's friend than her daughter.

My mother began, "We grew up in the same small town, he four years older than I," and before the conversation was over I knew more than I cared to. This conversation squelched my curiosity for the time being. I remembered why I had waited so long for this day of reckoning. I needed to make sure that my desire to track my father down was to find *this man*, not *a father*. This was very important to me since I had had such high hopes. I had to be prepared for anything.

They were married one year before I was born and were living in Philadelphia, where my father was attending medical school and my mother was working in a department store. She had postponed her education so she could earn money to put him through school (a far too common scenario). Some intuition warned my mother that my father was not being straightforward. After playing detective—following him and making several investigative phone calls—she discovered that he was not enrolled in school at all. After confronting him and having him deny her allegations, my mother knew that one of them was crazy. She also knew that for the sake of her and her soon-to-be child she would be better off without him.

She never knew what happened with his time or her money. Since the day my mother left my father, the only contact she has had with him was seeing his signature on their divorce papers. Although he was required to pay child support and alimony, she never saw any of it and was too discouraged (and probably disgusted) to pursue it. She later learned that he was remarried and had another child.

Eight months pregnant with me, my twenty-year-old mother went to her parents for help. Her father was a retired school teacher and her mother a sales clerk at J.C. Penney. They were willing to take in their daughter, but they were not able to be responsible for my mother and her child. They offered to help her arrange an adoption, but my mother was determined to have and care for her child. She turned to her sister, who was a flight attendant living in Virginia, for help.

We lived with my aunt for the first year and a half of my life, and then moved to my grandparents' house so my mother could take care of them and they could help with me. My grandmother was dying of brain cancer and my grandfather was about to undergo open-heart surgery with a ten percent chance of survival; luckily, he beat the odds. Despite my grandparents' earlier suggestion of putting me up for adoption, we became very close. They must have admired my mother for doing what she wanted, despite their apprehension, and for being a success at it. It amazes me that when my mother was my age, twenty-four, she worked full-time, went to school full-time for her B.A., cared for her dying mother and her sick father, and raised a very energetic three-year-old. Now I admire her for all of this, but when I was a girl my admiration was overshadowed by my longing for a "normal" family.

Although my mother fell into the inevitable role of Superwoman, traditional gender roles were minimized in our household. My mother left every morning for work, and my grandfather walked me to and from school. His grandfatherly affection was the way fathers should be, but unfortunately, this care was lacking in some fathers I knew. During these early years my mother worked in a variety of jobs. She was an elementary school teacher, a caseworker for the Pennsylvania Department of Mental Health and an associate director of the local YWCA, and she also attended a local state college, getting the degree she had earlier postponed for my father. My grandfather helped with the grocery shopping and other household errands. As I remember, cooking and cleaning were always egalitarian efforts. This way of life continued for about ten years until my mother and I went out on our own.

My Pennsylvania town typified the class divisions of the United States. The rich people (all white) dominated the town with their posh houses on top of the hill; the middle and working classes (mostly Italian and Irish immigrants) filled in the middle section; and the poor families (African American and white) were pushed to the bottom. Religious diversity was lacking—Catholics were the overwhelming majority—but this mattered little to my mother and me; we occasionally amused ourselves on Sundays by trying out churches of any denomination. All of these worlds converged in my elementary school.

My grandfather's house was in a middle-class neighborhood. I was surrounded by families with two working parents. In most cases the wives were waitresses and the husbands were police officers, firefighters or other civil servants. I spent my weekends and summers with their kids playing kickball in the streets or, if it rained, trading baseball cards on someone's back porch. If these fathers had ever left their families, the mothers would most likely turn to welfare and be pushed to the bottom of the hill.

I related most closely to my poorer classmates, the majority of whom were also being raised by single mothers. The only reason my mother and I evaded these poorer conditions was that my grandfather had made his home ours. My grandfather's generosity gave my mother an advantage these women had never been afforded. I rarely spent time with these friends after school, because they had to spend their free time caring for their younger siblings or their older sisters' children. In these families, there were few men in sight over the age of eighteen, and the women had barely enough money to put food on the table and clothes on their children's backs.

My mother worked at the YWCA, so I was able to take gymnastics—a privilege usually reserved for the richer children. Every day after school, I escaped my reality and entered a middle-class world from the fifties. Everyone's parents were married, with two or three children, the family dog, the family station wagon and a membership in the country club. Everyone's father was a professional and everyone's mother a homemaker—probably more out of duty than desire. It was the early seventies and many of these women had not yet been introduced to the women's movement (some still haven't), so they fell into a rut of assuming rather than defining their roles. They were always decked out in the latest styles. Their houses were complete with pools and refrigerators that were stuffed with food. I wanted my family to live like this. In our culture, all classes are taught to idolize the richest. I saw a glimpse of this world through my aunt, my "other mother," who would visit frequently with gifts from around the world and who would occasionally take me on trips. I had also created an extended family. I became a third or fourth child in some of my richer friends' families and I was an "adopted" daughter to older friends who had no children of their own. These families provided me with many opportunities, like going to fancy restaurants and not-so-fancy stock-car races. I also learned the meaning of filet mignon, Waterford crystal, Cadillac and the like. However materialistic it may sound, it gave me a great sense of pride to know these things.

I perceived these families as perfect, because I equated material possessions with love. Now this sounds ridiculous, but as a young naive child, it was conceivable to me that the tangible and the visible were worth more than love, which has no monetary value. Because it was the fathers who financed these outings, paid for these dinners and gave their wives and children allowances, the only way I saw to have this "love" was through a father. Since I did not have one, I belittled myself and my experiences and continued living in denial.

Looking back, this all sounds so silly; my mother has always been there for me. I had all the love, respect and encouragement a child needs and deserves—and more. But this was overshadowed because I was too busy being embarrassed and yearning for the "perfect family." It was not until last summer that I reconciled these fallacies and rejuvenated my interest in finding my father.

At my high school reunion, I was catching up with friends I hadn't seen in five years. Among the routine questions was always one about my parents. When I spoke of only my mother, others remembered, "That's right, you don't see your father that often." It was interesting to hear my words coming back at me, and silly to think I had felt I needed to lie. When I finally told the truth, I was amazed that my friends were interested in this unknown side of my life. They didn't respond with the contempt I had expected. Buoyed by my friends' encouragement, I returned home eager to meet this man who had helped create me.

I started by calling his parents, with whom I had had no previous contact, though I knew where they lived. I was hesitant about calling these strangers, but I had nothing to lose. After fumbling over different introductions in my head, I finally said, "Hi, this is Amy Richards—your granddaughter." My grandmother wasn't half as surprised as I had expected. We had a great conversation, and she was excited that after all these years we finally had contact. She had thought about meeting me when I was a little girl, but was not sure how my mother and I would react.

After telling her about myself and hearing about her and her husband, I was anxious to get to the point of my call. "I am very eager to meet my father, and I thought you would know how I could get in touch with him." "Actually, I don't," was her response. This shocked me, but nothing like the shock that was to come. "Your grandfather and I haven't spoken to him since he was let out on parole." Parole, I kept repeating in my head. Before I had time to respond, she interrupted my thoughts: "Oh, I am sorry, you probably didn't even know he was in prison." No, I didn't. As our conversation continued, I felt as if I were listening to a TV drama— forgetting this was my father I was hearing about.

About eight years ago, my father kidnapped his son. He took him to New Hampshire (they had been living in Florida), established a successful psychiatric practice—though he was not a licensed psychiatrist—and educated his son at home. He could not enroll him in the public schools for fear that they would be discovered. They lived this way for three years. He then kidnapped a patient of his, another nine-year-old boy, and attempted to take the two boys to Canada but fortunately was caught at the border. Both boys were returned safely, and my father went to prison for kidnapping. Although kidnapping was the only charge, I can't help wondering if he wanted more from these two nine-year-old boys.

That could have been me, was my first thought. My mother was right—one of them was crazy. Hearing this story scared me, but it also lifted a huge weight off my shoulders. It all seemed so perfect. Here I had spent my life feeling incomplete because I didn't have a father, when all along he was a horrible person. The "perfect family" I had yearned for had been there all along; I just needed this discovery to see it.

I now have a new fantasy for our introduction: I will see him on the street or in a restaurant. I can observe him from a distance and decide whether I want anything more than a glimpse.

Everything had come full circle. Now I could begin celebrating and sharing the unique relationship my mother and I had—and continue to have. I am only beginning to realize the advantages I had because I was raised by a single mother. The term "two-parent family" is often a misnomer, because mothers have always been the primary caregivers, whether they have chosen this role or not. (Have you ever heard a father asked how he combines his career with child rearing?) In fact, single-parent families are far more common than society—especially the media—would like us to believe. According to the Census Bureau, they represent thirty-four percent of all families, and eighty-five percent of these thirty-four percent are families headed by single mothers.

In my observation, single-parent families are more egalitarian. Most two-parent families I know are based on hierarchies—with the father reigning from above, the mother acting as the mediator and then the children, who are usually relegated to the lowest level. On the other hand, my family has always been a partnership between my mother and me. *We* make the decisions about where to live, how to spend *our* money and how *we* spend our time. In other words, I am her "better half" and she is mine. This respect has afforded me greater independence and self-esteem. Sometimes this freedom did not work to my advantage—for example, when I picked out my own wardrobe or when I developed the habit of parading around with long pants on my head, sometimes even pulled back with ribbons for special occasions. This was my way of having long hair, since I didn't have the patience for my short hair to grow. This strange sight might well have been an embarrassment to my mother, but if so, she never let on. Maybe she just found other ways to get back at me, like when she taught me that "I Am Woman" was the national anthem. When my teacher asked my first-grade class, "Does anyone know the national anthem?" I proudly responded "yes" and proceeded to sing "I Am Woman" to my class. Their laughter was an indication that not everyone used this song to express their feelings of patriotism. Although I can now tell this story and laugh, at the time I was humiliated.

At a young age, I discovered that my equal household, unfortunately, was not standard. In the classroom and in other households, I learned that most adults were not willing to listen to me and my opinions in the way I was accustomed to. At friends' houses for dinner I was always relegated to the kids' table. Adults called me "Amy" and I expected to use their first names in return. I also assumed that I could talk with adults as I talked with my friends. This, I was quick to learn, was not acceptable. For a long time I viewed this confusion as my fault, never realizing that although what I expected was not the norm, it was better than the hierarchal option.

I also had the advantage of having a "working mother." Although I lived in a neighborhood where most of the mothers were in the paid workforce, my rich friends' mothers occupied their days by carpooling, playing tennis or volunteering at the Junior League. This I, of course, envied. My rich girl friends had fantasies of being actresses, ballerinas or professional tennis players, careers where there were female role models. My goal was to become the first woman president of the United States. Other friends raised by single mothers shared my ambition and dreamed of being politicians, pilots or news anchorwomen. We were determined to be pioneers.

My mother's various occupations, which went on to include working with displaced homemakers and being a consultant to AT&T, taught me that I did not need to choose only one career path. So when I am asked, "What do you want to do?" it is no wonder I frequently can't stop with one answer. These frequent job changes, combined with waiting in a few unemployment and welfare lines, also took us to various cities. This exposure taught me a lot about diversity and about the United States, and even boosted my self-esteem, as I frequently had to make new friends.

Probably the greatest benefit to having a "working mother" was that since my mother was the breadwinner, I grew up seeing women have control of money and therefore knew that money was not a "male thing." I am always amused when people ask, "How did you pay for college [or anything else for that matter]?" I always proudly respond, "My mother." This response never seems odd to me, but others always question, "How did *she* afford it?" If you replace "mother" with "father" it would never be questioned.

While I had previously assumed that the only passport to opportunity was a father, I later learned through my own experiences that mothers were just as capable of providing these benefits. In my family, it was my mother who paid the rent, who treated us to dinner and whom I asked for money. Unfortunately, my mother's financial stability is uncommon for women. Most women are thwarted financially by limited access to higher paying jobs and by the lack of equal pay for equal work.

I also wasn't exposed to family violence or incest, which are more likely to occur with males in the house. And I was able to have a great relationship with my mother, a friendship, which I can't imagine would have been as true had someone else been a part of our lives. My list could go on and on. I know my experience is unique, but I hope other children of single parents do not live in the denial that I did and that they too have learned to celebrate these relationships.

Reflecting on my mother and her life, I realize that we all come to feminism in our own way and under our own terms, whether it's because of opinions, visions or personal experiences. It was my mother's experiences that made her a feminist and planted the seeds for my own feminism. She is a role model to me, to other single mothers and to all women. She did what was right for herself and me, even though it defied a tradition embedded in our culture—the nuclear family. I knew that my feminism had sprouted when I began to appreciate my mother for taking this giant leap into what was then the unknown.

Abortion, Vacuum Cleaners and the Power Within

Inga Muscio

One of my mottoes for the nineties, a little saying I hope to see made into bumper stickers motoring down the nation's byways, is ABORTION SUCKS. That's right, I, a young lady, being of sound feminist mind and undeniably womanly body, am adamantly against clinical abortions.

"Abortion Sucks" is a literal statement, made in reference to the machine employed in ridding a woman of her unwanted pregnancy. This machine is a vacuum cleaner. In theory, if not design, it's quite like the Hoover upright, the Dustbuster or the Shop-Vac in your closet at home.

Vacuum cleaners are useful for cleaning up messes, and in our society, a pile of kitty litter on the floor is treated much the same as an undesired embryo. The main difference, though hardly recognizable to Western science, is that kitty litter is sucked from cold linoleum and an embryo is sucked from a warm-blooded living being's womb.

Women and linoleum floors, sure is hard to tell us apart, ain't it? Maybe I sound bitter, and maybe I feel that I have every right to, for I've been on somewhat intimate terms with that appliance. That's right, 'cause good ol' childless me has been knocked up not once, not twice, but three times in my dear life. While this may be a testimony to my previous irresponsibility and ignorance regarding available methods of birth control, that is another fly in the ointment of women's health care and fertile ground for another essay altogether.

The first time I got pregnant, I was nineteen. I lived in California and was within weeks of moving away from home for the first time in my life, to Seattle, Washington. The idea of making such a major move with a tiny human growing inside me seemed a pretty contradictory way of setting off on my own, so I went to Planned Parenthood.

In the waiting room were fifteen to twenty other women. Each had a horror-stricken look on her face. It was one of those situations where you can assume that you have the same expression as everyone else without having to look in the mirror. I sat there for an hour and a half, nervously leafing through *People* magazines in a desperate attempt to give a rat's ass about the lives of Daryl Hannah and Princess Di.

When they called my name, I probably would have shit my pants if there had been any digestion going on in my intestines, which there wasn't. It's hard to eat when you're pregnant with a child you do not want.

My boyfriend accompanied me into the exam room. I was told to strip and lie on the table, feet in the stirrups. I still remember the ugly swirl designs and water marks on the ceiling. After a while, the nurse came in and explained what would be happening. She said, "Are you sure this is what you want?" I think she asked because I was crying uncontrollably. What other goddamn choice did I have? I'm sure. What an idiot. I wasn't crying from indecision, I was crying from fear. I muttered, "Just do it, please."

With the ugliest needle I had ever seen, she shot something into my cervix. I don't think my cervix was residing under the belief that it would someday have a large needle plunged into it, so it protested accordingly. The pain was overwhelming; my head swam into the netherworld between intense clarity and murky subconscious.

Then I heard a quiet motor whirring.

The lady told me to recite my ABCs.

"A, B, C, D, E..." Something entered my vagina, deeper, deeper, deeper than I imagined anything could go.

"F, G, H, I, O, W..." The walls of my uterus were being sucked, felt like they were gonna cave in. I screamed "O, P, X, X, D, VOWELS, WHAT ARE THE VOWELS? R? K? A! A's A VOWEL!" And then my organs were surely being mowed down by a tiny battalion of Lawn-Boys.

"S, did I say S?" My boyfriend was crying too and didn't tell me whether I had said S or not.

There was a two-inch-thick pad between my legs, and blood gushing out of me. The motor had stopped whirring. I was delirious. I asked, "What do you do with all the fetuses? Where do they go? Do you bury them?" The lady ignored me, which was fine; I had to puke. She led me into a bathroom, and I vomited bilious green foam. Then I went to a recovery room, lay down and cried. There was another nurse in there. She patted my hand and said, "I know just how you feel." I said, "You've had an abortion before too?" She said, "No, but I know how you feel." I told her to get the fuck away from me.

For two weeks, there was a gaping wound in my body. I could hardly walk for five days.

And then, stupid me, a couple of years later, I got pregnant again. I still lived in Seattle but was just about to move to Olympia, Washington, to begin school at the Evergreen State College. Since I thought this was no way to begin a college education, I had to face the reality of going to that machine once again. This time I was even more petrified, 'cause I knew what that rectangular box and its quiet motor had planned for my reproductive system. Have you any idea how it feels to willingly and voluntarily submit to excruciating torture because you dumbly forgot to insert your diaphragm, which gives you ugly yeast infections and hurts you to fuck unless you lie flat on your back? I had to withstand this torture because I was a bad girl. I didn't do good, I fucked up. So I had the same choice as before, that glowing, outstanding choice we ladies fight tooth and nail for: the choice to get my insides ruthlessly sucked by some inhuman shit pile, invented not by my foremothers, but by someone who would never, ever in a million years have that tube jammed up his dickhole and turned on full blast, slurping everything in its path.

On one of Olympia's main thoroughfares is an abortion clinic. I passed it every day on my way to and from school. Almost always, there were old women, young girls and duck hunters standing on the corner outside the clinic, holding signs that showed pictures of dead fetuses. The signs often had words to the effect that this aborted fetus may have been the next president of the United States of America.

Whenever I saw those people out there, especially the young girls, I'd see myself yanking the bus cord (in all probability snapping it in two), vaulting off the bus, crossing the street and turning into a walking killing machine, kicking in faces, stomping on hands. There were times when I gripped my wrist so I wouldn't yank that cord.

Upon examining my desire to physically mutilate individuals whose convictions were in direct opposition to mine, I realized I had to get hold of myself. I had studied different kinds of medicines and healing methods in the past, and I decided that now would be a perfect time to immerse myself in histories and applications of medicines far and wide. Maybe if I better understood the situation, I'd feel less of an inclination to beat up duck hunters.

I found one thing that was a constant: Healing starts from within. It appeared to be some kind of law, no, more than a law. Is breathing a law? Is waking up every day a law? If so, maybe the notion of healing coming from within is a law as well. At any rate, this concept is completely alien, even deviant, in our culture. In this society, we look to the outside for just about everything: love, entertainment, well-being, self-worth and health. We stare into the

TV set instead of speaking of our own dreams, wait for a vacation instead of appreciating each day, watch the clock rather than listen to our hearts. Every livelong day we are bombarded with realities from the outside world, seemingly nonstop. Phones, car alarms, pills, coffee, beepers, ads, radios, elevator music, fax machines, gunshots, bright lights, fast cars, airplanes overhead, computer screens, sirens, alcohol, newspapers. One hardly has the opportunity to look inside for peace and love and other nice things like that.

Western medicine, that smelly dog who farts across the house and we just don't have the heart to put out of its misery, is based on a law opposite the one the rest of the universe goes by, namely, Healing Has Nothing To Do With You; It's Something Only Your Doctor Can Control.

In the U.S., we don't (and we're also not encouraged to) look inside ourselves for healing or for finding truths or answers. If you want to know something, you find out what the Person In Charge Of This Area says. The weather is not to be discerned by looking at the sky or the mountains in the distance or by listening to the song of the wind. You will find it in the Report of the Meteorologist. Likewise, if you are pregnant and don't want to be, you don't look to yourself and the resources in your immediate world, you pay a visit to the Abortionist, who will subsequently predict the climate in your body for nine days to two weeks, guaranteed. And so, la dee dah, once, twice, three times a lady . . . I got pregnant again.

It was the same boyfriend as the other two times, only now we were breaking up. It was the stupidest one of all because I didn't want to be with this man and I shouldn't have fucked him, but it was his birthday and he was fun to romp with and blah dee blah blah blah. No force on earth could make me feel that I wanted this child, and furthermore, I promptly decided there was to be no grotesque waltzing with that abhorrent machine.

So I started talking to my girlfriends. Looking to my immediate community for help led me to Judy, the masseuse, who rubbed me in places you aren't supposed to touch pregnant ladies. She also did some reflexology in the same vein. Panacea told me where to find detailed recipes for herbal abortifacients and emmenagogues. Esther supported me and stayed with me every day. Bridget brought me flowers. Possibly most important was the fact that I possessed not one single filament of self-doubt. With that core of supportive women surrounding me and with my mind made up, I was pretty much invincible.

So, one morning, after a week of nonstop praying, massaging, tea drinking, talking and thinking, I was brushing my teeth at the sink and felt a very peculiar mmmmbloommmp-like feeling. I looked at the bathroom floor, and there, between my feet, was some blood and a little round thing. It was clear but felt like one of them unshiny Super Balls. It was the neatest thing I ever did see. An orb of life and energy, in my hand.

So strange.

So real.

And Jesus H., wasn't I the happiest clam? It hardly hurt at all, just some mild contractions. I bled very little, felt fine in two days. I wore black for a week and had a little funeral in my head. This was definitely one of the top ten learning experiences in my life thus far. You know, it's like when Germany invaded Poland. I once read how in the ghettos of Warsaw, the people fighting the Nazis were amazed at first that a Nazi soldier would die if you shot him. They suspected that Nazis could die, but felt like they were somehow superhuman.

That's how I felt after I aborted a fetus without paying a visit to that sickening vacuum cleaner. I felt like I imagine any oppressed individual feels when they see that they have power, and nobody— not even men and their machines, nobody—can take that away.

I learned that the fight for human rights does not take place on some bureaucratic battleground with a bevy of lawyers running from congressional suite to congressional suite, sapping resources into laws. The war for peace and love and other nice things like that is not waged in protests on the street. These forms of fighting acknowledge the oppressor outside of yourself, giving that entity yet more life. The real fight for human rights is inside each and every individual on this earth.

While traversing along this line of thought, I realize that I just might sound like a young woman who has never experienced the unspeakable horror of back-alley abortions, and I am. I also realize that it might seem as if I'm ungrateful to all the women and men who have fought their hearts raw for equal rights and legal abortions, but I am not. I think of it like this: The fact that there now exists a generation of women who can actually consider clinical abortions to be an oppressive diversion to one's own power is based wholly upon the foundation that our mothers and sisters have built for us. I sincerely thank the individuals who have fought so hard for themselves and their daughters. I thank the people who bent over backwards so that I can have the luxury of experiencing the beliefs I now hold. Evolutionarily speaking, however, it is quite natural for this fight to progress into a new arena, since by no stretch of the imagination is this fight over. The squabble between pro-lifers and pro-choicers serves only to keep our eyes off the target: patriarchal society.

Concentrating on the power within our own circle of women was once a major focus of the women's health movement. I think we would benefit from once again creating informal health collectives where we discuss things like our bodies and our selves. If we believed in our own power and the power of our immediate communities, then abortion clinics, in their present incarnation, would be completely unnecessary. Let the fundamentalist dickheads burn all those vacuum cleaners to the ground. If alternative organic abortions were explored and taken more seriously, there wouldn't be much of an abortion debate. Abortion would be a personal, intimate thing among friends.

Can you say Amen.

Lessons from a Young Feminist Collective

Tiya Miles

for the women of the Rag with love and good wishes

The room overflowed with women. They stretched out across the floor, leaned against chair backs and chair legs, their faces open with excitement. I found a space among them and listened to the six who had called the meeting explain their plan to create the only feminist journal on the Harvard-Radcliffe campus. They stressed that although they had been the catalyst for the formation of the group, they did not expect or want to be the leaders. They proposed a method of consensus for decision making and suggested that the positions of facilitator, time keeper and vibes watcher (whose job it was to monitor the tension in the room and notice if people were being silenced) should rotate on a voluntary basis.

Our initial act of consensus was to decide on a title for the magazine. The final choice, after what seemed like hours of debate, was *The Rag: A Feminist Journal of Politics and Culture*. Soon the name outgrew the journal itself and came to refer to the group of women who constituted the collective. In those early weeks, we became fond of saying with a smirk, "I'm on the Rag."

Our first planned event was a discussion forum to generate ideas for the topic of our premiere issue. In the fall of 1991, we gathered in the Lyman Common Room to talk about the theme of "control." We sat in a wide circle and munched on snacks while we voiced personal experiences and observations. The conversation branched in several directions. We discussed issues ranging from the injustice of being perpetually vulnerable to sexual attack on the streets to oppressive societal beauty ideals. I felt invigorated by the energy, challenged by the ideas and supported by the words that echoed my own thoughts. It was in this forum that I was first able to voice and begin to transform my negative self-concept, which was rooted in my long-held belief that as a black woman, my hair and features were ugly.

The weekly Rag meetings forged an incredible bond among the twenty or so of us who attended regularly. Most of us were writing essays, and we would spend the time editing pieces, discussing current events on and off campus and sharing personal feelings.

At the end of fall semester, when it was time to distribute copies of our first issue, we met at Dunster House with charged expectation. Thrilled by the sight of our newly published journals, we picked them up, ran our hands over the covers and flipped through the pages rereading our words. We had caused a ripple of interest and criticism among our fellow students, some of whom flung the terms "lesbian" and "angry" as intended slurs. And now, as we prepared to tell them where we stood and where they could go, we felt formidable. We laughed and yelled as we dropped off stacks of journals at first-year dorms, upper-class "houses" and libraries. Our thoughts in print (particularly personal accounts of rape and a description of giving "Uncle Sam" a blow job) caused a messy splash in the Harvard sea.

Two semesters and two journals later, fifteen of us sat in a small room with angry mouths stretched across our faces and tears pressing out of our eyes. The energy we felt had a different character now—heavy, tense, rife with blame and defensiveness. The Rag was tearing from the pull of problems that had been so small at first, we hadn't noticed them. Resentment about cliques and an inner circle bubbled under the surface. Racial and class conflicts had crept up like weeds. During several meetings and informal discussions in the spring of 1992, we tried to talk out our difficulties and ended up drawing battle lines.

Our organizational problems seemed to have taken root at that very first meeting, while we were reveling in the creation of a supportive forum for our opinions. Although the journal's creators had attempted to disseminate power and control, their central role remained.

The journal creators and a few others handled the collective's business responsibilities outside of regular meetings. Discontent arose among other members of the collective who felt left out of such an important Rag function. The group discussed this problem at several meetings, but all attempts at change failed. When the business group incorporated its work into weekly meetings, our already drawn-out Thursday night sessions became hours long. And because the business group knew more about the subject than other Rag members, finance discussions often turned into reports. When the business crew scheduled open brunch meetings, no one attended. At the same time that some Rag members continued to feel excluded, those who handled business resented being blamed for doing more than their share of the work.

Somehow, a small group of Rag members had kept what seemed to be a disproportionate amount of responsibility and power. And although we all felt the problem, we did not know how to excise it. As more people joined the collective, the situation worsened. The journal creators and those who had attended the founding meeting were perceived to have (and perhaps took on) a possessive attitude, as if we owned the journal and were the only legitimate members of the group.

In the middle of the Rag's second year, racial strife developed out of what was intended to be an innocuous proposal. Another Rag woman and I were also members of the Association of Black Radcliffe Women. During a meeting of that group, ABRW members expressed anger at the title of an upcoming Black Students

Association dance—"The Boody Slam Jam." The ABRW women felt that the slogan reinforced negative portrayals of black women's bodies. The women argued that these portrayals, common in popular music videos and songs such as "Baby Got Back" and "Poison" (which includes the lines: "That girl is poison. You can't trust a big butt and a smile"), caricatured black women's behinds and emphasized them as sexual objects. Although this concern led to a discussion of ABRW members' wider interest in feminist issues, many of the women were opposed to joining the Rag and writing about their thoughts. They felt an aversion to the term "feminist," which they thought described a white, even racist movement, and they saw the Rag as a quintessential "feminist" group.

The other joint ABRW/Rag member and I related this discussion at a Rag meeting. We suggested that *The Rag* change its subtitle to a "Womanist" or "Feminist and Womanist Journal of Politics and Culture" as a signal to other black women that the collective was an open, welcoming space. The debate over this suggestion revealed Rag members' unspoken racial tensions and opened the floodgates of the group's internal conflicts.

When we introduced the idea of the subtitle change, a rash of impassioned reactions followed in the group of four black women (two of them biracial), two Asian women, and several white women. Some felt that womanism, as first defined by Alice Walker, was an admirable ideology, but others felt that it wasn't radical enough because it included a commitment to the liberation of oppressed men. Some white women rejected the idea that there could be legitimate reasons for not wanting to call oneself a feminist; one woman termed such people "wishy-washy" and implied that changing the subtitle would be an act of weakness.

The two of us who had suggested the change pointed out the self-oriented perspective of some white feminists, which blocked them from seeing the necessity of black women's and men's struggling together for survival in a racist society. We also argued that requiring women to identify themselves as feminists excluded like-minded, politically active black women and categorized them as weak. One biracial black woman, who called herself a feminist and explained how long it had taken her to gather the strength to do so, felt that we were excluding her by holding up a narrow black feminist authenticity that defined mainstream feminism as antiblack.

Class conflicts piggybacked racial discord. In other meetings that semester, a black woman who had taken a year off to work in order to fund the rest of her college education expressed resentment at what she viewed as the insensitivity of wealthy white women. A few Rag parents had donated hundreds of dollars to the magazine, and one Rag member had offered her family's summer house as a retreat site. The black woman, who had no such funds or house to offer the group, felt that her worth and strength as a group member were diminished by those women's obvious economic power. Other women pointed out that it would be impossible for us to publish without those funds. A white woman revealed her family's extensive wealth and said she felt both angry and hurt at being blamed for who she was and things she had no control over.

We never recovered from the accusations, resentment and tension that doused us. The spring of my senior year, *The Rag* was not published. The year after I graduated, remaining Rag members published the pieces that had been written the year before, and then the group dissolved. We had lasted only two years.

During those final meetings, I often tried to understand what had happened to us. Now, as I look back with the hindsight afforded by time, reading and many conversations, I can pinpoint a constellation of problems that have weakened many young feminist groups. Many of the women on the Rag had awakened to feminist consciousness only recently and were unfamiliar with feminist history and contemporary feminist theory. We were not aware of the need for individual self-analysis or for recognition of our own role in oppressing and silencing others. We were so focused on our individual development and liberation that we failed to reach out to women with different experiences and to plan group activism.

Perhaps the main problem was our ignorance of feminist history. We should have read the warnings, reflections and advice of the many older women who had already struggled with the dilemmas we faced. In fact, the importance of knowing history in the struggle against oppression is an issue in many of these women's writings. Audre Lorde writes in *Sister Outsider*, "By ignoring the past, we are encouraged to repeat its mistakes. . . . [H]istorical amnesia . . . keeps us working to invent the wheel every time we have to go to the store for bread."[1]

In *Daring To Be Bad*, Alice Echols traces the development of radical feminist groups in the late sixties and seventies. Over twenty years ago, the women Echols discusses fought and split over issues of leadership, hierarchy, race, class, sexual orientation and feminist authenticity—many of the problems that disintegrated the Rag. Like the women in those early groups, we strove toward an ideal of collective decision making and equal power but ended up with a certain degree of centralized power and internal strife. A group discussion of this historical account (as well as others) might have prepared Rag members for the difficulties we would face in the realm of organization and decision making.

An early awareness of the potential for these pitfalls would have forced us to rethink our organizational procedures (or lack thereof), rather than glossing over them with vague notions of sharing and inclusivity. We might have decided to collectively choose a small group that would handle business for the duration of a semester. In this way, important matters would be handled efficiently, but concentration of responsibility and power would not be arbitrary or static. Similarly, we might have chosen a structured means of incorporating new members into the group to lessen feelings of possessiveness on the part of old members and exclusion on the part of new members.

Our lack of historical knowledge also contributed to the racial tensions and misunderstandings between us. As Patricia Hill

Collins points out in *Black Feminist Thought*, black women have a longstanding feminist intellectual tradition, which has often been suppressed in feminist contexts as well as mainstream culture. Many black women are unaware that we have deep roots in feminist consciousness and that our foremothers have always been involved in feminist struggle. Our misinformation about feminist history—the false idea that feminist thought and activism in the United States have been exclusive to white women—led some of us in ABRW to reject feminism immediately and refuse to work with white women who claimed the label. White women's lack of knowledge about black feminist history led some of them to automatically deny black women's critiques of white feminist racism and to categorize womanism as a watered-down version of "real" feminism.

Black feminist theorists Patricia Hill Collins, bell hooks and Audre Lorde point to the necessity for all feminists to critically assess themselves to determine the ways in which they participate in systems of oppression. In *Feminist Theory: From Margin to Center*, hooks discusses black women's feelings of self-alienation, a result of living in a climate in which they are devalued: "Women of color must confront our absorption of white supremacist beliefs, 'internalized racism,' which may lead us to feel self-hate, to vent anger and rage at injustice at one another rather than at oppressive forces."[2] hooks encourages black women to affirm blackness and "decolonize" our minds to free ourselves from the restraints of oppressive ideologies.[3] Perhaps the black woman on the Rag who had taken a year off to work felt devalued not only because of the white women's actions, but also because she had accepted the cultural correlation between wealth and worth.

Middle- and upper-class white feminists must also examine their acceptance of racist and classist assumptions as well as their privilege in order for a group to flourish. Some white Rag members became defensive and resistant to dialogue when issues of race emerged and were insensitive to the ways in which their privilege and cross-cultural ignorance hurt women of color. The white women's offhand rejection of womanism as a viable theory and equation of their experiences with the oppression of black women might have been avoided if they had critically considered their own positions and assumptions. If the women whose parents funded the magazine had reflected upon how that deed might affect less privileged women, perhaps they would have thought about other options, such as having their parents donate anonymously.

At times black Rag members duplicated some of these mistakes as a result of not considering our individual positions in relation to other black women and other women of color. Some of us fell into the myth of the existence of what hooks calls "monolithic [racial] experiences"[4] and assumed that most black women shared our feminist perspective. We vehemently advanced the consensus of a few black women to the degree that a biracial black woman felt that she was excluded and that her experience was being defined as inauthentic. In addition to this, we contributed to other women's invisibility by making only a marginal effort to widen our discussion to embrace women of color who were not black. Audre Lorde's piercing words are applicable to all members of feminist groups: "The true focus of revolutionary change is never merely the oppressive situations which we seek to escape, but that piece of the oppressor which is planted deep within each of us."[5]

When the Rag women gathered at that first meeting, we all harbored burning issues that warmed or scalded us from within. The opportunity to voice and share these feelings motivated us to produce the journal and bonded us as a group. But this foundation of individual desire and need crumbled as time went on. Once we had expressed the thoughts that we had bottled up inside, our task seemed less urgent and our energy level waned. This static focus on our individual experiences and problems deterred us from seeking out and listening to other women's experiences. If we had stretched beyond the boundaries of our group, perhaps we would have invited older women in our community to join discussions and gained the opportunity to learn from their wisdom. Perhaps we would have attracted a variety of women to participate in the earliest stages of Rag development and combined all of our insights and energy to create a more dynamic collective.

If we had reached out to other women, we might have opened space for discussion of our differences before we were consumed by them. We might have learned about each other's specific life experiences and dismantled our assumptions about other groups. Early exploration of our differences and individual definitions of feminism might have forestalled our retreat into defensiveness and closed-mindedness when conflicts arose. As Audre Lorde envisioned, we might have been able to "recognize differences among women who are our equals, neither inferior nor superior, and devise ways to use each others' difference to enrich our visions and our joint struggles."[6]

bell hooks also emphasizes the danger of group members becoming so entrenched in the exploration of personal feelings and experiences that they do not move from consciousness to action. Although the Rag did produce four journals, we never published beyond that, and only once did we move into the realm of activism. If funneled into action, the consciousness that was developing in the Rag might have had a tremendous impact on our campus and beyond. As a group we might have participated in demonstrations for minority faculty hiring, lesbian and gay rights and divestiture. We might have planned clever actions against the all-male, elite Harvard clubs that offended many Rag members. We also might have participated in any of the many social service activities organized by other students on campus. For example, one Rag member who also did public service work gave a copy of *The Rag* to a mother who lived in the housing development where she volunteered. After reading an essay about popular animated films (such as *The Little Mermaid*) having a negative impact on the self-esteem of girls of color, the mother responded that she had never considered the subject and that she had not been aware that feminism was concerned with girls of color. Perhaps the Rag could have followed up on her interest and offered to work with mothers in that community to create greater awareness of the issue and to collect books and films that contained positive and inclusive portrayals of girls.

My experience in the Rag leads me to imagine the following picture of a vital, growing young feminist group. A commitment to encourage and a responsibility to challenge form the roots. The study of feminist histories, intergenerational communication, self-analysis, dialogue, activism and respect for diversity shape the branches. And the women—in their myriad textures and colors, in their possibilities for flying in the face of the wind—are the seeds, pods and blossoms.

1. Audre Lorde, *Sister Outsider* (Trumansburg, New York: Crossing Press, 1984), p. 117.

2. bell hooks, *Feminist Theory: From Margin to Center* (Boston: South End Press, 1984), p. 55.

3. bell hooks, *Black Looks* (Boston: South End Press, 1992), p. 10.

4. hooks, *Feminist Theory: From Margin to Center*, p. 57.

5. Lorde, p. 123.

6. Lorde, p. 122.

Don't Call Me a Survivor

Emilie Morgan

Please don't call me a survivor. I really don't feel like one. I still live my life as if I were raped yesterday. Essentially I was; it happens again every night in my dreams. I am not a victim either. I am just a woman—and a statistic.

I was thirteen the first time I was raped. It was a "classic" rape scenario: A young virgin from the suburbs is lured from a shopping mall into a room no bigger than a closet. The doors were locked, the room was dark. He held both of my hands above my head and then it happened.

I remember it hurting, but I don't remember crying until I got home. Looking back, it amazes me that I was able to accept it so well. Not once did I blame myself. I never thought it was my fault; I was too young to understand the political and social implications of rape. To me it was just a personal thing—a very, very disgusting thing that some dirty man did to me.

However, it wasn't long before certain messages began hitting me with a vengeance. My first mistake was telling a couple of friends at school. Junior high can be pretty tough when you acquire a reputation for being a slut. I was suddenly the most desirable girl in the school. It didn't matter that I still considered myself a virgin. I figured that technically I really hadn't had sex; rape didn't count. Yet, to all the boys in school I was "experienced," and to all the girls I was cheap.

The next mistake was telling my parents. I was a good kid; I rarely got in trouble. So when my parents yelled at me and grounded me after I told them, I knew that I must have done something horrible to deserve this.

Then came the trip to the doctor's office. Because I was grounded, I had to sneak out of the house and take a bus there. I had called around and found a clinic two hours away that would not charge me. I thought it was pathetic that anyone would try to make me pay for an exam. I didn't ask for a medical bill. I didn't ask for any of this!

Sure enough, he had given me a sexually transmitted disease. I wasn't surprised, but it scared me nonetheless. My only experiences in a doctor's office had been for the usual childhood ailments: strep throat, a sprained ankle, routine shots. I never dreamed I'd find myself being treated for chlamydia.

The doctors knew nothing more about me than my age and first name, but they lectured me as if I were their own child. Three of them came into the room: One had a prescription, another a pamphlet on the dangers of unprotected sex, and the third gave me a condom sample. I told them this wasn't necessary, but they didn't listen. Their response? "Obviously it is."

A couple of weeks later I found myself back in the clinic. I hadn't gotten my period, and I was beginning to get concerned. They remembered me as the thirteen-year-old with chlamydia. What an honor! This time, however, I wasn't going to put up with their condescending judgment.

"Look, I was raped," I told them. "I am not a little tramp. I have nothing to be ashamed of or educated about. I didn't do anything wrong!"

They gave me the pregnancy test and told me to come back later for the results. I never went back. I didn't go home that night either. I went to the parking lot of a liquor store and paid someone to buy me some alcohol, I didn't care what kind. Later that night, the police found me lying naked and drunk in the gutter. I had no idea what had happened, and to be perfectly honest, I really didn't care.

They brought me into the hospital and later sent me off to a detoxification center. When I arrived, I was put through one of the most humiliating experiences of my life: I was told to take off all of my clothes and take a shower. A woman from the staff was in the room, watching me, the entire time. Afterward, I was given some hospital clothing that included pants that tied together at the waist, a blue paper cap and a very loose-fitting shirt. All of my clothing had been taken away. I wasn't even allowed to wear underwear.

Having recently been raped, the experience of having a stranger stare at my naked body frightened me. And then, to be among thirty other kids (twenty-nine of whom were boys), wearing clothing that truly did not conceal a thing, furthered this paranoia. I felt even more vulnerable at that point than I had while I was being raped. To this day, I am afraid to close my eyes in the shower because I always wonder if someone will be standing there when I open them.

During my stay at the detox center, one of the employees molested me. I was completely vulnerable at that point and had no recourse. I did not have the privilege of calling the police or yelling out to anyone because he was the only one to yell to. He had all of the power and I had nothing. It made me sick. I was stuck in that place for seventy-two hours, and there was nothing I could do about it.

Two days after I left the center, I had a miscarriage. It happened while I was at my grandparents' house. I suppose my grandma just figured I had really bad cramps or something. She told me to take a warm bath and then drink some water. A few weeks after that happened, I called the clinic just to confirm what the results of my pregnancy test were: positive.

I tried to put the experience behind me and just move on. The rape itself wasn't what bothered me the most. I had basically come to terms with what had happened and considered it a part of growing up. What did bother me was always wondering what could have been. What might have happened if I hadn't gotten so intoxicated? I got drunk to avoid the thought of what might be inside me, not realizing how much my actions were threatening the fetus. What bothers me most is knowing that I could have a six-year-old child right now.

Ironically, it was nine months after the rape occurred that I went to the police. An officer came into my home ec class to talk about sexual assault. Afterwards, I asked if I could speak to him, and I told him what happened. Although he spoke with me a few times and even called my parents, nothing ever came of it. Finding the man who had raped me was a lost cause at that point.

I was sixteen the next time I was raped. I was sexually active at that point, and the rape occurred on a date. He didn't overpower me like the man who had raped me three years earlier. He simply didn't stop when I told him to.

Despite the fact that I was three years older and the rape itself was far less momentous, I was much more affected by it this time. In those three years, I had fully internalized the view that a woman is somehow to blame if she is raped, and this experience wasn't as clear-cut as the first one. Although I held him ultimately responsible, I couldn't help scrutinizing my own behavior. I had consented to everything up until that point. I knew what my limits were, but it's possible I didn't make myself clear to him. Maybe the word no wasn't enough.

This time I didn't go to the police. I knew it was rape, but I felt partially to blame. Why bother trying to explain it to anyone just so they could vindicate him and put me to shame?

What made the experience even worse was having to see him at school every single day. The way he looked at me made me realize that he knew what he had gotten away with. I know he told all of his friends. One day some guy walked up to me at my locker and asked how much I charged.

Later that year I switched schools. He graduated with honors and is a pre-law student right now.

I was raped again two years later, the summer before I was to go off to college. I don't remember everything about that night, but I do remember what I was feeling; I remember my thoughts. I am not sure which was harder: being gang-raped, or having the sudden realization that this is what it means to be a woman.

There was a clock, a digital clock on the shelf by the table. Having the clock there was very important to me. It was my only reminder that the world was continuing as usual, despite what was happening to me. It became a symbol, a tie to life. In many ways it represented the hope that my life would also continue, in time. . . .

I was at a party. I was playing cards with several men in one of the side rooms. One of them said to the others, "Does anyone feel like going on a train ride tonight?" They all exchanged glances and kind of nodded in agreement. Before I had a chance to realize what was happening, someone grabbed me from behind and threw me against the wall. One of them held me down while a couple of the others took off my clothes. They each proceeded to rape me, several times, and then invited their friends to do the same.

I didn't know when I would be able to leave—how long it would last. It was six hours and twenty-six minutes. I started to believe it was never going to end. It hasn't. It happens again every night in my dreams. Every night I see their faces, I feel the pain, the powerlessness. Every night I realize the control they have over my life, and I cry. This has been the longest six and a half hours of my life.

There was something else, something I will never forget. I couldn't escape it then, and it still continues today. The music. It was constant. It wasn't so much the act that was occurring, but the music that was playing that made me realize my status as a woman. The lyrics, from NWA's *Niggaz 4 Life*, told me who I was in their eyes:

In reality, a fool is one who believes that all women are ladies.
A nigga is one who believes all ladies are bitches and all bitches are
created equal.
To me, all bitches are the same. . . .
To me, all bitches ain't shit.

I couldn't escape the music. I tried to imagine other things, anything besides what was happening to me. Sometimes I could almost forget the physical pain I was in, but I couldn't escape the music. The volume was turned up just loud enough so that no one could hear me scream. The tape player was set on automatic reverse so that it would play over and over again. The sound penetrated my ears. The words fractured my soul. And the message shattered my life.

So fellas, next time they try to tell a lie, that they never would suck
a dick, punch the bitch in the eye and then the ho will fall to the
ground and you open up her mouth put your dick in it and move
the shit around.

When I was finally able to leave, I didn't have all of my clothes. I gathered together what I could and just ran. I got to my car and drove straight to the hospital. The waiting room was full of people, and everyone just stared at me. Children commented on my lack of clothing, which revealed the fist marks and scratches that marked my body. In that moment, I was transformed back to that thirteen-year-old child being watched in the shower. On no other occasion have I experienced that kind of vulnerability. I spent the night in the emergency room, telling my story over and over again to doctors, cops and social workers.

The next morning, I hardly recognized myself. I went home and looked at myself in the bathroom mirror. My face was swollen. My arms and legs were black and blue with bruises. My chest and back were burned from where they put out their cigarettes. I will always have those scars.

While I was standing there, I noticed that for the first time since the rape began, I was all alone, and there was no more music. Yet neither was there silence. I could still hear the words. I still felt the pain. I fell to the floor and cried. I knew my screams would never be heard, and the music would never fade away. . . .

It was four months later that I found myself at a Take Back the Night march. I was eighteen years old and in my first semester of college. That night I found myself surrounded by women, most of whom I hardly knew. Yet we all knew each other's story as if it were our own. It was. We were all there for the same reason. Our lives had all been affected by sexual violence, and we were ready to heal.

With candles in our hands and tears in our eyes, we listened to story after story of women just like me. We held hands and closed our eyes and asked for the healing to begin. . . .

We have heard the stories, the pain, the silence of women, who are all different, and who are just like you and me. We all need healing. We need healing of our memories, of our silence, we need healing of our bodies, of our minds.

I couldn't hold back the tears, tears I had held inside for so many years. When it came time to name the names of those who had been hurt by sexual violence, I remained silent. But I knew the healing had already begun. I listened as the names of countless women were shouted out as if it was roll call and I was back in elementary school. I was not alone. I was surrounded by strong women who were all surviving. The energy in that room could not be contained. We marched throughout the campus, releasing the years of pain and anger that we had held inside for far too long. We shouted into the air of the city and the ears of those who would listen, demanding that our voices be heard. I screamed the night I was raped, but nobody heard me.

≈

Please don't call me a survivor. I really don't feel like one. Not yet anyway. I have a lot more healing to do, and it's going to take time. I am just a woman who has a story to tell, and I am learning how to make it heard.

Why I Fight Back

Whitney Walker

"Take a look," he said.

My fingers stopped on my combination lock as I looked to my right to see a man, naked from the waist down, standing a foot away from my locker.

For years I'd heard about girls getting flashed near my suburban California high school. When it had happened to my sister a few years earlier, it had been broad daylight and she and her girlfriends laughed until the man ran away. It was not like that tonight. It was dark and we were alone.

All I could do for a moment was follow his orders and look at him. He carried his pants over his left arm, and his right hand was shoved into the pocket of his grey-and-blue running jacket. Was he holding a weapon beneath his jacket? Was he going to rape me? Did he move closer? Did I hear someone else?

"What do you want?" I finally managed.

"Just take a long look."

I stood frozen in front of him for a long time. I thought about running or yelling for help, but told myself it wouldn't work: He would be too fast, no one would hear. I was feeling desperate. My car keys were cutting into my hand. Were they a weapon?

"I could stab you," I warned him, gripping my keys.

"I'd like to see you try."

I recoiled, shaking with both fear and anger. He was right, I wasn't going to try. "All right, I saw you, just leave."

"Close your locker."

I did, and was relieved when the next order was to walk away slowly and not look back. When I began to run, he disappeared into a dark hallway and did not follow me. I went home and told my mother what had happened, and we called the police. To my knowledge, he was never caught.

It would be several years before I'd take my first self-defense class and stop seeing myself as a failure that night. I wanted to stab him, stop him, scare him the way he scared me. I wanted to be unafraid of him. But he overpowered me, ordered my obedience and received it. "I'd like to see you try." His words followed me long after I stopped hearing his voice. It was typical teenage insecurity that made me freeze up during tests, get tongue-tied during arguments, fumble the winning shot during soccer games. But I'm sure those words contributed. They taunted me, pushed me down, reminded me: He won.

As a kid with an equal-rights, athletic mom and a dad who wanted daughters rather than sons, I was raised on feminist children's books like *Free to Be . . . You and Me,* and I knew boys weren't better than girls. I also refused to believe they were stronger. When bullies picked on me or my friends, I hit them in the knees with my Holly Hobby lunch pail and that was that. But as with most girls, my self-confidence decreased as I grew. I continued to believe in equal rights, but—since I didn't excel on the playground and wasn't allowed to hit boys—I gave up on being athletic or tough.

My feminist awakening came at about the same time I discovered self-defense; it's hard to say which came first. I met strong women in college who weren't afraid to call themselves feminists. I also met women who had been assaulted, raped or molested. Some were victims of violent attacks from strangers, others from people they knew or even loved. I heard the statistic predicting that one out of four women in my age group would be raped in her lifetime and saw how it left many of my friends helpless with fear. During the day, we held discussion groups, gave speeches, led marches. But at night, we clutched whistles, carried Mace, looked in the backseats of cars before getting in—and still we didn't go out alone. When we thought about fighting back, we heard "I'd like to see you try."

That all changed my junior year, when I took my first self-defense class with Karla Grant. A fifth-degree black belt in karate who has taught self-defense for fifteen years, Karla explained to me how tradition and the media warned me not to fight back against men. She told me how I could fight back, where and when to strike and with what. She told me why I must fight back, both to save myself and to help stop the growing number of attacks on women every day. Then she taught me how to punch and kick; how to block a blow from a fist, a club, a knife or a gun; how to fight two attackers, or three, or five, or a gang. At the end of eight weeks, I broke a two-inch-thick wooden board with my fist, and Karla told me: "If you can break a board, you can break his nose."

I've carried that message with me ever since, through three years of martial arts and self-defense training. When I hear the words of my attacker attempting to push me down, the voices of my three feminist teachers—Karla, Kathy and Roberta—tell me to push back. I see that night in high school differently now: I was not a failure, I was brave. I did not risk my life. I got away.

Most girls growing up in the United States experience some level of sexual assault accompanied by feelings of insecurity and low self-esteem like the ones I experienced. But women of my generation had feminism and self-defense as a backdrop for our childhoods. We are making self-defense "popular" again only now, as adults, but even as a girl I was proud of the women's movement. It was a source of strength for me to know that women organized and fought for the right to legal abortion, equality in schools and an end to sexual harassment. Knowing that women were martial artists did the same thing for me. When I discovered that women were learning to defend themselves, I knew I had to be part of it.

Self-defense is becoming as important to my generation of the women's movement as it was to my mother's. Our mothers, too, learned that self-defense increases self-esteem, but the women I know didn't hear about it as we were growing up. Why weren't we told? Why didn't we listen? Maybe we thought it was just a phase our mothers went through in the sixties. Maybe they thought so. Women who studied martial arts thirty years ago usually did so in macho coed schools that resented their presence. Most classes were male-taught and focused on male strength. Women were expected to fight like men with men—if they were allowed to fight at all. Even though karate emphasizes targeting rather than strength, early coed schools stressed muscle-based techniques. And, while the women's movement helped women to be independent, these martial arts schools told women to follow orders without question, to submit their wills to a male sensei.

By the time my generation got into self-defense, our foremothers had already revolutionized the classes, even started their own programs. Discipline and obedience are still part of martial arts teaching, but the rigid rules of the earlier schools are gone. I feel more independent because of my self-defense training, not less so, and I am grateful for the female senseis who encourage questions and focus on women's strengths. Women's bodies are perfect for karate: We have more lower-body strength and tend to be more agile than men. Most important, our attackers do not expect us to fight back, so women have the element of surprise.

I've been a pacifist all my life, and yet I relish the knowledge that my front kick can reach someone's head, my punch can knock someone to the floor. These are not completely incompatible notions. Passivity does not mean submission—it means de-escalation. Fighting back does not mean warfare—it means handing over the money if I'm mugged, but going for the testicles if he grabs me. Equal rights means women should be equal to (not the same as, but equal to) men in all ways—including equal fighters.

Self-defense for women is an emotional topic, and when I think about potential attacks, the rage can boil up inside me with a power that is tempting to use. But rage is both unstable and blinding. I prefer to think of fighting in rational terms: You want to hurt me, I'll take you down. I won't allow it.

I do not hate men as potential attackers; I do not even hate attackers. I just know that if someone comes for me, I will not hesitate to take that person down. Karate means "open hands," and in every school, before sparring you bow and show your opponent that you come to her with open hands, without a weapon. I am taught to avoid a fight when it is possible. When it is not, I am taught to fight to protect myself, not out of anger.

Thankfully, I have not had to test my fighting skills on the street, but I am confident in them, and perhaps that has been my best protection. I'm more aware of my surroundings when I walk at night, and I know when someone is behind me on a deserted street. Once this would have made me feel helpless—and footsteps approaching from behind do still scare me—but now I can concentrate on how to handle a potential attack, plan my reaction and calculate the distance between my foot and his groin. Self-defense teaches responses appropriate to every point along the continuum of violence. Attempted rape and murder might require me to strike to the eyes or throat of the attacker, or to break his knees. But for an unwanted touch or verbal harassment, confronting the perpetrator, or simply looking at him, may stop an attack before it even starts.

Women who study martial arts say they are calm in the world and that they wear their training like an extra layer of protection, a warning: I can take care of myself. Women have long been striving to say that with confidence on an economic level. Self-defense provides the strength to reinforce it on a physical level. Living with the fundamental knowledge that I can protect myself against a man has changed my life completely, inside the dojo and out. I no longer question my instincts. I know them to be good when my arms block a punch before my eyes see it. I don't apologize for being in the way; I have seen the usefulness of my body. Knowing that I am strong, I refuse to be weak.

It's self-confidence that doesn't come from a gun or a can of Mace, and it won't leave you fumbling through your purse in a dark alley. It's not surprising that women have responded to the marketing tactics of gun manufacturers and deterrent-spray dealers. Cultural "wisdom" has always held that women's bodies were not made to fight, and that we are constantly vulnerable to sexual violence. With that kind of setup, movies supply the ending: She beats his chest and hysterically pleads for mercy; he doesn't grant it. She runs away but trips; he walks slowly and still catches up. Even if she's a strong female character and lands a swift knee to the groin, he's the Terminator; he stumbles for a millisecond, smiles and then keeps coming.

These are ridiculous scenarios, but they've made their way into the consciousness of every woman and still succeed in scaring us and preventing us from fighting back. So does this warning: Don't fight back, you'll only get him angry. Everyone's heard it from the most well-meaning of sources, like the high school sex education teacher or the cops who speak to first-year female students in the dorms. The idea is that if you submit to brutal rape and torture, you may get away with your life. May. But as Karla explained to my first self-defense class, an attacker is already angry and not very trustworthy as a bargainer. He may say, "Don't scream and you won't get hurt." But he's already breaking the law; why should he keep his promise? The best time to fight back is when he's least expecting it—when he puts down the gun or the knife to assault you, when he gets the rope to tie you up. After that point, you don't know what he's going to do. And then there's the double standard that comes from the same sources that advise against self-defense. If you get raped, the first question is "Did you fight back?" "No." "You must have wanted it."

No other crime victims are accused of encouraging the attack. As Karla told us, the male robbery victim does not get blamed for keeping his wallet in his back pocket. No one says, "You must have wanted to get robbed." And—even if the male victim doesn't know how to defend himself, even if doing so would make his assailant angry, even if his assailant is bigger and stronger—male victims are never expected to submit without fighting back.

When I began seeing the hypocrisy of these messages from male authority figures, I also began to see the hypocrisy in all of patriarchal society. My self-defense training became connected to my awakening as a feminist. The questions began to sound the same and have similar answers. Why is a woman's right to control her body constantly threatened? Whether referring to reproductive rights or sexual violence, the answer is to take control back. With self-defense, I am in control.

Karla also told my class that the one-in-four statistic left something out—the possibility that women can successfully take down their attackers and get away. It should read: One in four women between eighteen and twenty-four will be targeted for rape in her lifetime. And every time a woman isn't attacked because she defends herself, this statistic is whittled down even further. The National Women's Martial Arts Federation estimates that women make up thirty percent of all martial artists in the United States. To me, that's not enough, but it's up from ten percent ten years ago and one percent twenty years ago. When rapists are thwarted because women fight back, attackers will stop assuming their victims will be intimidated into obedience.

I was flashed again recently, on the subway in Manhattan. An older man stood next to me, his coat draped over his arm to hide his fly, which was open to expose his penis. He was trying to show only me, but I didn't notice for a while. When I finally saw what he was doing, I immediately thought about all I could do to take him out. His knee was in a perfect position for me to break it with a kick. I could smash his elbow with a punch, or karate chop his neck. And I could certainly knee him in the groin. We were in a crowded, well-lit car, and he was no threat to me. Instead I looked to his face and showed him that he had not succeeded in frightening or arousing me, whichever his purpose might have been. At the next stop, he covered himself up with his coat and exited the car. I laughed to myself.

Woman Who Clears the Way

Lisa Tiger

I have found my purpose. I am living out my dream. I was twenty-nine summers in 1994 and I am doing what I was meant to do.

In the spring of 1992 I was taking college classes. I was feeling a restlessness, an energy that I knew I needed to apply wholeheartedly to some sort of cause. It was driving me crazy. Over and over I asked my professor, an African American man of strong Christian beliefs, "What is my purpose? What am I here to do? I am ready."

"Lisa, you are impatient," he said. "You may not be ready. God will let you know when the time is right."

I argued, "I am ready!"

He said, "You may not even want to know. If you could look into the future and see what you will be doing, it might scare you to death. Just be patient."

A few months later I tested HIV positive and found my purpose.

My father was Jerome Tiger, a nationally respected Native American artist. He died of a self-inflicted accidental gunshot wound when I was two years old. I don't remember my father, but I have been told I was Daddy's little girl and my older sister, Dana, was Momma's girl. My brother, Chris, was only two weeks old when Daddy died. My dad made a fine living as an artist. He was amazed that he could make a living doing something he would do anyway. Jerome Tiger was a spiritual man; it shows in his paintings. When I look at his art, it can move me to tears.

My mother, sister, brother and I were a very close family. In 1970 Mom and her cousin Molly started the Jerome Tiger Art Company in Muskogee, Oklahoma. They had to act as if the company was run by a man. They said the owner was M.A. Babcock, which was really Molly Ann Babcock. Mom acted like the secretary, using her maiden name, Richmond. Molly assumed her maiden name, O'Reilly, and acted as the salesperson. This was acceptable to gallery owners, and Mom had a successful business reproducing the beautiful art of Jerome Tiger.

When I was fifteen years old someone told me the average age for a girl to have sex was sixteen. I thought that was pretty young. I knew sex would be a big responsibility. I hung around with a lot of guys, and they would tell me all about their relationships with their girlfriends. The lines they would use! I couldn't believe girls would actually fall for those lines. I didn't trust guys, and I knew that if I had sex with one, he might use it against me. A lot of guys I knew started to be disrespectful and abusive toward their girlfriends once they had had sex with them. And I didn't want to even think about birth control or unwanted pregnancy.

I made a bet with my friend Billy. I told him, "I'll graduate a virgin, and I'm not going to drink, either." Billy said he would buy me a steak dinner if I graduated from high school without drinking or having sex. Now, when I speak to high school students, I can say I won the steak dinner. I learned that young people can have good and fulfilling relationships without sex. And I now know that the stakes are even higher than unwanted pregnancy.

After high school I didn't have plans to go to college or to even get a job. I don't know what I was thinking. I ended up getting a job as a new-car salesperson at a local Oldsmobile-Cadillac dealership.

In the meantime, I started drinking. I planned only to try it, then I thought I would do it only for the summer of my eighteenth year, but I drank for three years before I realized that I had a really big problem. Just before my twenty-first birthday, I realized that I had become the kind of person I didn't like and couldn't respect. An acquaintance of mine totaled her brand-new sports car. My reaction upon hearing the news was laughter. Later that night I thought, "What could be funny about a serious car accident?" I became very sad as I realized I must have been jealous of that woman. I cried at the person I had become. Alcohol had destroyed my self-esteem and made me unsympathetic, and even worse, amused by the misfortune of another. That night I began a struggle for sobriety.

I replaced drinking with exercise. I spent hours at the Muskogee High School track. I lost the weight I had put on in three years of drinking, and as my physical condition improved, so did my self-image. I established a routine. Up at five, I jogged three to five miles, went to the fitness center and rode the Lifecycle twenty to thirty minutes. I started working at our family business, choosing to do hard labor in the warehouse behind the gallery drying our Indian-design, hand-silk-screened T-shirts. After work it was back to the fitness center for an hour of Jazzercise, an hour of aerobics and a session of weight lifting.

I loved working with my family and friends at Tiger Art. Chris worked in the silk-screening department and was establishing himself as a painter, showing his art in Oklahoma and other states. Dana had chosen to paint the strength and courage of Native American women and was on her way to becoming a leading contemporary Native American artist. With the encouragement of my family, I started my own framing and matting business. Eventually, I began taking college courses. I had turned my life around, and I felt good about myself. During my three years of drinking I had lacked the confidence to even think of a relationship. For the three more years it took to rebuild my self-esteem, all my energy was directed toward dealing with my own problems. But now I felt good enough to think of beginning a relationship.

There has always been a side to me that my mother refers to as the "sympathetic social worker." I had made such an improvement in my own life that I knew I could work the same miracle in the life of another. I started dating Ronnie, a young man who, like me, had been popular in high school. He was a great athlete and had even been offered a baseball scholarship. After high school, he started hanging around bars, drinking, and wasting his life. He seemed to be following the same misdirected path that had nearly destroyed my life. I knew I had a lot to offer; I knew I could help him. I gave this relationship all of my newly rediscovered energy. I truly believe that my constant effort and attention helped him to give up drinking. Ronnie really turned his life around, and we moved in together a year after we started seeing each other.

On my twenty-fifth birthday, I got calls and presents all day. My one disappointment was that, of all people, my brother seemed to have forgotten. Finally, at the end of the day, I said, "Chris, aren't you forgetting something?" As soon as he realized, he jumped up and ran out the door. He came back with a present and a giant cookie with the words "HAPPY BIRTHDAY LISA." It turned out to be a perfect day, one of the best of my life.

That night I lay in bed, reflecting on the day and on my life. Twenty-five years. I knew I would live at least another twenty-five years because I was such a careful person. I thought of how lucky I had been. I even thought I was lucky that I had lost my dad while I was still too young to remember him. I thought of my mother. At my age she had already lost her husband and had just lost her mother to cancer. I thought of the next twenty-five years, and I was scared my luck would run out.

Two months later my best friend, Randy Hawkins, knocked on my door to tell me that Chris had been shot to death. I had to identify my baby brother's body at the hospital. My twenty-two-year-old brother had been shot at point-blank range by a man he had met earlier that night. I was very strong at the funeral. I don't know where the strength came from—or where it went for the two years following Chris' death.

Chris' killer was convicted of first-degree manslaughter in February 1991 and sentenced to forty years in prison. Soon after the trial ended, Ronnie began to make it known that he could not understand how I could continue to cry myself to sleep night after night. I knew there was no way he could understand my pain. I ended my three-year relationship with this man who I had thought would always be there for me.

Growing up and attending public school in Muskogee, I was happy because I was able to reach my goals. But my goals were those of the typical mainstream "all-American girl," not a young Native American woman. I was proud to be Native American but didn't know what being Native American meant. It wasn't until I was in college and had suffered through two years of unhappiness after losing my brother that I began to realize that there was another way far different from the way I had lived my life.

During the spring of 1992, for the first time in my life I made it a priority to seek out Native people who could teach me the ways of my ancestors. By summer I was following the Oklahoma pow-wow circuit, hanging out with full-bloods and reading books written by Indians about Indians like Dee Brown's *Bury My Heart at Wounded Knee* (a book I believe should be required reading in every high school in America). I finally made the decision to major in Native American studies.

I ran into Ronnie that summer in a convenience store and was shocked by his appearance. Ronnie had always been the big, athletic type, but now he was underweight and puny. Two weeks later a gay friend confessed to having had a brief affair with Ronnie while we were still together. Until that time I had not suspected that my ex-boyfriend was bisexual—or that he had ever been unfaithful. In 1988, when our relationship began, I thought AIDS was on the West Coast and on the East Coast, but AIDS was not here in

Muskogee, Oklahoma. I had considered myself very low-risk. I had never used drugs or had a blood transfusion, and in the past seven years I had had only two relationships, both long-term and, I thought, monogamous. But now I was concerned.

I arranged to take an HIV-antibodies test. The week after I took the test I was at a Fourth of July powwow in Quapau, Oklahoma, about three hours from home. I called my answering machine and there was a message from my doctor. "Lisa, you need to call me," she said. "I'll be in my office all day." Something in her voice scared me. It was late at night, and I wanted to be at home with my mother, but it was storming so severely that I couldn't drive home. I stayed all night in a tent listening to the storm. The next day was beautiful, and I started the long drive home. I called my mom from the road and told her I was worried about the test. I asked her to phone the doctor. My doctor is my mother's cousin, so I know she could get the results, and I preferred to hear the news from my mom. Throughout the rest of the ride I thought about the test. What would I do if it was positive? I thought, "If I'm HIV positive, things will change; people won't want to be around me." I was scared and lonely. Then I thought of Chris, and for the first time since his death, I felt his love and strength was with me. I was filled with overwhelming peace. I knew if the test was positive, it would be okay.

When I walked in the front door, I saw my mom and I knew. It was hard for me to see her devastated by yet another tragedy. All she asked from her creator was what all mothers ask: "Please let me go before my children." Two years after her beautiful twenty-two-year-old son walked out of the house for the last time, her daughter tested positive for HIV, the virus that leads to AIDS. Dana and her boyfriend, Donnie Blair, came to the house. Mom and Dana were trying to be strong for me. I told them they didn't have to be strong for me; somehow the strength that had gotten me through Chris' funeral had come back. We held each other and cried together.

The next day I had tests to determine how much the virus had affected my immune system, and was told that my T cell count was in the normal range. While Mom, Dana, Randy and I were at the doctor's, Donnie decided to do a little investigating. He went to Ronnie's house and learned that he had been rushed to the hospital and was in intensive care. Later that week Ronnie's sister called and told me she needed to talk to me. I said, "It's about your brother—he has AIDS, doesn't he." She asked me how I knew. I told her I had tested positive. I asked her if he was going to die. She said, "I think so." I said, "I'm sorry you are going to lose your brother, but I'm pretty pissed off right now and I don't know what I'm going to do." I learned that he had tested HIV positive twice in 1988, months before we began our relationship. He didn't die, and several weeks later I saw him driving his truck. I still see him around town occasionally, but we never speak. Sometimes my anger at him feels overwhelming.

I knew immediately this wasn't something I could keep secret. Before Dana, Mom, Randy and I went to Tulsa for my first round of tests, I asked Mom to go to work and tell the people there. Mom said, "Lisa, I don't think this is a decision you should make today. You just found out last night, and I think you need more time to think about it. Even at the gallery with our close friends, this isn't something you can change your mind about later. Once we tell even a few people, this is going to be all over town." I said, "Go and tell them now. I know I won't change my mind." Later that same evening Dana and I talked to as many close friends as we could by phone so they could hear it from us. One of the first people Dana called was the great Principal Chief of the Cherokee Nation, Wilma Mankiller.

Wilma later phoned me and shared some of the struggles she has had with her health, and I talked to her about my plans of being open about my condition. Wilma arranged a press conference the following week. My hometown newspaper, the *Muskogee Daily Phoenix*, wanted to be first with the story. We invited Betty Smith, a reporter there whom we knew and trusted, to come to our gallery and spend the afternoon.

The morning of the press conference the *Phoenix* carried a big color photograph of me, accompanying an article headlined: AIDS ACTIVISM JUST SEEMS RIGHT. LISA TIGER LEARNS SHE IS HIV POSITIVE." All the big state newspapers and television stations showed up for the press conference, and for the next several days it seemed to be the number one story.

I am one of an ever-growing number of HIV-positive women. Women with AIDS get sick faster and die sooner than men. Women make up eleven percent of all people with AIDS in the United States, but by the end of this century most new infections will occur in women. Women do infect men, but according to recent studies, a woman is seventeen and a half times more likely to be infected by a man than a man by a woman. Yet many doctors don't associate HIV with women, so women are not encouraged to be tested. In women AIDS has different symptoms, so often women are not diagnosed early enough to benefit from early treatment. Almost all research has been done on men. After a woman tests positive for HIV, she is dealt a second blow when she learns her doctor cannot fight to prolong her life with the same knowledge that is available to treat men.

At the press conference held on July 24, 1992, I stated that I planned to take good care of my health, exercise, eat right and speak out at every opportunity for myself and others living with this virus. Soon I was being asked to speak at schools, colleges, clinics and conferences, first in Oklahoma and later throughout the nation. Now I am given an honorarium for many of my presentations and have turned over my framing and matting business to Donnie Blair, who is now my brother-in-law. Like my father, I feel very lucky to be able to make my living doing something I love to do and would do anyway. It is fortunate that I can't be fired because some of the more conservative people nearly fall out of their seats when I speak—like the administrators at the junior college where I told students that there are other ways to satisfy yourself besides having intercourse. "Try sex toys," I recommended. "A man can't satisfy you the way they can anyway."

When I talk about sex toys, sexually transmitted diseases and condoms, I see the kids sneaking looks at their teachers. Later they tell me they can't believe I talked about penises and genital warts in front of the teachers. My subjects are the same in a junior high as in a college. I get a lot of laughs when I make comments such as "You guys love your penises so much, I'd think you'd want to learn how to protect them."

Some of the teachers and parents in the schools where I speak are homophobic, and I feel it is important to educate young children before they become like their parents. I have told kids as young as kindergarten that someday most little boys will dream of little girls and most little girls will dream of little boys, but some little boys will dream of little boys and some little girls will dream of little girls, and when this happens, it's okay.

Once, I was walking through the halls of a school to the auditorium where I was scheduled to give a presentation. Some of the kids were talking, and I overheard, "There's a woman with AIDS coming. I'm out of here!" My feelings were hurt, and for a second I didn't feel like talking, but there is always the hope that I may be able to change someone's mind or heart. Getting to know me gives AIDS a face, and it's harder to fear someone once you get to know them. That day I began by repeating what I had heard and ended by saying I hoped getting to know me would make a difference.

When I step up to a stage and the kids see that they can't tell by looking, they are really shocked. Then when I tell them that HIV has no signs or symptoms, I scare them even further. Right after I finish speaking, the kids rush up and around me and shake my hand and hug me. They ask for my address and write me letters. I always stay until every person with a question or comment gets a chance to speak. A few times sessions have gone on six or more hours.

My message and my goals have changed, strengthened and grown since July 1992. At first I shared my own story as a way to warn others, especially Native Americans and women in general, about

HIV/AIDS. Now I learn so much from the people I meet that my presentation changes from day to day and from week to week. I have come to believe it is important for us to stay within the red race when we decide to become parents because we are so few in number we could easily be gone forever. We have gifts that our people must recognize and share. We are a very spiritual people. If our religion had to be described in just one word, the word I would choose is respect, and respect could also be called spirituality. Our respect for all the gifts of the Creator can be seen in our traditional songs, our dances and the sweat lodge as well as in our medicine, which respects and treats the spirit as well as the body.

The Cherokees have a view of life that Wilma Mankiller calls having a good mind. A person can choose to go one of two paths. The path most people take, unfortunately, is the path where they only see the negative in life. A person with a good mind chooses the path where they see the positive in all people and all situations. More than anyone I know, Wilma has chosen the path of having a good mind. Whenever I feel I'm losing focus, I go see Wilma and her husband, Charlie Soap.

Sometimes I am given eagle feathers, which I carry with me wherever I go. My first eagle feather was a gift from Charlie. The prayers, generosity and good will from women and men of many tribes are in the feathers. Sometimes I wear a feather when I speak, and sometimes at night in motel rooms I take out my feathers and feel where I have been. Then, even if I'm tired, I have the strength to go on. Sometimes I say to myself, "You can't get sick because you have to be in South Dakota tomorrow, Santa Fe the next day, and then you have a week at the pueblos around New Mexico." And so far I have never gotten sick when I'm traveling. If I have a cold or some other sickness, it waits until I have a few days at home. Having a life-threatening illness makes it easier to put aside distractions and work consistently.

One of my desires is to shake the hand of every Native American in this country—not an impossible goal, since there are only 1.8 million, and only an estimated 700,000 of us are a quarter blood or more. I share this desire with my audiences and tell them I'd appreciate it if they would help me to accomplish this goal by taking the time to shake my hand at the end of my presentation. I mentioned this to the students at Lodgegrass on the Crow Reservation. They all ran toward me, nearly crushing me against the stage. It was beautiful, especially since I had been told of their reaction before I came to Crow: One student was seen looking at my poster and backing away, saying, "Ooh, scary."

When speaking to Native American audiences, I emphasize our heritage. Our traditions call for us to laugh easily and often, to take pride in *not* killing our enemies and to strive for spiritual and physical health. I make the point that sexism, homophobia, and violence against women and children were introduced to us by European men. I address our number one problem, alcoholism. Drinking leads to risky behavior—a drunk person doesn't worry about sexually transmitted diseases. We drink because we have low self-esteem. We have low self-esteem because we are still in culture shock from being forced to live like the Europeans. I set goals with my audiences—like complete sobriety by the year 2000, sobriety to the point that if you see a drunk you'll know that person can't be a Native American. I remind my audiences that Native Americans see life as a sacred circle where no one is above or below anyone else. I make the point that our tribes and other minorities must teach each other and learn from each other and support each other's goals.

In my story I believe other Native Americans can find hope for their own lives. They too know the pain of losing someone you love. Living on the reservation, they have seen plenty of death. Yet they see me as a happy person with big dreams.

As a Native American woman, I am afraid the AIDS epidemic could wipe our people out. Lots of Native Americans still don't know that AIDS has reached Indian country. But awareness of AIDS won't do any good until we know our lives are worth saving. We suffer disproportionately from murder, suicide, poverty, fatal accidents, fetal alcohol syndrome, alcoholism and drug addiction. Our young people attempt suicide in record numbers and do not fear a virus that may not show symptoms for years. The answer to AIDS will come after we have learned self-esteem. Caring enough to practice safe sex will come when we have our own heroes back.

I am also a feminist, which to me means respecting my sisters' and brothers' dreams. There should be no room for jealousy in a feminist heart. As a Native American feminist I have only to reach back to our traditional ways, before the European influence, to find a feminist culture that flourished for hundreds of years.

I think of myself as Lisa Tiger, a member of the Muscogee (Creek) Nation, and I am most comfortable when I am addressing Native American groups. I went through school without learning about a single Native American hero. I was not taught the Indian way (the Red Road) that says if you contribute and give back to the earth and your people, especially the very old and very young, you will be sustained. After decades of living with the myths made up by white male historians, we, the people of the first nations, have lost confidence in ourselves. I now find the truth and beauty of my Indian people not in books, but in sharing my story on reservations and in Native communities and receiving in return instant, deep and lasting friendships.

The lives of the people I meet are now a part of my life story. I have learned many things. I know young people on reservations who have been able to quit drinking when they begin traditional dancing. I know alcoholics who have quit drinking after entering a sweat lodge for the first time. I have been blessed with seeing the power of the Red Road and have been given the name "Woman Who Clears the Way" by Marsha Hunter, the sister of Phil Hunter, a man from the Tule River reservation in California who has become my spiritual guide.

What do I look forward to in my life and my work? Truly trying to make a difference. I look forward to fighting this virus and beating it—it will have to be awfully powerful to get me. I look forward to maybe having a child of my own and adopting and housing many young Indian people. I look forward to my life experiences, to learning and loving all of the Creator's creations. The more I give the more I get, which makes me love life and want to give even more.

I am now living the happiest days of my life. Every day is satisfying beyond any of the dreams I once had. In August 1993 I traveled around the Navajo Nation with the great President Zah. The next week I traveled throughout North and South Dakota, across the Sioux Nation to Eagle Butte, Turtle Mountain, White Shield, Trenton and Sisselton. I exercised at night by running on a stretch of highway in North Dakota so deserted no humans were within miles except for my friends, who followed me in their car. I stood in a field near my home at sunrise while my Hopi friend Wil Numkena placed an eagle feather near the crown of my head, nearest my creator. I spent a week with Gloria Steinem, and accompanied Prairie Band Potawatomi producer Nedra Darling when she accepted a Peabody for *Surviving Columbus*, the story of the Pueblo people. And on September 1, 1993, I watched as my sister gave birth to Hvresse Christie Blair Tiger. Hvresse is the Creek word for moon. For Dana the moon cycle represents the fullness of a life well lived. The moon goes through its phases, changing from a sliver in the sky to a half moon that says, "Everybody look at me. I'm proud and complete. I've been through all my phases and I'm back to what I was meant to be."

I am not yet what I am meant to be, but I am trying. I still have dreams. I dream of reminding my people of just how beautiful they are. Of seeing my niece grow up. Of seeing an end to homophobia. Of all Indian tribes, as proud and sovereign nations, forming an alliance to preserve the health, history and culture of each and every Native American. I dream of living in a world where there is peace and respect among all races. And I dream of growing old and wise. I have a lot to live for, but I do not fear death because when it is time for me to go, I have a lot to go to.

Beyond Bean Counting

JeeYeun Lee

I came out as a woman, an Asian American and a bisexual within a relatively short span of time, and ever since then I have been guilty of the crime of bean counting, as Bill Clinton oh-so-eloquently phrased it. Every time I am in a room of people gathered for any reason, I automatically count those whom I can identify as women, men, people of color, Asian Americans, mixed-race people, whites, gays and lesbians, bisexuals, heterosexuals, people with disabilities. So when I received the call for submissions for this anthology, I imagined opening up the finished book to the table of contents and counting beans; I then sent the call for submissions to as many queer Asian/Pacific American women writers as I knew.

Such is the nature of feminism in the 1990s: an uneasy balancing act between the imperatives of outreach and inclusion on the one hand, and the risk of tokenism and further marginalization on the other. This dynamic has indelibly shaped my personal experiences with feminism, starting from my very first encounter with organized feminism. This encounter happened to be, literally, Feminist Studies 101 at the university I attended. The content of the class was divided into topics such as family, work, sexuality and so forth, and for each topic we studied what various feminist paradigms said about it: "liberal feminism," "socialist feminism," "radical feminism" and "feminism and women of color."

Taking this class was an exhilarating, empowering and very uneasy experience. For the first time I found people who articulated those murky half-formed feelings that I could previously only express incoherently as "But that's not fair!" People who agreed, sympathized, related their own experiences, theorized, helped me form what I had always known. In seventh grade, a teacher made us do a mock debate, and I ended up arguing with Neil Coleman about whether women or men were better cooks. He said more men were professional chefs, therefore men were better. I responded that more women cooked in daily life, therefore women were better. He said it was quality that mattered, not quantity, and left me standing there with nothing to say. I knew there was something wrong with his argument, something wrong with the whole issue as it was framed, and felt extremely betrayed at being made to consent to the inferiority of my gender, losing in front of the whole class. I could never defend myself when arguments like this came up, invariably with boys who were good at debates and used to winning. They left me seething with resentment at their manipulations and frustrated at my speechlessness. So to come to a class that addressed these issues directly and gave me the words for all those pent-up feelings and frustrations was a tremendously affirming and empowering experience.

At the same time, it was an intensely uncomfortable experience. I knew "women of color" was supposed to include Asian American women, but I could not find any in the class readings. Were there no Asian American feminists? Were there none who could write in English? Did there even exist older Asian American women who were second or third generation? Were we Asian American students in the class the first to think about feminism? A class about women, I thought, was a class about me, so I looked for myself everywhere and found nothing. Nothing about Asian American families, immigrant women's work patterns, issues of sexuality and body image for Asian women, violence against Asian

American women, Asian American women in the seventies feminist movement, nothing anywhere. I wasn't fully conscious then that I was searching for this, but this absence came out in certain feelings. First of all, I felt jealous of African American and Chicana feminists. Their work was present at least to some degree in the readings: They had research and theories, they were eloquent and they *existed*. Black and Chicana women in the class could claim them as role models, voices, communities—I had no one to claim as my own. My emerging identification as a woman of color was displaced through the writings of black and Chicana women, and I had to read myself, create my politics, through theirs; even now, to a certain extent, I feel more familiar with their issues than those of Asian American women. Second, I felt guilty. Although it was never expressed outright, I felt that there was some pressure on me to represent Asian American issues, and I could not. I felt estranged from the Asian American groups on campus and Asian American politics and activism in general, and guilty about this ignorance and alienation.

Now mind you, I'm still grateful for this class. Feminism was my avenue to politics: It politicized me; it raised my consciousness about issues of oppression, power and resistance in general. I learned a language with which I could start to explain my experiences and link them to larger societal structures of oppression and complicity. It also gave me ways that I could resist and actively fight back. I became interested in Asian American politics, people of color politics, gay/lesbian/bisexual politics and other struggles because of this exposure to feminism. But there is no excuse for this nearly complete exclusion of Asian/Pacific American women from the class. Marginalization is not simply a politically correct buzzword, it is a material reality that affects people's lives—in this case, my own. I would have been turned off from feminism altogether had it not been for later classes that dealt specifically with women of color. And I would like to name names here: I went to Stanford University, a bastion of privilege that pretends to be on the cutting edge of "multiculturalism." Just under twenty-five percent of the undergraduate population is Asian/Pacific American, but there was no mention of Asian/Pacific American women in Feminist Studies 101. All the classes I took on women of color were taught by graduate students and visiting professors. There was, at that time, only one woman of color on the feminist studies faculty. I regret that I realized the political import of these facts only after I left Stanford.

I understand that feminists in academia are caught between a rock and a hard place—not too many of us hold positions of decision-making power in universities. And I must acknowledge my gratitude for their struggles in helping to establish feminist studies programs and produce theories and research about women, all of which create vital opportunities and affirmation. But other women's organizations that are not constrained by such explicit forces are also lily-white. This obviously differs from group to group, and I think many of them are very conscientious about outreach to historically marginalized women. But, for instance, in 1992 and 1993, at the meetings I attended of the Women's Action Coalition (WAC) in New York City, out of approximately two hundred women usually fewer than twenty women of color were present.

But this is not a diatribe against feminism in general. I want to emphasize that the feminism that I and other young women come to today is one that is at least sensitive to issues of exclusion. If perhaps twenty years ago charges of racism, classism and homophobia were not taken seriously, today they are the cause of extreme anguish and soul-searching. I am profoundly grateful to older feminists of color and their white allies who struggled to bring U.S. feminist movements to this point. At the same time, I think that this current sensitivity often breeds tokenism, guilt, suspicion and self-righteousness that have very material repercussions on women's groups. I have found these uneasy dynamics in all the women's groups I've come across, addressed to varying degrees. At one extreme, I have seen groups that deny the marginalizing affects of their practices, believing that issues of inclusion really have nothing to do with their specific agendas. At the other extreme, I have seen groups ripped apart by accusations of political correctness, immobilized by guilt, knowing they should address a certain issue but not knowing how to begin, and still wondering why "women of color just don't come to our meetings." And tokenism is alive and well in the nineties. Those of us who have been aware of our tokenization often become suspicious and tired of educating others, wondering if we are invested enough to continue to do so, wondering if the overall goal is worth it.

In this age when "political correctness" has been appropriated by conservative forces as a derogatory term, it is extremely difficult to honestly discuss and confront any ideas and practices that perpetuate dominant norms—and none of us is innocent of such collusion. Many times, our response is to become defensive, shutting down to constructive critiques and actions, or to individualize our collusion as solely a personal fault, as if working on our individual racist or classist attitudes would somehow make things better. It appears that we all have a lot of work to do still.

And I mean *all*. Issues of exclusion are not the sole province of white feminists. I learned this very vividly at a 1993 retreat organized by the Asian Pacifica Lesbian Network. It has become somewhat common lately to speak of "Asian and Pacific Islanders" or "Asian/Pacific Americans" or, as in this case, "Asian Pacifica." This is meant to be inclusive, to recognize some issues held in common by people from Asia and people from the Pacific Islands. Two women of Native Hawaiian descent and some Asian American allies confronted the group at this retreat to ask for more than lip service in the organization's name: If the group was seriously committed to being an inclusive coalition, we needed to educate ourselves about and actively advocate Pacific Islander issues. And because I don't want to relegate them to a footnote, I will mention here a few of these issues: the demand for sovereignty for Native Hawaiians, whose government was illegally overthrown by the U.S. in 1893; fighting stereotypes of women and men that are different from those of Asian people; decrying U.S. imperialist possession and occupation of the islands of Guam, the Virgin Islands,

American Samoa, the Marshall Islands, Micronesia, the Northern Mariana Islands and several others.

This was a retreat where one would suppose everyone had so much in common—after all, we were all queer API women, right? Any such myth was effectively destroyed by the realities of our experiences and issues: We were women of different ethnic backgrounds, with very different issues among East Asians, South Asians, Southeast Asians and Pacific Islanders; women of mixed race and heritage; women who identified as lesbians and those who identified as bisexuals; women who were immigrants, refugees, illegal aliens or second generation or more; older women, physically challenged women, women adopted by white families, women from the Midwest. Such tangible differences brought home the fact that no simplistic identity politics is *ever* possible, that we had to conceive of ourselves as a coalition first and foremost; as one woman on a panel said, our identity as queer API women must be a *coalitional* identity. Initially, I thought that I had finally found a home where I could relax and let down my guard. This was true to a certain degree, but I discovered that this was the home where I would have to work the hardest because I cared the most. I would have to be committed to push myself and push others to deal with all of our differences, so that we *could* be safe for each other. And in this difficult work of coalition, one positive action was taken at the retreat: We changed the name of the organization to include "bisexual," thus becoming the Asian Pacifica Lesbian and Bisexual Network, a name that people started using immediately.

All this is to say that I and other young women have found most feminist movements today to be at this point, where there is at least a stated emphasis on inclusion and outreach with the accompanying risk of tokenism. I firmly believe that it is always the margins that push us further in our politics. Women of color do not struggle in feminist movements simply to add cultural diversity, to add the viewpoints of different kinds of women. Women of color feminist theories challenge the fundamental premises of feminism, such as the very definition of "women," and call for recognition of the constructed racial nature of *all* experiences of gender. In the same way, heterosexist norms do not oppress solely lesbians, bisexuals and gay men, but affect all of our choices and non-choices; issues posed by differently abled women question our basic assumptions about body image, health care, sexuality and work; ecofeminists challenge our fundamental ideas about living on and with the earth, about our interactions with animals, plants, food, agriculture and industry. Many feminists seem to find the issues of class the most difficult to address; we are always faced with the fundamental inequalities inherent to late-twentieth-century multinational capitalism and our unavoidable implication in its structures. Such an overwhelming array of problems can numb and immobilize us, or make us concentrate our energies too narrowly. I don't think that we have to address everything fully at the same time, but we *must* be fully aware of the limitations of our specific agendas. Progressive activists cannot afford to do the masters' work for them by continuing to carry out oppressive assumptions and exclusions.

These days, whenever someone says the word "women" to me, my mind goes blank. What "women"? What is this "women" thing you're talking about? Does that mean me? Does that mean my mother, my roommates, the white woman next door, the checkout clerk at the supermarket, my aunts in Korea, half of the world's population? I ask people to specify and specify, until I can figure out exactly what they're talking about, and I try to remember to apply the same standards to myself, to deny myself the slightest possibility of romanticization. Sisterhood may be global, but who is in that sisterhood? None of us can afford to assume anything about anybody else. This thing called "feminism" takes a great deal of hard work, and I think this is one of the primary hallmarks of young feminists' activism today: We realize that coming together and working together are by no means natural or easy.

Two Jews, Three Opinions

Robin M. Neidorf

*Who is Jewish? Perhaps it is the person who, never quite sure of it, by and
by discovers Jewishness in the probability.*[1]

—*Edmond Jabès*

I am what is known as a lapsed Jew. It almost sounds like an ortho-
pedic condition—she visited the doctor to have her lapsed Jew re-
aligned. But being a lapsed Jew can be serious business where other
Jews are concerned; I have read more than one enraged polemic
written by an overzealous rabbi, denouncing my kind as taking
up where Hitler left off. After all, I hold no Sabbath day as holy, I
keep no kosher kitchen and the recent death of my grandfather
occasioned my first visit to a synagogue since the Reagan administration. To people like these righteous rabbis, we lapsed Jews are
burning our own history.

Yet if I were to describe myself, the word "Jewish" would certainly be among the top five adjectives I would use, somewhere
below "feminist," somewhere above "argumentative" and "slightly
neurotic."

The process of becoming an argumentative Jewish feminist is
a sort of deliberate accident, a combination of family choices and

individual choices, circumstances both beyond and within one's control. The synagogue to which my family belongs is unusual in its approach to Judaism. As one of half a dozen Humanist synagogues in the country, Congregation Beth Or of Deerfield, Illinois, has given me the tools—and the permission—to be Jewish *and* whatever else I want to be. Jewish and feminist, for example. The choice of synagogue was deliberate; the fact that such a place existed in the Chicago suburbs near our home was circumstantial.

Choices and circumstances can cultivate only what is already there, however. Seven years of Sunday school, unwillingly and impatiently attended, cannot manufacture determination or outspokenness. Nor will those years develop an interest in Jewish women's history, not unless that interest is ready to be developed. By the age of twelve, when I selected a research topic for the service presentation I was to give at my Bat Mitzvah, I was apparently ready; my presentation was based on several months of study of the social constraints placed on women in Israel. I challenged the myths of the liberated Israeli women who participate fully in the military and kibbutz culture of Israel. I explained the discoveries of my research—that Israeli women are oppressed by social mores that narrowly define their roles as wife and mother, second to men in a distinctly masculine culture. "Israel's public image is connected to activities of masculinity, such as the military and kibbutz life," I told the congregation gathered to celebrate my passage into womanhood. "Yet women are expected, even encouraged, to be feminine. This presents a conflict of stereotypes for the Israeli woman. She is torn between being identified as a woman or an Israeli." Rereading my speech eleven years later, I am amazed to see what I had already observed at the age of thirteen. I definitely raised a few eyebrows. My Torah reading to mark the occasion was from Genesis; I read passages that described the early days in Eden when Eve was Adam's equal partner.

But the Books of Moses definitely go downhill from there, as far as women are concerned. "Eve has simply been used to explain sorrow and sin without any of the blame going to men," I said on the day of my Bat Mitzvah, and the Fall overshadows everything in Jewish theology and commentary for the next five thousand years. I attended three more years of Sunday school classes after my Bat Mitzvah, and my chosen major in college was religion. I had ample time to look for the hidden female in Jewish tradition.

This was my cultural heritage, after all. I wanted to know where I stood, who I was as a Jew, as a woman, as a feminist. I observed closely what was said and practiced at the Jewish gatherings I periodically attended, those of my family and those of the Jewish Association on campus. There was a lot of God the Father, a lot of women arranging and planning the meals, and essentially a lot of what you'd expect from the culture that invented patriarchy.

Letty Cottin Pogrebin, one of the founding editors of *Ms.* magazine, has written a beautifully articulate and comprehensive book, entitled *Deborah, Golda, and Me,* about her life as a Jew, as a feminist and as one who combines the two. In a passage recalling the Passover seders of her childhood, the yearly celebration of the liberation of the Jews from Egypt, Pogrebin hits on a crucial point in the character of Judaism. The topic at hand is *charoset*, a mixture of apples, walnuts, cinnamon and grape wine, but the statement reaches far beyond the edible. She writes:

> The mixture, which we spread on pieces of matzah, was a dual symbol: first, of the mortar made by Jewish slaves under the Egyptian lash, and second, of the sweetness of God who remembered the Jewish people and put an end to such labors. The bitter/sweet contradiction confounded me. When I asked my father how one thing could represent such opposites, he answered that it typified Jewish experience and I'd better get used to it.[2]

It typifies Jewish experience to be living out a paradox, a contradiction. It is a paradox to survive in the face of centuries of hate, to pray "I believe in the coming of the Messiah" while marching to one's death. It is a contradiction to live in an age of secularized Judaism, in the split between enraged rabbis on one hand and us unobservant yet still Jewish types on the other. It is a contradiction to see the strength of women within the traditions of the oldest patriarchy in the world.

To be sure, there is much for a feminist to argue with in Jewish theology and tradition. And yet in how many communities can a thirteen-year-old girl-woman stand before a congregation and speak out for women's equality in a distant land?

Judaism is a culture that speaks two languages, the Hebrew of liturgy and the vernacular Yiddish. And if Hebrew is the language of admittedly misogynist rituals and prayers (the most infamous of which is the daily prayer of Orthodox men: "I thank you, God, that I was not born a woman"), then Yiddish, in my mind, is the language of my foremothers. It is the language that my aging grandmother has begun to return to more and more since the death of my grandfather. ("We return to the things that give us the most comfort as we age," my mother said to me when I pointed this out to her.) It is the language I imagine my namesake, my great-grandmother Rose, speaking as she single-handedly brought her family out of pogrom-ridden Russia to come to the United States. It is a language I came closer to in my studies of German; when I overhear it in another's conversation, my ears burn with the attempt to understand.

I do not mean to suggest that this margin between Judaism, the Religion, and Judaism, the Community is an easy one to navigate. It is frequently more than I can handle. Is this why I avoid synagogues? Why, in spite of my facility for languages, I have not learned Hebrew? Why I have yet to visit Israel, my Bat Mitzvah research notwithstanding?

Several years ago, I spent a few days during Passover with distant cousins. At the same time, some friends of theirs, a young man and his teenage sister, were visiting from Israel. The Israelis and half the family were observing closely the laws of *kashrut*, forbidding the consumption of bread products during Passover. The other half of the family, including me, were reaching for bagels at breakfast.

"How can you do that?" the Israeli man asked me on the second day of my stay. "How can you turn your back on Judaism?"

I tried to explain to him something of the untraditional approach to Judaism offered in a Humanist upbringing, the questioning I was going through at the time and my discomfort with what I had seen as an unwillingness on the part of Jewish traditionalists to accommodate women in their prayers.

To this man, my reasons were unimportant in face of the fact that I was eating bread during Passover, a practice that even many liberal Jews would not condone.

He turned to his sister and spoke to her as if I were not in the room, as if I were barely worth ignoring. Yet he spoke in English, and his comments were clearly meant more for me than for her. "You see?" he said. "You see what she does? I guarantee you—her children will never know they are Jewish."

That still stings. Because I do not believe it is true. Because I am still a Jew of Yiddish conversations and memories, if not of Hebrew ones.

It is a difficult contradiction to live out, to be sure, this simultaneous embracing and rejecting. And yet I continue to call myself a Jew, in spite of the unease of my position as a woman, as a feminist in such a community. Reading what Pogrebin has documented in *Deborah, Golda, and Me* is not unlike reading my own story as a work-in-progress, although I did not start at the same place as Pogrebin, and I will not finish where she finishes either. But the template, the story, the contradictions are there, written down for me to study. It makes me feel very Jewish to do so; we are a people of the written word, of study.

But Jewish feminists of my generation are not merely the heirs of Pogrebin's generation. It is easier, I think, for my generation to be both Jewish and feminists. While women like Pogrebin, like Judith Plaskow, like Ellen Umansky and others are undoubtedly valued pioneers, there are factors that have softened the edge of contradiction between these two aspects of my life.

Many more Jews of my generation have grown up in secular-yet-Jewish households than our older counterparts. In the American Judaism of the first half of the twentieth century, there was Conservative or Orthodox life, and there was completely assimilated life, but there was not much in between. Jewish feminists of my generation have the advantage of existing alternatives. We have models of Jewish communities that are not traditionally observant and yet continue to call themselves Jewish. We have grown up with the powerful reality of women rabbis. We have celebrated our Bat Mitzvahs without the pressure of being the first in our congregations to do so.

And yet there are still the contradictions, the centuries of misogyny that we continue to contend with, the polemics against assimilation or what is perceived as assimilation, the not-so-subtle put-downs that suggest that a Jew who eats bread during Passover is an invisible Jew.

I am hardly alone among my peers in my perception of these contradictions, in conversing in the two languages of Judaism. I would say that, without exception, the women I met at Jewish Association functions at college would have called themselves feminists. Perhaps many of the men would have as well. Some of these young feminists, like me, chose to make themselves peripheral to JA activities, perhaps attending a Rosh Hashanah dinner and a Yom Kippur service at the beginning of the school year but otherwise keeping their distance. We were what has been scornfully referred to as "twice-a-year Jews." We were the lapsed. And we were isolated. We missed the vitality of the community.

There were others, however, who attempted and continue to attempt to bring about some reconciliation between their feminist hearts and the rituals of Jewish tradition. The Association brought feminist theologian Ellen Umansky in to speak one night, and several JA women made a project of writing their own feminist service for the Passover seder. I attended both events. While I found Umansky's theology intellectually intriguing, I could not respond to it emotionally; it felt too intellectual, too stiff. And I enjoyed the seder very much. But I noticed that it was still the women who did all of the cooking and preparations.

Two ways of coping, each with its disadvantages. One group tries to reconcile and continues to fall short; one group withdraws and thus misses the rituals of Jewish life that give the comfort of familiar community.

It was only after college, when I moved away from the home I'd grown up in, that I found the Jewish ritual in which I could fully participate, in which I fully celebrated my ties to Jewish culture and yet made room for my feminist consciousness and drive for social change.

My move to Minnesota, my mother's childhood home, was inspired by my desire to be on my own and yet near something familiar. My mother's brothers, their families and my grandmother all live in and around the Twin Cities, and I began to join them for their holiday gatherings. I soon discovered that I was looking forward to these gatherings, though certainly not for the brief service that always preceded the meal.

No, it was something else that attracted me, something as traditionally Jewish as matzoh ball soup, as Friday night dinners.

It was the fights. I have enjoyed such engaging, enriching, enraging fights at dinner with my Jewish family.

Question: You've got two Jews, and what have you got?

Answer: Three opinions.

Jews fight. We have to. It is born in us. It is demanded of us if we are to survive. For a young feminist, this is a rich legacy, one that provides a model of social behavior that values confrontation.

The taste for argument, however, is by no means automatically bestowed at Bat Mitzvah. Opinionated stubbornness is a muscle that must be developed and exercised; sibling spats and parent-child blowups are valuable training ground for the adult who joins my family for dinner.

I consider myself in argument, as in many things, my mother's apprentice. I learned my taste for argument at her knee, when others were learning sewing (which I taught myself in the third grade) or cooking (which I taught myself after college).

But the legacy goes back farther than that. My mother's only match for opinionated stubbornness was great-grandmother Rose. Rose and her stubbornness brought my family here, and only my mother ever dared to argue with her. Rose is a strong, valued namesake; she is far enough in my past to circumvent any rebellion I might feel against an authority figure, yet near enough that I feel a true connection to her. My grandmother talks of her, flavoring her descriptions with a sprinkling of Yiddish phrases, and I see glimmers of Rose's personality, flickers of who I will become, who I have been. I am proud to have such a heritage, to have been so taught.

And so every time I visit my uncles and their families for High Holidays or Passover, I am well prepared. After all, no Jewish holiday with my family is complete without an hours-long, blood-pressure-raising argument at its centerpiece.

A typical evening with my uncles and cousins goes something like this: We inadvertently select a theme. Someone mentions, for example, a news item, an ongoing public lawsuit or a scandal of some sort. Then someone makes an inflammatory statement.

And the fur flies. We take sides and shout at each other. We pause for the presentation of the entrée and regroup. We begin to repeat ourselves and grow sullen. Then dessert is served, and we are suddenly refreshed. Most important is that the question at hand is never resolved; the point is the argument, not the winning.

But we are not shouting simply for the singularly perverse pleasure of it. We are taking our places in the history of Judaism, with its Talmudic scholars and respect for the opinion gracefully phrased. Or not so gracefully phrased. I recently heard a story about a bloody fist fight that took place outside of a synagogue; several men came to blows in the parking lot over the placement of candlesticks on the altar.

Make no mistake, though; our themes are hardly limited to religious matters. Anything from legalized gambling to Woody Allen's intrafamilial affairs to the advertising policies of the Stroh's Brewing Company is fair game. Anything on which we are collectively guaranteed to disagree.

And at these explosive dinners, these rituals of Jewish life as old as the Sabbath and as venerated as circumcision, there are no repercussions for losing my temper, for becoming emotionally involved in the argument, for stating my opinions and refusing to back down. These are not skills; they are gifts from my family, from my mother and great-grandmother; they are gifts from the Jews.

Where would I be in this world without them?

1. Edmond Jabès, *The Book of Shares*, trans. Rosmarie Waldrop (Chicago: University of Chicago Press, 1989), p. 22.

2. Letty Cottin Pogrebin, *Deborah, Golda, and Me* (New York: Doubleday, 1992), p. 116.

Weaving an Identity Tapestry

Sonja D. Curry-Johnson

The Negro is a sort of a seventh son, born with a veil, and gifted with second-sight in this American world—a world which yields him no true self-consciousness, but only lets him see himself through the revelation of the other world. It is a peculiar sensation, this double-consciousness, this sense of always looking at one's self through the eyes of others, of measuring one's soul by the tape of a world that looks on in amused contempt and pity. One ever feels his twoness—an American, a Negro: two souls, two thoughts, two unreconciled strivings; two warring ideals in one dark body, whose dogged strength alone keeps it from being torn asunder.[1]

—W.E.B. Du Bois

These words, written in 1903, eloquently capture the duality that was and still is the African American experience. Yet as much as every African American has felt the "two unreconciled strivings," it seems to me that Dr. Du Bois' description applies more to black men than black women. Could Du Bois ever imagine the multiplicity that defines the existence of the contemporary African American woman? Could he fathom the dilemma of being both inwardly and outwardly torn among many factions in the quest to become a complete woman? As an African American, I feel the duality. But I suffer from more than duality. As an educated, married, monogamous, feminist, Christian, African American mother, I suffer from an acute case of multiplicity.

Each identity defines me; each is responsible for elements of my character; from each I derive some sustenance for my soul. But they do not peacefully coexist within me any more than the duality does in the lives of black men. These elements are in constant conflict, questioning my loyalties, my convictions, my love. How can you love, honor and cherish your husband, yet keep your last name and high personal aspirations? admonishes my Christian ethic, critical of my feminist dogma. How can you subscribe to a faith that was once used to enslave your people? demands my African American heritage, inspired by the heady themes of black nationalism, suspicious of anything without marked African origins. Why do you buy into the male-dominated media myth of feminine beauty? cries my feminist credo, condemning my quest for a "better" body and lamenting my trivial affinity for high fashion. At times one voice can pull stronger than the others; yet, as I struggle to find my place in the world, I am always aware of each presence.

In spite of my inner turmoil, I am not in need of psychotherapy, nor am I wandering through my life constantly confused, nor do I lack self-confidence. But in my dark hours, and frankly I have many, these voices of multiplicity rant and rail against each other; most often it is many voices struggling with my feminist voice. For self-preservation's sake, I desperately try to blend them together harmoniously like one cooks a soup or weaves a tapestry. My efforts, however, sometimes seem to be in vain, because as it is in the world around me, there is always sediment left in the bottom of the pot or a loose thread dangling at the seam.

But surely I am not the only woman, African American or otherwise, caught up in this dilemma. Once we decide to raise and carry the feminist banner, we may feel some sort of loss as we abandon traditional ways of thinking and living. Like it or not, our society forces us to make sacrifices in many aspects of our lives if we assert our feminist beliefs. For example, whether we are raised Islamic, Baptist, Catholic, Jewish or Mormon, we may miss something when we reject, for the sake of our own integrity, the religion of our parents solely because of the positions women hold (or don't hold) within its doctrine. Must we now be without spiritual guidance because the people within our religions are afraid to change? If the purpose of organized religion is to touch as many souls as possible, I believe that purpose is undermined when sanctioned hypocrisy alienates women, who make up a significant portion of the congregations. Similarly undermined are the noble crusades of the movements dedicated to the advancement of those under siege in a racist society, when they allow this same pervasive hypocrisy to taint their inner workings. If we are part of a maligned and disenfranchised minority, and we object to devoting all our energies to the uplift of the males in our group, our priorities are suspect. We deserve to have a place as women and as feminists within our religious institutions, social change movements or any other group that means something to us. We should be able to bring our whole selves to the table.

As long as we can't be our full selves, we will feel a need to hide parts of ourselves. In order to get a job or get ahead in her career, for example, a woman may feel a need to repress those aspects of herself that she fears will cause her to appear too "feminine." This same type of phenomenon is found in minorities trying not to appear too "ethnic," even to the point of changing their surnames. In either case, I find the results tragic and abhorrent, yet I myself fell victim to this syndrome when I allowed my pregnancy to derail my confidence while looking for a job.

Even though I knew full well that there are laws specifically prohibiting discrimination on the basis of pregnancy, I felt that the first thing a prospective employer would see was not my résumé but my ample abdomen, and that he (or maybe even she) would summarily dismiss me in his mind. I imagined all the possible excuses that would be used to put me off: that my familial responsibilities would not allow me to give my all to a job, or that I would be too distracted by home ties to give my undivided attention to my work, or that I would take a lot of time off for children's illnesses and appointments. So I never even attempted to set up one measly interview. I still don't know what infuriates me more, the fact that I allowed myself to be cowed, or the fact that, unfortunately, a lot of my fears were probably well-founded.

Rest assured, these issues would have never come up for my husband if he had been the one job-hunting, although he, too, was expecting this child; he just wasn't carrying it. And so I pose the question: Is it necessary that we sacrifice a good career because of society's expectation that a proper wife and mother is chained to her family, condemned to live out a nightmare of domestic martyrdom? Conversely, must we let go of our dreams of marriage and family because workplaces refuse to accommodate women— or men—who are committed to their families? When we consider ourselves intelligent, competent and confident, we answer these questions with a resounding "No," but deep within ourselves these answers can sometimes ring hollow. Simply put, theory and practice often yield very different outcomes. In reality, when a woman is committed to asserting herself as a valuable, independent member of society, unwilling to be ignored, disrespected or dominated, she can find herself thwarted by the inflexibility of societal expectations.

I believe that children should, whenever possible, be nurtured and raised at home with a parent until they enter elementary school. But why does that parent always have to be the mother? Women are expected to stay at home, but then often find it difficult to re-enter the workforce. Meanwhile, most fathers are trapped in the workplace because if they ask for the time to really help raise their children, it could mean a death warrant for their careers. Until these destructive attitudes change, women will face impossible choices, and men will remain cut off from their children.

I believe I was born a feminist, because I can't remember a specific point in my life when I can say I was "enlightened." I read

Betty Friedan's *The Feminine Mystique* in high school, but it didn't bring me to a dramatic revelation. In my mind Friedan was only stating a logical fact that should be obvious to any logical being: Men and women are equals and should be treated as equals. Indeed, for me the revelation was that the society I was living in did not truly believe that women and men were equal creations. Somehow women came out on the losing end of things simply because we are able to give birth. I was incredulous that we were being penalized for ensuring the continuance of human existence, and I was floored when I realized that many women structured their lives around this ignorant train of thought. The idea of being trivialized because of my gender infuriated me almost as much as being marginalized because of my race. I remember feeling quite strongly that the administrators at the single-sex prep school I attended were bent on our finding not career goals and colleges but husbands with secure futures, and I begged my friends not to fall into this limiting mental trap. I constantly warned my classmates about the subtle messages that lurked behind the well-meaning faculty's lectures, counseling and advice. Some of my classmates shared my concern, but I was puzzled and angered when others seemed calm in the face of this sinister plot to turn us into smiling domestic sponges who would lay our lives at the feet of the false idol of some antiquated view of "family values." Only when I recognized that the deep religious undertones of the school (a religion that I did not share) were largely responsible for my friends' apathy did it start to dawn on me just what kind of conflicts would face me if I continued to openly declare myself a feminist.

I was and am a deeply religious person, and although my Baptist church has no official catechism, most sermons and lectures make it clear that women can best do their part in the advancement of the Word by being good wives and mothers and by not using our feminine wiles to tempt upstanding men to sin. Women are not encouraged to preach the doctrine unless we do it in a demure manner, such as singing in the choir, rather than the dramatic, largely male performances in the pulpit. If I were not convinced that God had actually touched my soul, and if I had not felt from an early age that basic Christian doctrines and legends are true, I would have separated from the church. But as it is, I know, because of the spiritual connection I have with God, that these patriarchal influences are of man, not God, and in time, the universal truth will be revealed to all in an event that has been promised to be the "great equalizer." I still attend church and observe traditional holidays, and I frequently challenge those who have the audacity to question my commitment to Christianity.

In college, conflicts did not lessen, but rather grew, both around me and within me. Here I had to decide what meant more to me, the attention and admiration of men, or my integrity as an independent woman. Unfortunately, there were times when my willingness to find and keep a boyfriend outweighed my desire to live my life honestly as my own person. During these times, I often placed the needs of the relationship over my own. It took a few years and a few broken relationships for me to reassess the importance of romantic love and to realize that there was no fantasy that was worth my denying any part of my identity. I decided not to become involved with a man unless I was sure he was the type of person that would not only accept my feminist ideals but also support my execution of them in my personal and professional lives. That type of man, in my mind, was a rare bird indeed. No sooner had I resigned myself to a life without romance, than I met such a bird and, in perhaps the least-debated decision of my life, married him.

Of course, marriage and the raising of a family have presented their own problems, but most of the discord can be attributed to the adjustments any two people must make when they decide to share living space on a long-term basis. Within our family it is clear that Mom and Dad are partners, and neither is concerned about who is wearing trousers. Finances, discipline and in fact all major and minor decisions in the household are handled jointly.

Outside of the family hub, however, are the old familiar rumblings. Because of the traditional facade of our relationship, friends and family tend to comment on what they assume is my abandonment of my feminist beliefs. At this time in our lives, my husband is working outside the home while I stay at home with our son and daughter, a joint decision arrived at after consideration of financial, geographical and time-frame conditions. My high school friends tease me constantly, amused at the firebrand feminist turned "little mother." They conveniently forget that my husband was the primary caregiver for our son when he was first born, enabling me to finish the first semester of my last year of school with peace of mind. They also fail to recall that when my husband had to relocate because of his military career and I could not immediately join him because I was still in school, I single-handedly cared for the baby while finishing my last undergraduate semester in a blaze of grade-point glory. They don't hear my husband urging me to get into a graduate program and to finish the "Great American Novel" I've been working on for eons.

Strangers who ask me about my career often frown at my glib descriptions of life as a domestic engineer. They usually don't bother to examine me a bit closer and would rather cluck about the "waste" of my college education. Nor do they care that their comments stir guilt, doubt and fear within me about my decision. Will this time away from professional activity rob me of my talent, instincts, competence? If I am as smart as I once thought I was, am I wasting precious time as the world revolves quite well without my being in the thick of things? Am I too concerned with making my family's laundry brighter and softer, my kitchen floors shiny and disinfected, my meals healthy and exciting? Maybe, but when I cannot pull myself out of the vortex of the fear of becoming June Cleaver, my husband becomes a mirror that reflects the image I'm afraid of losing. She's still there, the "firebrand" feminist, the independent, self-assured woman who is doing something just as important as running a company or educating the masses: raising sensitive, moral, self-aware children. Soon the career will evolve, the advanced degree will be obtained and I will truly have it all.

These days, as our threat to the old order increases, stereotypes about feminists seem to be more and more negative. Even among women peers, I find myself defending my feminist identity. I challenge them with three questions: Do you believe women should earn equal salaries for equal jobs? Do you believe women should defend other women if the need arises? Do you believe a woman should have the right to choose if and when she wants to raise a family? When they answer yes, I tell them simply, "You, too, are a feminist."

I am tired of feeling as though I must sacrifice parts of myself, and so I fight daily to meld my life into a celebration of womanhood, Christianity and the African American experience. What helps me most in the struggle to achieve inner harmony is my understanding that to call oneself a feminist need not be to offer oneself up as a martyr for the "cause," as many may think it must be. It is to celebrate and explore all that is woman, not to defame or emasculate all that is man. When a woman insists upon being treated as a living, thinking human being, while also standing up for the rights of all her sisters, how can this be interpreted as threatening by anyone but the most ignorant of people?

I now know that it is not necessary to shun marriage and family. Instead we must redefine these concepts and break the narrow traditional encasings of a mother, a father, a wife and a husband. We can make the roles fit our own identity instead of deriving our identity from these labels.

I suspect many of my sisters, women of all races, feel the same way I do about the concept of multiplicity and how it drives our lives, but we tend to try to manage one element at a time; to address the entire package can be overwhelming. Maybe multiplicity is like Du Bois' duality, in the sense that we can create a cohesive whole by nurturing and addressing each force within us singularly. We must hold on to the hope that in our quest to successfully merge the many forces that affect us so deeply, we will become stronger and more adroit. All the aspects of our identities can be sources of strength within ourselves and sources of understanding among us. Women can make sure that as long as we are leaning on each other, we are also protecting and celebrating one another. I like to think that if enough of us subscribe to this theory, maybe the wars within us will cease and we can forge a definition of what it means to be a woman that incorporates our whole selves.

1. W.E.B. Du Bois, *The Souls of Black Folk* (New York: Bantam, 1989), p. 3.

Reality Check

Aisha Hakim-Dyce

The woman's voice on the other end of the phone was low and sexy; I imagined her to be a classy agent, casually beautiful with an air of sophistication. After arranging to meet her in a few weeks, I felt shaken by my nerve-racking decision to pursue an opportunity that felt less liberating and more restrictive as the appointment day drew closer.

Our meeting was a jarring and almost surreal experience. I expected a fashionable woman living in a swank and stylish apartment. Miss Sweet—her stage name—of the syrupy voice was in actuality a streetwise woman in her mid-sixties, judging by the thinning hair that lay tousled atop her scalp. She wore an old, faded housedress and whispery slippers that made hissing sounds against the chipped wooden floor as she led me to the sitting room.

Miss Sweet's apartment was crammed full of boxes, old furniture and toys, making an already small space appear even tinier. The apartment had a scattered feel to it, as if random objects had been thrown haphazardly around to make space and then left to rest wherever they fell.

In my backpack were the two laced thong bikini panties that Miss Sweet had informed me I would need to perform in. She noticed my backpack and asked if I was a student. My nod of affirmation didn't seem to faze her, so I assumed that she booked quite a few college women to perform as seminude go-go dancers in sleazy after-hours clubs. My presence in her stuffy apartment wasn't an anomaly.

I had never thought that my underemployed status would lead me to seriously consider a stint that would require me to shake my breasts and gyrate my hips to the catcalls, whistles and sexually explicit suggestions of men. I believed that my identity as a politically astute and active woman would somehow protect me from exploitative situations, that having a politically correct worldview would somehow translate into tangible economic benefits. Reality check, anyone?

As a student at the prestigious Music and the Performing Arts High School in Manhattan, my activism was characterized by seemingly never-ending demonstrations in front of neighborhood food markets to demand employment of community residents; protest marches in white enclaves like Bensonhurst and Howard Beach to demonstrate outrage and demand justice for the murders there of young African American men; and petition signings like the successful drive to incorporate a black literature class into the Music and the Performing Arts school's curriculum.

I went on to attend Fisk University, a small, historically black institution in Nashville, where I devoured the work of bell hooks, Alice Walker and Gloria Anzaldúa. Off-campus women's groups helped me to deepen my sense of the richness, fullness and sensuality in being a woman. Simultaneously I was learning about the interconnectedness of sexism and racism. I made these discoveries with the help of a few close women friends I met at school, all of whom were also exploring questions of identity.

Despite my friendships there, I felt that Fisk's overall environment was not conducive to my personal growth, so I returned to New York City after one year. Struggling with late rent, unpaid bills and an echoing refrigerator became a constant in my life. None of my attempts at self-development translated into employment opportunities.

I was constantly depressed and often thought of dropping out of school in order to hold down a full-time job to cover my living expenses. Most of my women friends could offer only words of encouragement and empathy, since they found themselves in similar situations.

I was always on the go, sending out what I was sure were unread résumés, answering newspaper advertisements of potential employers who never returned my calls and going to pointless interviews. The *Village Voice* became my sacred Bible. Each week I'd spend one precious dollar to scan the Help Wanted section. It seemed that any and every type of job was available in those pages, from phone-sex operator to tour guide on one of those two-tiered trolley-esque monstrosities that crawl through the city filled with gaping tourists. I looked into these and other non-mainstream jobs. I answered one ad for an on-call clown for children's birthday parties, sent résumés to P.O. box addresses in response to ads for "Gal Friday" and was interviewed by dozens of distracted receptionists in employment agencies.

The process of looking for work began to aggravate, tire and terrify me. Either I didn't have enough years of experience (though in my early twenties I've held more jobs than a lot of people more than twice my age), or the pay was inadequate on a purely survival level, or the hours were in conflict with my school schedule. Being a young, underemployed, independent college student, politically aware or not, leads to very few job opportunities.

Conversations with friends at school about the high wages of "alternative" work sparked my initial interest in go-go dancing. I was given the number of a young woman dancer who raved about the ease with which she could make up to one thousand dollars in one week. Her job included such activities as lap dancing, which requires the dancer to sit on the lap of a man and grind, gyrate and otherwise stimulate him. It also included going into back rooms for "private audiences," which consisted of men watching the women dance around entirely naked.

The more depressed I became because of my economic situation, the less manipulative such work seemed. After all, I began to reason, if silly men want to give away their money in order to watch my breasts and hips jiggle, why not? I tried to remove from my mind the stigma attached to such activities by shifting my perception of the work: Instead of viewing it as being inherently exploitative, I started seeing it as being simply a job that conjured up negative connotations for people, another example of the sexual double standard that allows men to strip and be sexy studs, while women who do the same are viewed as dirty or somehow less than other women with "real" jobs.

The irony, of course, is that those "real" jobs often pay next to nothing, while sex work carries considerably higher wages. As an African American woman, I faced a particular quandary in that I understood I would be viewed not only as an object of lust but as exotic *other*, wild and unattainable, with just a hint of the jungle lurking somewhere between my thighs.

I succeeded with this reinterpreted analysis of go-go dancing for a while and placed my concerns about being exoticized on a back shelf. My rent was late again, and morbid fantasies of living in subway cars or on park benches had a fairly strong pull on me. While in a department store purchasing (with borrowed money) the thong panties that were to make up my costume, I considered stage names I could use. The process of desensitizing myself had begun. I tried not to think too deeply about the step I was about to take, choosing instead to dwell on surface issues like the pay. A distancing between myself and my activities took shape in my psyche in order for me to deal with the decision I had reached. I wanted to feel as uninvolved as possible without splitting myself entirely in half.

I even visited a go-go dancing club in midtown Manhattan to familiarize myself with the atmosphere. The interior of the club was all heavy red curtains with silver flashing strobe lights. There were several women of various ethnicities on a stage practicing for the night's show. They all wore glittering and shimmering pieces of cloth that did more to highlight their nakedness than cover it.

Every few minutes an announcer would call out their names—stage creations like "Mistress Butterfly from Asia" and "Laila the Caribbean Tigress"—and the appropriate woman would gyrate her way center stage and perform acrobatic maneuvers with her legs and hips. I felt extremely uncomfortable in the club. There were several men milling around, and I felt acutely aware of my gender even as I felt that my presence was ignored. It was as if in all of that flesh, or perhaps because of it, I was a nonentity, real only to the degree that I was on show for the sexual excitation of men.

Only a few of my women friends and acquaintances knew of my decision. With one exception (a friend who told me a horror story about the double murder of two young strippers), they all empathized with my situation and offered suggestions to help me—everything from using a minirecorder to keep track of my thoughts to viewing the experience as anthropological and sociological research that I could later write a paper about, for credit, of course.

I went with the minirecorder idea and, borrowing one from a friend, began keeping daily verbal notes. After a few days of rumination over my words, I realized that I was indeed being profoundly affected by my decision. My words held a hint of resignation, and I constantly spoke of school as being a luxury I couldn't afford. My words were angry and resentful tirades about the near impossibility of attending school full-time and meeting my basic living expenses. I sputtered irrationally about "imbeciles" who turned school into a fashion showcase, received low grades and lived at home, while we "serious" students strove to maintain impressive G.P.A.s, wore run-down sneakers and lived on rice and beans for weeks on end.

I cursed the government for financial aid fiascos that penalized working students by denying them needed federal aid. I growled nastily about the unfairness of paying rent: "Housing should be an inalienable fuckin' right!" These feelings were directed at myself for being in this predicament; my mother, who put me out of the house to begin with; and friends who could say no more than the well-intentioned "I know what you mean."

My sense of confidence in being an intelligent and capable woman faltered. When I tried to envision myself prancing around semi-naked, shaved, and wearing high-heeled shoes (I could barely put my feet into those contraptions, much less dance in them, and had never shaved any body hair and was afraid to experiment), I balked.

I wondered: Is this really what I had to do? Weren't there some other viable options? My mind could only think of canvassing for a nonprofit organization—physically and mentally exhausting door-to-door fundraising work in privileged hideaways throughout elite New York neighborhoods—and telemarketing, which is essentially the same thing but residents are harassed over the phone. I had tried both types of work and hated them passionately.

At these jobs I was required to guilt-trip people into paying loads of money for some worthy cause. They were basically sham operations that played on the vulnerabilities of otherwise common-sense folk. I could barely stomach the thought of work like that, much less engage in it. Go-go dancing, if I could only get my mind around it and my heart in it, seemed to be the perfect way to make a sizeable amount of money in the least amount of time.

I kept that thought in my head and pushed away all conflicting feelings and my desire to earnestly re-evaluate my resolution. I would shave my armpits, legs and crotch, teeter precariously on a pair of heels and not think about it. I would ignore the unsavory surroundings and sweaty outstretched palms holding out bills.

I had psychologically prepared myself for this type of scenario—or so I thought until the meeting with Miss Sweet. The protective bubble I'd surrounded myself with quickly deflated as I sat in an overstuffed chair listening to Miss Sweet talk about what to expect from this kind of work. She cautioned that many of the dancers turned tricks and that some were also involved in drugs, thus increasing the risk of danger for other dancers. Miss Sweet highlighted the importance of stringent sanitary precautions due to the condition of many of the clubs.

A flood of sordid images inundated me. The reality of what I was about to do hit me full force, and I could no longer steel myself against what I knew would be, for me, a humiliating, degrading and spiritually depleting experience. Up until that meeting, I had managed, just barely, to convince myself that I could go through with it. But now my resolve was disintegrating.

As I scrutinized my surroundings—if the women who dance make so much money, how is it that the agent providing club bookings lived in such a shabby apartment?—a full awareness of how painful the preceding weeks had been washed over me. I realized that I had been shocked into cognitive numbness by the decision to objectify myself for a price.

I sat there, contemplating the enormity of the mental, spiritual and emotional healing I would need after engaging in such a depersonalizing activity, one that would surely require me to become distant and removed from my body. In fact, a detachment was already in swing, beginning with my purchase of tacky and diaphanous panties to parade around in.

My internal struggles came to a head in Miss Sweet's cluttered living room. Though I still listened to her introduction to the world of go-go dancing, a battle of conflicting messages was being waged in my head. One side told me to simply inform the woman I'd changed my mind—thanks, but no thanks—and leave. Meanwhile, the other part of me kept repeating that it was all about perception, and if I didn't take it seriously, the work wasn't a big deal. After all, I didn't have to do it forever. Just long enough to pay off my mounting debts.

I listened to the length of Miss Sweet's spiel and answered her questions. Miss Sweet mentioned that I would need to audition for her and gave me all the particulars—where, when and what she'd be looking for (sexiness, body rhythm, firmness)—and that was the end of the meeting. I left her apartment weighed down by my dilemma.

I knew I needed to back out of this. There was no way I could subject myself to such an unhealthy experience, underemployed or not. The decision was obvious enough in some ways, but I could not bring myself to follow through. As mentally drained as I was, some part of me continued to rationalize my commitment to Miss Sweet. I began to try to figure out why it was that I felt that go-go dancing was so unhealthy. As far as its being an impersonal and emotionally abusive way of working, the same could be said for most jobs in a capitalist country like this one, where the profit motive is the driving force of the economy.

I was not able to draw any neat conclusions or take decisive action about the dancing. I phone-dodged Miss Sweet for a while, feeling inexplicably and irrationally wary that she would somehow get me to change my mind. Maybe the temptation to generate what could be a comfortable income would still be too strong. As the days progressed and she stopped calling, I felt more relaxed and less pressured. I was still grappling with all of the complex emotions surrounding the decision when an unbelievably timely and, in my eyes, symbolic event occurred.

I was scheduled to audition for Miss Sweet on a Tuesday night. That morning I received a call from the local community college offering me an English tutorial position I had applied for several months earlier and had long since forgotten about. This extraordinary event left me feeling that an unseen hand had intentionally reached out with another, more comfortable option. This fortuitous offer also released me from having to face Miss Sweet. I still cannot say for certain what choice I would have made had this opportunity not come along.

After settling into my tutorial position, I tried to make the memory of my go-go dancing experience dissipate, but it didn't. I was troubled by how close I had come to what would have been, for me, a traumatic ordeal. Although in too many instances poor and working-class people are faced with demoralizing and dehumanizing work, most of that work does not explicitly revolve around sexual objectification the way that go-go dancing does.

At one point I talked with several go-go dancers. They expressed satisfaction with their income but were cynical about people in general and men in particular. The work had cost them something vital, and I could see that happening to me. I would be a dispassionate woman "just doing my job," becoming cut off from my feelings in order to make ends meet. I came extremely close to shutting off a part of who I am, that part of me that is spontaneous, creative, open and empowered.

More than a year later, I still grapple with the issues raised by this experience. Under- and unemployment has caused many of my women friends to consider dehumanizing work. Conversations about these "options"—call girl, nude dancing, cage dancer—are usually discussed half-jokingly, but there's a hard edge lying just beneath the surface of our words. Our reality simply is that we are sometimes faced with crucial choices that are limited—and that are neither easy nor simple to make.

WAC-ing Operation Rescue

Melissa Silverstein

I ran through Penn Station early that steamy Monday morning looking for Operation Rescue (OR) members who were supposedly exiting a Long Island Rail Road train. I had no idea what any of these people would look like or even what train they were coming in on, but I knew my goal: Prevent Operation Rescue from shutting down an abortion clinic in New York City. It was the summer of 1992, and I was part of a citywide mobilization to prevent OR from disrupting the Democratic National Convention.

I have always been interested in clinic defense and other pro-choice activities. While I was attending Brandeis University, I helped organize Brandeis' presence at the 1989 pro-choice march in Washington. Because we wanted anyone to be able to go to the march, even if they couldn't afford the bus fare, I raised money from professors and administrators. I had never done anything like this in my life. I practically stormed into the offices of the school administrators, even the president, and demanded that they give me both personal and school funds to send a large delegation to Washington. I managed to raise several thousand dollars, and the trip was a huge success. Around that time we also organized a group to respond to calls from clinics in Brookline, Massachusetts that were being harassed by OR. Somehow, the calls for help often came after a long night of intense partying. When they did, everyone, even the people who had not gone to sleep yet, would haul their butts up and get in a car to go defend the clinics.

Protecting the Brookline clinics in 1988 and 1989 provided my first exposure to OR. The pro-choice people would stand in front of the clinics with signs, peacefully demonstrating and chanting, while the OR people would lie down in the middle of Beacon Street and stop traffic. I was outraged by the way in which OR forced their religious views on others, particularly women. They showed a flagrant disregard for a woman's constitutional right to privacy. The cornerstone of their philosophy was the belief that the rights of a fetus outweigh the rights of the woman carrying that fetus; these people were willing to go to jail to protect the rights of a fetus.

No one should have control over my body but me. For me, this was a clear-cut issue. They were wrong and I was right.

In the fall of 1989, I came to New York to attend graduate school. My schedule soon relegated any activism to a back burner. What pushed me into becoming active again was a combination of my oppressive job environment, my awareness of the escalation of OR's efforts and the fear that my rights were slowly but surely being chipped away. I was ready to fight back and began religiously attending Women's Action Coalition (WAC) meetings.

WAC was started by women in New York City in 1992 as a response to the Anita Hill/Clarence Thomas hearings. At WAC meetings any woman could suggest an idea to the group and request interested people to call her. At one meeting, a woman from the Fund for the Feminist Majority got up to announce that OR had threatened to disrupt the convention and block women's health clinics, and that the Fund was organizing clinic defense training to mobilize against OR. WAC united with other reproductive choice organizations like WHAM (Women's Health Action Mobilization) to gather large groups of people willing to give up their summer vacations in order to make sure OR did not take over New York.

From what I could tell, the operation was massive. I was trained to be a co-caravanner—one of the people who would stake out certain locations away from clinics and report if there was any OR activity. Because we were a mobile unit, when we got news that OR had hit a clinic we had to rush to help hold OR back from taking it over. In addition, groups of people were posted at all the major clinics to block OR. There were site leaders at each location who communicated by walkie-talkie with each other and with "Central." Central was the place where the leaders of this effort planned strategy and tracked OR.

OR was being monitored not only in New York City but throughout the region. I really did not understand how complex this effort was. It seemed like an antiterrorist movement. We were defending ourselves in the only way we knew how against the enemy. I think that was part of the reason I was drawn to it—we were in a war and I was contributing to the cause. I have always been upset that I missed the protests of the sixties and seventies. Lots of women in my generation have felt that there was no way to actively fight for our rights. Many, many strides have been made over the last twenty years to secure equal rights for women, but my generation has not had as many options for action. This was my chance to be involved in a protest for social justice.

Saturday, July 11, 1992 (Two days before the beginning of the Democratic National Convention)

We had to be at our meeting point on the corner of Park Avenue and Thirty-third Street at four-thirty in the morning. Saturday is always a big day for OR because they can get a large turnout at their "rescues." We were prepared to be called to any clinics that were hit by OR, but it turned out to be a slow morning, and we had no intelligence saying that there were going to be any hits that day. I think we were a little disappointed with the lack of action. I can't really say what we were expecting; there was a mixture of excitement and nervousness. Part of the energy was fueled by the upcoming Democratic convention. I thought that, finally, we had a chance to have a Democratic president in the White House, one who actually believed in reproductive freedom. The last pro-choice president was Jimmy Carter. I had barely entered puberty when he left office. A Clinton presidency would be my first opportunity to see a person who shared many of my political values lead this nation.

Monday, July 13

Forty people assembled at the designated site at four-thirty in the morning. Weekdays were always a big test because people have to go to work. (Since I had arranged with my workplace to take two hours off each morning, I had to carry my work clothes with me each day in a knapsack.) Most of the people in my group were artists and students. Someone asked if anyone knew anything about the Long Island Rail Road (LIRR). Being from Long Island, I volunteered my services. We were told that a meeting of Franciscan monks had been infiltrated the previous evening, and they and others were planning to take the LIRR to Manhattan to hit a clinic. I was impressed that our operation was clever enough to infiltrate OR meetings.

I can only imagine what the commuters of New York City thought of us. The leaders had their walkie-talkies and wore yellow pinnies (like the kind we wore in fifth-grade gym class). The average clinic defender wore an orange pinny, and the real power people wore yellow pinnies with green sashes, which meant that they could go anywhere they wanted, even in front of the police barricades. All of us orange pinnies wanted to throttle the yellow pinnies at times—they were so stuck up with the power of the pinny. When we were away from the clinics, we removed our pinnies and avoided those who were wearing them so as not to blow our cover. It's ironic that although we were fighting against the patriarchy and hierarchies, our system of operation was clearly hierarchical.

When we arrived at Penn Station (where LIRR trains enter and

leave Manhattan), we immediately inquired about th
arrivals from Freeport, Long Island. We split up anc
the different tracks. But no one had any idea what w(
ing for. We were told that they were monks, and my
that these guys in robes would walk off the train. W
that the potential rescuers were usually in their sixties, walked in
groups of two or four, carried Bibles and sometimes carried a gym
bag. (Gym bag? I asked. To carry their Kryptonite locks, I was told.
Later I learned that carrying Kryptonite locks is a fairly common
practice with OR. A group will enter a clinic and use the locks to
attach themselves to equipment inside the clinic so that it's very
difficult for the police to remove them from the premises.) We followed people coming off the trains to see where they were going,
and if they looked suspicious we would follow them all the way to
their destination. Everyone looked suspicious. We monitored Penn
Station for several hours. We then got information that the monks
had eluded us by changing trains.

We were getting ready to leave the station and reassemble
when we noticed two white-haired women (with the suspicious-
looking gym bags) and an older man walking around Penn Station looking a little perplexed. The big crosses hanging from their
necks were dead giveaways. They waited around the ticket area
for a while. Out of nowhere, I heard someone yell, "This woman is
a member of Operation Rescue—she wants to rule our bodies!"
Chanting was one of the tactics used to embarrass the OR members by exposing them to the public. I wondered how this pro-
choicer could know for sure that this woman she was yelling at
was OR. She did. It seems she had done surveillance before and
remembered the woman's face from previous encounters. She had
pictures of OR's local and national leaders, which she showed us
so that we would also be able to recognize them. We were told to
call Central right away when we saw anyone who was a leader. It
was very important to keep track of the leaders because they could
lead us directly to a potential hit sight. We blended in and followed
this group out of Penn Station to see where they were headed.

As we walked, we knew we had hit the jackpot. There were about ten of us and six of them. They split up and so did we. Two other women and I followed two women across Thirty-third Street. At that point we thought we were headed to a rally at Eastern Women's Clinic. As we got closer, they split up and we followed one of them downtown. She eventually met up with another woman. Suddenly there were two of them and two of us. They knew who we were and we knew who they were. They split up and each of us followed one of them. I was not too pleased to be by myself because one of things we were told was never to follow anyone on your own—you never know where you will end up. This woman just took me on a walk around the block. We were practically walking next to each other, but neither of us ever said a word. All of a sudden one of my groupmates came running toward me, shouting, "They've taken the doors, hurry!"

I started screaming, "Shit, shit, shit!" I was excited and frightened at the same moment. I came around the block and was startled to see that there were fifteen of them and three of us, including me and one guy on the inside of the wall of OR people. The other woman ran to call Central to get reinforcements while I screamed obscenities at the OR people. They stared at me and prayed. We were panicking and furious that OR had gotten the door and that there had been no clinic defenders at this location in the first place.

The cops and the TV cameras began to arrive. The police told the OR people that they had to get away from the door, and after a while they did. Once our reinforcements arrived, the police set up two pens in the street, one pro-choice and the other anti-choice. The two sides began screaming at each other for media attention. Our leaders arrived with the news that this clinic was closed on Mondays and that was why it had been left unprotected. All we knew was that OR had the door and we could not get it back.

Tuesday, July 14

This morning I went to Penn Station again. After about an hour, I saw a suspicious woman (whom I thought I recognized from the day before) get on a subway and go downtown. One other woman and I followed her and played cat and mouse for a while. We got down to the Wall Street area and lost her. To this day I think that she was OR. (During that week I would have thought my grandmother was OR.) We turned around and headed back uptown. As we left Penn Station on our way to our meeting place, we got a call that a hit was in progress on the Upper East Side. Finally, some action. I will never forget the image of twenty of us running through the streets to the subway hoping that we would get there in time to protect the clinic doors.

We bolted uptown. My back really hurt from running everywhere with a backpack full of work clothes. When we got to the door, there were no cops or cameras—just us and them. Five small pro-choice women had managed to hold the door, but they were being crushed by the wall that OR had formed around them and were screaming for help. We all huddled and decided to go in and try to get the door back. This was the point when I realized that I could get hurt or hurt somebody. I also thought, This is the day I'm going to go to jail. I figured that I would call my lawyer friend from jail and have him call my mother and tell her. I could only imagine my mother's reaction.

Thankfully, there were several big guys in our group this morning, and we all threw our bodies at the wall of OR people in a section that looked weak. We threw ourselves in and at the same time tried to pull the OR people out. We wanted to get them out of there before the cops and the media arrived. I will never forget the moment we rushed the line. I was pushing with all my might, and the guy next to me was just peeling people away. Tempers flared. People were beginning to get hurt. The cops arrived while some people were involved in a fist fight. I had managed to slither in and infiltrate OR's line. We had broken their hold. I was frustrated that there were only five people at the site covering the door and upset at how long it took to get more people to respond. This was not a sign of an efficient operation. The women who had been holding the door were bruised and shaken. Volunteer lawyers came to talk with them to see if we could press charges. One of OR's tactics that day (which they use a lot now) was to bring young children to the rescues. A boy of about eleven wound up getting hurt, and he really knew how to work the cops and the press. He had definitely been trained. His mother said that we should be arrested. We all thought she should be arrested for bringing her child to an illegal activity that could end in violence.

The crowd dispersed, and we noticed a woman across the street observing the scene very carefully. As she started to move away, several of us followed her around the block. We realized she was one of the regional directors of OR. As she got on a pay phone we walked up and stood right next to her and tried to get the number she was dialing and eavesdrop on her conversation. We were not subtle. Had she not been OR we would have been embarrassed, even arrested. But she was. She talked about the rescue and the arrests and tried to feed us misleading information about another rescue.

A prayer vigil was being held at St. Agnes' Church on East Forty-third Street, and I decided to go after work. When I got there, a group of women from Refuse and Resist (an extreme left-wing, feminist group) had blocked the entrance to the church. They were fighting fire with fire. I had never seen such radical women in my life. They said that if we were going to be blocked from entering the clinics for abortions and health care, the OR people were going to be blocked from having their prayer meeting. These women were prepared to get arrested. I actually thought about joining the line, but I was too afraid. The OR contingent was furious that we were able to prevent them from praying. Members of their leadership were walking up and down the street, fuming. I stood next to Patrick Mahoney (one of the national leaders) and realized how much I hated him. One of the OR people walked over to a table where someone was selling socialist literature and kicked the table up in the air in a fit of anger.

After an hour the women were arrested, and OR entered the church. We decided that someone had to go in to listen to their strategy. Since I still had my work clothes on, I volunteered. I was petrified. I knew that if they let me in they would watch me, and, as a Jewish woman, I had no idea what to do when I entered a church. But I wanted to get information about their rescues for the rest of the week. I knew that the OR people were really upset because they had been outnumbered in the streets and were not getting the kind of media attention they wanted. Also, the same week, a crony of Randall Terry (the founder and leader of Operation Rescue) presented Bill Clinton with a dead fetus in a jar and was arrested. This meant more bad publicity for OR.

After being given instructions on what to listen for, I walked over to enter the church and was stopped at the door by OR and the police. I stated that this was a public place, and I was free to go in and worship whenever and wherever I pleased. The police begged to differ and wouldn't let me in.

Wednesday, July 15

We were sent to monitor the apartment of a local OR member who was believed to be housing the leadership of OR. When she realized we were watching her, she called the police and tried to have us evicted from the street. The police were sympathetic to us. Once we explained what we were doing, they usually warned us to be careful and left us alone. But this woman was nuts, and her craziness did worlds of good for our side. She kept calling the police and said we were harassing her while we were just standing on the street waiting for the OR leaders to start their day. They were hoping to wait us out, and since there was other activity all over town many of our group filtered away over the hours.

My two friends and I stayed until someone finally left the apartment. He got in a taxi, and we got in our car and literally chased him down Lexington Avenue. When there was a red light, we tried to get next to the taxi to let him know that he was pegged. He arrived at his destination, Fifth Avenue and Thirty-first Street, which was the legal headquarters of OR. We staked out the street and told anyone who passed by that the lawyers for Operation

Rescue were in that building. People were very intrigued by our public humiliation tactics. We got the phone number of the office and repeatedly called and hung up. Many different thoughts went through our minds: vandalism, sneaking onto the floor and watching the office, and even storming the office. Several days of sleep deprivation were starting to get to us. We were beginning to act like OR. That was very scary.

We beat OR, and they left town as the convention continued. They had not been able to take over any major clinic, and they had gotten only bad press. Our operation had some sophistication and was run by wonderfully dedicated people. However, the effort was not well-run. Neither the leaders nor the foot soldiers were well trained; had OR been more organized, we could have been in serious trouble. My group of co-caravanners got antsy many times and were ready to go our own way and storm some church that we were sure was holding an OR prayer/planning meeting. Logic prevailed, and we grudgingly listened to our leaders. Because of the potential for infiltration, we had problems with sharing information, so we never knew where we were going until we got there. At my level of participation, I could tell that there were no lists of the people expected or present each morning; people were invariably missing, and OR members could have easily gotten in.

Spending the week running around New York City made me realize several things about myself. I realized that I could make a difference with my actions. I think this is what a lot of people in my generation don't understand—each person can make a difference. Each voice counts. My week as a pro-choice soldier led me to define myself differently. I acknowledged that I was an activist and proud of it. There are certain things that are worth fighting for. I am proud of what I've done, and I am committed to continuing the battle.

Bloodlove

Christine Doza

Every morning during high school I wake up pissed off, screaming "goddammit" at the top of my lungs, envisioning the hallways
filled with lockers and kids and hate, envisioning my own invisibility and the institutionalized invisibility of us all. It's pointless
really, because no one hears that scream but me.

I read lots of feminist texts. I read *Ms.*, flip through its pages
like a tornado, throw it down and pick of a copy of *Radical Feminism*, my eyes scanning the pages, searching. The floor of my bedroom is littered with books and magazines, the bodies of mangled
prey. But somehow, I'm still empty.

Once when I was thirteen my stepfather cornered me in the
kitchen, his face red and his eyes crazy, to set me straight on The
Rules In His House. I was up against the refrigerator, its constant
hum pressing along my spine, and he was yelling: "You fucking
bitch, how do you think it looks when you walk around like a slut?
Stop wearing that red lipstick—what do you think people think?
I'll tell you what they think. They think you're easy, they think
you'll fuck anybody. Is that true? Tell me, is it?"

I was crying because I wanted to say, Who are you? Who the
hell are you? but the words were a dry pellet in my throat. I fixed
my eyes on my mom, standing behind him the whole time in

silence. Then my brother came in and asked our stepfather what he thought he was doing. As soon as he looked away, as soon as those bloodshot eyes were off my breasts, off my body, I shrieked like mad. I braced myself against the refrigerator and screamed until I couldn't.

It's Friday night, it's Saturday night, it's every night of the week. I'm at home, behind a closed door, writing. At four in the morning I fall into bed, exhausted.

> Highschool is the single most dangerous place for a girl to be. . . . Once we hit 13 or 14 we realize that in this world the men we are associated with, not our own actions, make us who we are. . . . We learn, because wimmin are never spoken about except in social history side items, that we have never accomplished anything. . . . People might say we are part of The Third Wave of American Feminism, but the fact is there are no "waves"—only an endless ocean of feminists patriarchy has chosen to ignore. . . . Male teachers treat girls like property, like victims, like last-class citizens and no one seems to care. . . . We dont go to school to learn, we go to be indoctrinated. There is no room for free and individual thought. . . . Nowhere is competition between girls more intense than it is in high school. . . . After 12 years of learning that we dont matter, what else can you fucking expect? The 'education system' has taught us little else but to hate ourselves.

I go to a club tonight to see a band. I go by myself because I don't have any friends, really. The club is an abandoned warehouse, a meat-packing plant. There is no ventilation, and I can smell the blood, and skin and tissue slashed open. I am wearing a bra and shorts, and my skin is slippery with sweat from the heat of the people pressed all around me, bustling and jumping and elbowing each other to the beat. I am almost at the front, and the boy between me and the stage looks back, looks at my face, my shaved head, my breasts, in that order. He turns back around and I glare at the back of his neck. A boy behind me rubs his hands all over my head, gripping my short hair in his palm. I grab his wrist hard. "Excuse me," I say, and thrust his hand back at him. I turn around and the other one is there, staring at my breasts. "Gotta problem, dickhead?" He turns back around and the next song comes on, and I kick and punch everyone near me, to the beat of the music and the smell of the blood.

My English teacher is elitist, racist and sexist. He has us, his "honors" students, teach his "lower" classes because he can't be bothered. He wants to sleep with me. In my dreams at night, he stares at me until my clothes fall off and then pins me to the blackboard. I've complained to the administration three times, and every time they promise, they *promise*, that something will be done. They ask for my advice. "Fire him," I say through clenched teeth. "How about that?" I know I'm not the first. I'm not the first one to go to them for help. Of course, I can't prove a thing. No one ever can. There are no marks, no revealing comments overheard by other students. Only stares, touches, standing too close, inviting me over to his house to look at a book, untraceable attitudes about power. I know only what I see. I know they'll never fire him because we all score high on standardized English tests, and they need that to look respectable.

It's Friday night, it's Saturday night, it's every night, and I'm at home, behind a closed door, writing.

I'm learning to connect the dots. One dot for woman-hate, one for racism, one for classism, one for telling me who I can fuck. When I connect all the dots, it's a picture of me, a picture of privilege and the way it's disguised behind pretty white smiles.

I'm watching television, and the screen is filled with pretty white girls, long-haired teenagers who are supposed to be me. They are me—they're blow-up dolls, Barbie dolls, they're blank pieces of paper waiting to be filled with someone else's handwriting. They're impostors—where are the people I'm not seeing? I run to the bathroom and cut all my hair off, ripping and tearing it out with kindergarten blunt-tipped paper scissors, the only ones I have.

I take the first issue of my zine, *UpSlut*, to school and give it away free to all the girls I know. I expect to be punched, crushed, ground underfoot and left to bleed below them while they play party games and knife each other with wide eyes. But, amazingly, instead of being punched in the mouth I get kissed, and for once I've done something right.

My English teacher insists on seeing a copy; going against my wishes, he gets one. The next day he calls me into the storage room next door to his classroom. I'm sure I'll throw up in there alone with him, and I tell him to leave the door open. Sitting down across from him, I make myself stare at his face while he tells me that he is unhappy and disappointed about the crude comment I made about him in my zine. He demands a written apology in the next issue and threatens that he will sue for libel. I tell him the comment was only the truth, and we both know it, and I'm not going to sit here and play psychological warfare with him. I tell him he's a piece of shit, and I'll apologize the day hell freezes over. I tell him he better think again if he thinks he can tell me what to do with my zine. I leave. He never looks me in the eye again.

When I was little I wanted to be the president, a firewoman, a teacher, a cheerleader and a writer. Now all I want is to be happy. And left alone. And I want to know who I am in the context of a world full of hate and domination.

I pick up a copy of *Sassy* magazine and read it cover to cover, then toss it in the trash. I really can't believe, looking at the beautiful, thin, white models and the articles about finding the right boyfriend, that it masquerades as some kind of alternative teen magazine, that it purports to be profeminist, pro-girl, pro-intelligence. This is what it means to be an intelligent girl? Listening to bands with female members and wearing a more natural shade of lipstick?

I feel like we've been forgotten, I feel like we're all dying of anorexia and heartbreak, and everyone—you—you just turn the other way. I read *Ms.*, flipping through its pages like a tornado, looking for anything but what's there. I don't have a career, I don't have a husband, I don't need to know how to raise my son. I need to know what to do when I stop wanting to be an astronaut and start wanting to be Bobby's Girlfriend.

I don't need help in recovering from being raped when I was a kid. I am a kid; I need to know how to tell my English teacher to get his fucking hands off of me. I need to know what to do the first time I fall in love with another girl.

I don't need to be told what band is the cutest, what hairstyle is the most fashionable, what brand of clothes is the coolest. I need to know that every minute of every day I am being colonized, manipulated and ignored, and that minute by minute I am doing this to others who are not shining white and middle class. There's a system of abuse here. I need to know what part I'm playing in it.

Sometimes I'll be talking, and I'll hear myself blame the rape victim and congratulate the rapist. When I do that I go into my room, close the door and write. I write about the men who yell at me on the streets, the way language is all tied up in the wrong meanings, the racism of mainstream feminism, why I cried today—anything that will force the colonizer one more step back. Anything that will help me see myself more clearly.

How "liberal" can those oh-so-rebellious liberal boys be if they dont realize that patriarchy is the meat-eating, xenophobic, wife-beating system we all must impale if we want to bring the white male capitalist fucks down to spitting level? Even worse, if they think that male supremacy does not exist, or it does and is justified?

Strong girls, remember that sensitive liberal boys are our secret enemies. They disguise themselves with the androgyny of long hair and quiet thoughts, but underneath they are just as much BOY as the young republican of your choice. Be careful, beautiful girl, be strong—just because he holds your hand and looks you in the eye when you talk to him doesnt mean he respects your body or your mind.

My friend Denise tells me she's having a fight with her boyfriend. When I ask her why, she is vague about any particular incident, but tells me he's an asshole, calls her names, gives her orders. She says that once, while they were kissing, he said, "You could suck my cock now." It wasn't a suggestion, it was a fact. I hold her hand and tell her she's worth more than that. She tells me she doesn't want to hear any of my feminist shit and walks away.

> hey guess what? this is a flyer about a thing called riot grrrl press. what that is (hopefully) going to be is a distribution service for girl made/girl power fanzines. we know there are a lot of them out there, but we also know that it's often difficult to get a hold of and/or distribute them. . . .

Once I felt totally alienated from other girls. I wasn't one of Us or one of Them. I was an alien. And even though I knew I was right about everything, somehow everyone else thought I was wrong. So through writing and distributing, I discovered this whole other world out there and became part of a dialogue that included anyone who had anything to say. I took a bite out of the cake that said Eat Me, and now I'm growing and growing and growing.

My mother has certain problems with my feminism. "Just what is it about boys you don't like, Christy?" she asks. "They're not all the same, you know." I've tried to explain to her hundreds of times that girls and boys are socialized differently, and there's nothing exact I don't like about some boys, except for the way they interrupt me when I talk and take up too much room when they sit. These conversations usually begin rationally, my mom looking worried that I'm growing up freakish and me looking irritated that she's asking again. And they always end in one of two ways: with me screaming at her to get the hell out of my room, I don't even want to talk about it anymore; or with me finally just agreeing. Yeah Mom, you're right about everything; you're so right I'm speechless. I'm trying to radicalize her, and it's working slowly: She stopped eating meat last year. But some things we'll never agree on. For example, she'll never understand that I'm bisexual, she'd rather just pretend.

The only truth I can ever know is my own truth, meaning life gets filtered through my body meaning there is no such thing as objective truth. (a mask for life filtered through a man's hands) so why do I have to give you a reason for every statement I make? so why cant I just let you read my diary entries instead of writing a three page essay on power imbalances in sexual relationships and how they are reinforced by silence, and being all cool and detached like I was never there?

No matter how many women's studies classes I take in college, and no matter how many papers I write for those classes, I'll never be able to write what I want to write in the way I want to write it—by screaming it out. I'll never get past the elitism of the academic club. All I'll be able to do is spit out rhetoric. It probably wouldn't be acceptable to write anything but a nice, linear, calm and collected five-page essay on an assigned subject due on a specified date. Which means nothing.

Two weeks ago I went to a club to see a band. I went with my friend Chris, who's putting out a split issue with me: my girlzine *UpSlut*, his queerzine *ComeUppance*. We went to see two girl-positive bands at a little club in Manhattan that probably used to be a sweatshop, wimmin stooped at machines shoulder to shoulder, sewing stitch after stitch, paid next to nothing. I stand packed in with the girls at the show, and all of them feel like my sisters, all of them smile and look me in the eye when I talk and then get up on stage and shriek like mad. And when the music starts I see all the ghosts, my own and everyone's, rise up and dance, kicking and punching.

I put myself through tests to make sure I'm strong. If I need to call, I don't, and if it's cold outside I don't shiver. It was a long time before I would call myself a feminist, a long time before I thought I was strong enough to deserve that name. But I still have doubts: Can I call myself a feminist if I say mean things about other girls, even if they were mean to me first? If I don't always explain myself, if I don't correct everyone who calls a girl a bitch?

When I get upset I don't eat. Then that becomes a strength game, too. I want to know how long I can go without eating, how long I can go before I collapse. Sometimes I can't stay awake because my body is hollow, so I sleep sixteen hours a day to prove that I can be in control, that I am powerful. After a while I don't even feel hungry anymore.

The line between us and them is etched in stone and diamond and sinew & muscle & bone, always and forever.

I write this with certainty, as if I know where that line is, as if it exists anywhere but inside my own body. Colonizer and colonized, the piece of candy with the razor blade in the middle.

I worry sometimes that I'm too angry and I'll for sure explode if I don't do something—like kill someone quick. I worry that I scream and scream and we make a wailing wall, all of us screaming at the tops of our lungs, screaming for our lives, and no one is listening, nothing is changing. Everything is staying inside me. I worry sometimes that I'm losing my anger. I worry that I'm forgetting and ignoring and becoming apathetic. But I think I don't have to fight so hard now, because I know I'm not the only one fighting, I'm not the only one up against the wall.

It's Friday night, it's Saturday night, it's every night of the week, and I'm here, behind a closed door, writing. Or I'm not—I'm out there, watching you, listening to your words and watching your face to see what you really mean. Or I'm not—I'm with my friends, planting another bomb, holding hands, planning the revolution just by being together. I could be anywhere.

The revolution of little girls is bloodlove.
You bleed life and the blood is in my hands.
Smear that fucking blood.

I learned one thing of value in high school. I learned how to make a bomb. I would hide out in the lab all day, skip all my classes, make bombs and plant them. I have a little lab set up with me now, and I try to make at least one bomb a day, thrown at someone new, detonated by a different force. The only people who get hurt are those who won't confront their ideas about safety, those who laugh at the flames.

Contributors

Lisa Bowleg is a juggler of many trades who hopes to master a single trade some day. She: (1) is a research associate at a clearinghouse for state health legislation where she monitors and analyzes legislation related to HIV/AIDS and women and children's health; (2) is a doctoral student in the Applied Social Psychology program at George Washington University; and (3) teaches "Women, HIV/AIDS and Public Policy" in the Women's Studies Program at Georgetown University.

Veronica Chambers is a story editor at the *New York Times Magazine*. She has written articles for several national magazines, including *Essence, Glamour* and *Premiere*. She is coauthor with director John Singleton of the book *Poetic Justice: Filmmaking South Central Style* and is working on a family memoir about black women and mother-daughter relationships for Riverhead Books.

Abra Fortune Chernik grew up in Manhattan and on the beaches of Fire Island. She now shares a brownstone in Washington, D.C., with her partner, Derek, and their two cats. Abra frequently speaks about eating disorders at schools and women's organizations. She has optioned her first screenplay, *Portrait of an Invisible Girl*, and is currently working on her second feature-length script.

Sonja D. Curry-Johnson was born September 15, 1968, in Needham, Massachusetts. She graduated from Tuskegee University with a B.A. in English. She currently lives in Virginia with her husband, David, and two children, David III and Imani, and works on "the Great American Novel" between diaper changes.

Jennifer DiMarco, a Seattle native, is a twenty-one-year-old lesbian daughter of lesbian parents and the author of fourteen novels. *At the Edge* was released from Pride Publications in 1994. Jennifer, who now lives in Ohio, works in construction part-time and travels around the United States speaking on tolerance and feminism before school and community groups.

Christine Doza is currently working her way through Sarah Lawrence College. She is writing a zine called *Construction Paper* that talks mainly about systemized abusiveness in U.S. society and the ways it exists within her. She used to do a zine called *UpSlut*.

Laurel Gilbert is working on a Ph.D. in American cultural studies at Bowling Green State University in Ohio. She lives with her two daughters, two roommates, two dogs, a cat and a horse. She is currently teaching English at a medium-security men's prison.

Cheryl Green is pursuing her Ph.D. in social psychology at the Ohio State University in Columbus, Ohio, concentrating on issues regarding disability, ethnicity and feminism. After graduating with honors from an inner-city high school in Houston, she attended Yale University and graduated with distinction and honors in psychology. She is a paralegal and a member of the Americans with Disabilities Act Training and Implementation Network.

Aisha Hakim-Dyce was born in 1971 in Brooklyn, New York, where she currently shares a spiritually energized house with two housemates and a black cat. She and her housemates frequently sponsor poetry readings. Aisha has worked at more odd jobs than she cares to think about and gains her inspiration from listening to the music of Native American wind instruments, singing from the depths of her abdomen, arguing all night with great friends and successfully completing exercise regimens.

Anastasia Higginbotham lives with her similarly queer and feminist brother in New York City. She's the creator of "Lengthy and Squiggly," a radical bisexual cartoon duo devoted to truth, justice and a steady stream of both blatant and subversive attacks on the patriarchy. Higginbotham wants three things: to live, breathe and work feminist magic; to spend as much time as possible in the company of her family; and to run with Clarissa Pinkola Estés.

Nomy Lamm lives in a one-room apartment in Olympia, Washington with her friend Amanda. She's lived in Olympia for almost her entire life and now attends the Evergreen State College there. Nomy does a zine called *i'm so fucking beautiful* and, theoretically, is in a band called see-n-say with her two good friends, Val and Amanda. Someday they hope to practice. She also likes to spend her time with her family, who recently dug a pit in their backyard to create a homemade swimming pool.

JeeYeun Lee is a graduate student in the Ethnic Studies Ph.D. program at the University of California at Berkeley. Her focus is cultural studies, and she is trying to understand the ways in which power works in this society. Born in Japan and raised mostly in Chicago and its suburbs, she is a proud, out, 1.5 generation (migrated to the U.S. as a child) Korean American bi woman gradually learning more about her relative privileges.

Sharon Lennon was born and raised in suburban New Jersey and happily resides in New York City. Her work as a playwright (*Grace, Honey, Alone Time, Tea and Chocolate*), director, screenwriter and writer of educational programs has addressed issues such as sexual harassment, sexual assault, domestic violence and girls' and women's self-esteem. All this rolled into one lesbian.

Bhargavi C. Mandava's music criticism has appeared in *Alternative Press, Creem, Spin* and the *Village Voice*. Since relocating to Los Angeles from New York City in 1993, she has kept busy peddling her screenplays and writing fiction and poetry, some of which has appeared in *Poison Ivy Magazine* and *The Rockford Review*. Her short story "Under the Guava Tree" will be included in an anthology of Asian American erotica, to be published by Anchor Books/ Doubleday in 1995.

Tiya Miles lives in Atlanta, Georgia, with five plants and two cats. She is a graduate student at the Institute for Women's Studies at Emory University. In 1992 she graduated from Harvard-Radcliffe, where she majored in Afro-American Studies. She was born and raised in Cincinnati, Ohio, and her family still resides there.

Emilie Morgan is the pseudonym of a recent graduate of Metropolitan State University in St. Paul, Minnesota. She is a foster parent of an infant with special needs and hopes to begin work on a novel about a young woman's discovery of her sexuality.

Inga Muscio is a writer in Seattle. Her work appears regularly in *Blue Stocking* and in the *Stranger*, Seattle's critically acclaimed weekly newspaper. She also does spoken word performances and is currently working on her first novel.

Jennifer Reid Maxcy Myhre lives happily in Berkeley, California, and is pursuing a graduate degree in sociology. She admits to a fondness for reading social theory, chopping vegetables, getting her hands dirty and devouring fiction in her spare time. As an activist, she has been involved with literacy work, rape education and rape crisis counseling and is currently interested in the intersections between the cancer activist and environmental justice movements.

Robin M. Neidorf is a writer of essays, articles, book reviews, short stories and the occasional poem. She is a regular contributor to *Melpomene: Journal of Women's Health* and the *Minnesota Women's Press*, and her work has also appeared in *Iowa Woman*, the *Minneapolis Star Tribune*, *Ms.* and *Women's Review of Books*. She is a member of the inaugural class of the Bennington Writing Seminars' MFA program. E-mail her at rmneidorf@delphi.com.

Ellen Neuborne, twenty-eight, is a reporter for *USA Today*, covering retailing for the Money section. Before joining *USA Today* in 1990, she worked as a business reporter for the *Burlington* (Vermont) *Free Press*. She graduated from Brown University in 1988 with a B.A. in classics. She and her husband, fellow journalist David Landis, live in Alexandria, Virginia.

Amelia Richards is a twenty-five-year-old activist living in and loving New York City and the world of women. She works for Gloria Steinem and Voters for Choice, and serves on the board of the Third Wave Direct Action Corporation. She hopes to be doing the same for many years to come, and to someday spend a year working with women in India or Africa.

Melissa Silverstein is the manager of individual giving at the Ms. Foundation for Women, where she is currently working on a project on young women and feminism. Melissa graduated from Brandeis University in 1989 and Columbia University in 1993 with a master's degree in theater management. She worked for several New York City theater companies before becoming a full-time activist for women and girls.

Curtis Sittenfeld was born in 1975 in Cincinnati, Ohio. She graduated from Groton School in Massachusetts and is currently a student at Vassar College. She won first place in *Seventeen*'s 1992 fiction contest and third place in *Sassy*'s 1993 fiction contest, and has had writing published in *Ms.*, *Seventeen* and the *Washington Post*.

Sonia Shah works as an editor/publisher at the South End Press collective in Boston. Her work has appeared in magazines and anthologies, including *The State of Asian America: Activism and Resistance in the 1990s* (South End Press, 1993). She promises not to embarrass her sister any more than necessary.

Lisa Tiger is a member of the Muscogee Nation and is of Creek, Seminole and Cherokee descent. As an HIV/AIDS activist, she travels to reservations and Native American communities, speaking about AIDS prevention. Lisa's most cherished wish is to see a day when all tribes are in alliance to preserve the health, history and culture of each and every Native American.

Alisa L. Valdés is a twenty-five-year-old Cuban American writer and musician born and raised in Albuquerque, New Mexico. She graduated from Berklee College of Music in 1992 with a major in jazz performance, tenor saxophone. Since then she has worked as a free-lance writer, a staff writer for *Cuba Update* magazine, and an editorial intern at the *Village Voice*. She received a master's degree in journalism from Columbia University in 1994 and is currently a reporter for the Living/Arts section of the *Boston Globe*.

Rebecca Walker was born in Jackson, Mississippi, and grew up in San Francisco and New York City. She is a cofounder of the Third Wave Direct Action Corporation, a national nonprofit organization devoted to cultivating young women's leadership and activism. Her writing has been published in *The Black Scholar*, *Harper's*, *Ms.*, *Sassy* and various women's and black studies anthologies.

Whitney Walker grew up in northern California and now lives in the East Village of New York City with her partner, Eric Reyes. Whitney has studied martial arts for five years and is a purple belt in Kempo karate and a green belt in Tae Kwon Do. She is a freelance journalist and an editor at *Mirabella* magazine.

Amy Harrison

Barbara Findlen is the executive editor of *Ms.* magazine, where she started as an intern in 1985. Prior to joining *Ms.*, she was a student and activist in the Boston area. She became a part of the feminist movement in 1975, as an eleven-year-old growing up in Dedham, Massachusetts. Barbara now lives outside New York City with her partner, Kristen Golden.

Selected Titles from Seal Press

THE THINGS THAT DIVIDE US: *Stories by Women* edited by Faith Conlon, Rachel da Silva and Barbara Wilson. $10.95, 0-931188-32-6. Sixteen feminist writers present vivid and powerful short stories that explore difference and commonality between women.

CLOSER TO HOME: *Bisexuality and Feminism* edited by Elizabeth Reba Weise. $14.95, 1-878067-17-6. A dynamic anthology of essays by and about women who are bisexual, this collection breaks new ground in feminist and queer discourse.

THE BLACK WOMEN'S HEALTH BOOK: *Speaking for Ourselves*, expanded second edition, edited by Evelyn C. White. $16.95, 1-878067-40-0. More than fifty black women write about the health issues that affect them and the well-being of their families and communities. Contributors include Faye Wattleton, Byllye Y. Avery, Alice Walker, Angela Y. Davis, Audre Lorde, Lucille Clifton, bell hooks and Toni Morrison.

THE SINGLE MOTHER'S COMPANION: *Essays and Stories by Women*, edited by Marsha R. Leslie. $12.95, 1-878067-56-7. In their own words, the single mothers in this landmark collection explore both the joys and the difficult realities of raising children alone. Contributors include Barbara Kingsolver, Anne Lamott, Linda Hogan, Julia A. Boyd and Senator Carol Moseley-Braun.

SHE'S A REBEL: *The History of Women in Rock & Roll* by Gillian G. Gaar. $16.95, 1-878067-08-7. Packed with interviews, facts and personal anecdotes from women performers, writers and producers, *She's a Rebel* tells the fascinating story of the women who have shaped rock and pop music for the last five decades.

EGALIA'S DAUGHTERS by Gerd Brantenberg. $11.95, 1-878067-58-3. A hilarious satire on sex roles — in which the wim rule and the menwim stay at home — by Norway's leading feminist author.

NERVOUS CONDITIONS by Tsitsi Dangarembga. $10.95, 0-931188-74-1. A brilliant debut novel, this is both a moving story of a girl's coming of age and a compelling narrative of the devastating human loss involved in the colonization of one culture by another.

IN LOVE AND IN DANGER: *A Teen's Guide to Breaking Free of Abusive Relationships* by Barrie Levy. $8.95, 1-878067-26-5. An important, straightforward book for teens caught in abusive dating relationships.

SEAL PRESS publishes many feminist books under the categories of women's studies, fiction & poetry, mysteries, translations, young adult & children, self-help, recovery & health, and sports & the outdoors. To receive a free catalog or to order directly, write to us at 3131 Western Avenue, Suite 410, Seattle, Washington 98121. Please add 16.5% of the book total for shipping and handling.